THE RISE OF THE PROFESSIONS
IN TWENTIETH-CENTURY MEXICO

Statistical Abstract of Latin America
Supplement Series, Volume 12

Cycles and Trends Research Series, Volume 2

STATISTICAL ABSTRACT OF LATIN AMERICA

Supplement Series Editor

James W. Wilkie

INTERNATIONAL ADVISORY BOARD

CYCLES AND TRENDS RESEARCH SERIES

The Cycles and Trends in Twentieth-Century Mexico Project, directed by James W. Wilkie and Sergio de la Peña and coordinated by David E. Lorey, is a large-scale effort to examine the process of change in Mexico in the international context. The research series, which involves the development of historical statistics, is sponsored by UCLA and the Universidad Autónoma Metropolitana, Unidad Azcapotzalco. Project participants include scholars and institutions in Mexico and the United States.

The project and the publication series are funded by the William and Flora Hewlett Foundation.

Volume 1, *Industria y trabajo en México*, edited by James W. Wilkie and Jesús Reyes Heroles G.G.

Volume 2, *The Rise of the Professions in Twentieth-Century Mexico: University Graduates and Occupational Change since 1929*, by David E. Lorey.

THE RISE OF THE PROFESSIONS

IN TWENTIETH-CENTURY MEXICO

University Graduates and Occupational Change since 1929

DAVID E. LOREY

UCLA Latin American Center Publications
University of California, Los Angeles

UCLA Latin American Center Publications
University of California
Los Angeles, CA 90024–1447

Library of Congress Cataloging–in–Publication Data

Lorey, David E.
    The rise of the professions in twentieth-century Mexico:
university graduates and occupational change since 1929 / David
E. Lorey.
        p.   cm. — (Cycles and trends research series ; v. 2.)
Statistical abstract of Latin America. Supplement series ; v. 12)
    Includes bibliographical references.
    ISBN 0-87903-254-5
    1. College graduates—Employment—Mexico—Statistics.
2. Professional employees—Mexico—Statistics.   3. Education,
Higher—Economic aspects—Mexico—Statistics.   I. Title.
II. Series : Statistical abstract of Latin America. Supplement
series ; 12.
HD6278.M6L67   1992
331.7'12'09720906—dc20   92-15245
                                                                 CIP

*To Laura Meyer
for the "500 times"*

CONTENTS

Continued on overleaf

PREFACE

Despite considerable scholarly interest in the Mexican university system, analysts have not attempted to develop long-term quantitative data on the demand for and supply of the university's most important economic and social contribution: professionally skilled persons. Writers on the Mexican university have tended to base quantitative analyses (as far as they go) on enrollment statistics, certainly misleading for a system in which half of all students leave universities without achieving a degree.

Not only do we not have reliable information on how many students graduate from Mexican universities, or in what professional fields, but we have little idea of what sorts of jobs await them upon graduation. Almost no research has been devoted to developing statistics on Mexico's changing occupational structure over the course of the twentieth century. Some students of the Mexican economy have developed data on sectoral shifts in the economically active population. But a glaring gap exists in knowledge about the historical development of modern occupations defined functionally (as opposed to sectorially): professionals, technicians, and managers; street vendors, unskilled industrial laborers, rural *peones*.

These two topics—university graduates and occupational change—are closely related. A university system does not operate in a vacuum, but rather is fundamentally shaped by the supply of jobs for professionals; the form and function of a university system are in large measure determined by economic trends. And the creation of employment positions at the professional level is in turn related to at least two other extremely important phenomena: social mobility and political conflict.

The data developed in this study allow us for the first time to analyze the relationship between trends in university graduates (and their fields of study) and trends in employment opportunities for professionals. How has the market for university graduates developed in Mexico? What do patterns in the development of that market indicate about Mexican economic development? What has been the impact of economic development since 1929 on the university system?

The volume focuses on the development of statistical data on graduates and occupations, carefully reviewing appropriate methodologies for linking data sets and for making statistical series on diverse topics comparable with one another. The task of working out such problems is central to the effort to move analysis forward because the data (and the sources from which they are drawn) have themselves constituted the major stumbling block for past analysts attempting to make use of them. We can explain this obstacle easily: none of the numbers used as the basis for data development here were originally compiled for the present purposes; they were not tallied for historical or comparative analysis. It is the aim of this book to turn a mass of unorganized data into a useful tool for historical inquiry.

Clearing through the methodological thickets allows for a new and exciting view of some of the main themes in the historiography of twentieth-century Mexico. For the first time we can gauge the historical ability of the Mexican economy to produce employment for a crucial segment of society. For the first time we can approach sticky questions such as historical social mobility from the inside, from the perspective of people trying to make their way into the Mexican middle classes.

This book has been designed as a companion volume to my *The University System and Economic Development in Mexico since 1929* (forthcoming from Stanford University Press). Its principal aim is to provide a sourcebook for scholars interested in Mexican universities and their articulation with policy and economic development in the twentieth century. While it presents in skeletal form the basic arguments of *The University System and Economic Development*, it focuses on the strict quantitative basis of those arguments. Non-quantitative evidence as well as the broad meaning and implications of my analysis are offered in *Paradox*, and the reader is encouraged to refer to that book for treatment of issues that I have been unable to address here. The researcher will want to consult both works.

Acknowledgments

Many Mexicanists contributed helpful comments at different stages in the elaboration of the data and analysis presented in this study. Manuscript drafts or selected sections were read by Roderic Camp, Enrique Cárdenas, John Coatsworth, Barbara Geddes, Stephen Haber, Raúl Hinojosa, José Moya, Silvia Ortega Salazar, Sergio de la Peña, José Angel Pescador, Jesús Reyes Heroles, James W. Wilkie, and Sergio Zermeño. Kenneth Sokoloff, John Coatsworth, and James Platler advised me on statistical methodology.

Several sources of financial support helped make the study possible. Grants from UCLA's Program on Mexico and the UCLA Latin American Center provided support for early research trips to Mexico. A UC MEXUS grant provided funds for research and write-up during the final stages. Clint Smith of the Hewlett Foundation has been generous in his support of UCLA's Cycles and Trends in Twentieth-Century Mexico project, which provided a stimulating intellectual environment for the completion of this book.

I am grateful for research support in Mexico. Licenciada Ader and her staff at the ANUIES library in Guadalupe Inn were generous with their time, copying machine, and coffee. Dr. Juan Casillas, Ing. Ermilo Marroquín, and licenciado Jesús Barrón of ANUIES helped me out in many ways, large and small. Ing. J. Alberto González I. of the Dirección General de Profesiones gave me access to DGP archives and invaluable informal information in a year-long series of short conversations. The staff of the Banco de México library efficiently found hard-to-find books and manuscripts.

For research support in Los Angeles, I am particularly indebted to Christof Weber, my Program Assistant at the UCLA Program on Mexico since 1989, who checked the data and calculations and made innumerable trips back and forth to the University Research Library. Finally, thanks are due Colleen Trujillo, the Latin American Center's Publications Director, who has provided invaluable counsel on this volume and related projects from their inception.

D.E.L.
Los Angeles
December, 1991

ABBREVIATIONS

Abbreviations Used in Text, Notes, and Bibliography

ANUIES   Asociación Nacional de Universidades e
                Institutos de Educación Superior
CONACYT   Consejo Nacional de Ciencia y Tecnología
D.F.   Distrito Federal (Federal District)
DGE   Dirección General de Estadística
DGP   Dirección General de Profesiones
EAP   Economically Active Population
GDP   Gross Domestic Product
PNR   Partido Revolucionario Nacional
SEP   Secretaría de Educación Pública
UCLA   University of California, Los Angeles

Symbols Used in Tables

~   Data not available
#   Zero or negligible

Abbreviations for Sources Used in Tables and Notes

AE   Dirección General de Estadística, *Anuario
                estadístico.*
ANUIES-AE   ANUIES. *Anuario estadístico.*
ANUIES-ESM   ANUIES. *La educación superior en México* (1967)
                and *La enseñanza superior en México* (1968-76).
CE   Dirección General de Estadística. *Compendio
                estadístico.*
Census   Mexican Decennial Census.
DGP   Dirección General de Profesiones, unpublished
                data.

EHM	Instituto de Estadística, Geografía, e Informática (INEGI). *Estadísticas históricas de México*. México, D. F.: INEGI, 1985.
FU	Attolini, José. *Las finanzas de la universidad a través del tiempo*. México, D. F.: Escuela Nacional de Economía, UNAM, 1951.
HEU	González Cosío, Arturo. *Historia estadística de la universidad, 1910-1967*. México, D.F.: UNAM, 1968.
NAFINSA-EMC	Nacional Financiera, S.A. *La economía mexicana en cifras.*
OELM	*Obra educativa de López Mateos*. N.p.: n.p. [ANUIES], n.d. [1965].
PROIDES	ANUIES. *Programa integral para el desarrollo de la educación superior*. México, D. F., 1986.
QMCS	Mostkoff, Aída, and Stephanie Granato. "Quantifying Mexico's Class Structure." In James W. Wilkie, ed., *Society and Economy in Mexico*. Los Angeles: UCLA Latin American Center Publications, 1989.
SALA	*Statistical Abstract of Latin America*. Los Angeles: UCLA Latin American Center Publications.
SEP-EBSEN	SEP. *Estadística básica del sistema educativo nacional, 1971-1972*. México, D. F.: SEP, 1972.
SEP-EPM	SEP. *La educación pública en México 1964/1970*. México, D. F.: SEP, 1970.
SEP-ESM	SEP. *La educación superior en México.*
SEP-OE	SEP. *Obra educativo, 1970-1976*. México, D. F.: SEP, n.d. [1976].
UNAM-AE	UNAM. *Anuario estadístico.*
UNAM-CEAL	Dirección General de Administración, Departamento de Estadística. *Cuadernos estadísticos año lectivo 1979-1980*. México, D. F.: UNAM, n.d. [1980].
UNAM-CU	UNAM. *Primer censo universitario*. México, D. F.: UNAM, 1953.

UNAM-EAE	UNAM. Dirección General de Administración. *Estadísticas del aspecto escolar, 1970*. México, D.F.: UNAM, 1970.
UNAM-PP	UNAM. *Presupuesto por programas.* Various years.
UNESCO-SY	UNESCO. *Statistical Yearbook.*

Abbreviations for Mexican Universities

Anahuác	Universidad Anahuác
Ibero	Universidad Iberoamericana
IPN	Instituto Politécnico Nacional
ITAM	Instituto Tecnológico Autónomo de México
ITESM	Instituto Tecnológico y de Estudios Superiores de Monterrey
MICHSN	Universidad Michoacana de San Nicolás
UABC	Universidad Autónoma de Baja California
UACH	Universidad Autónoma de Chihuahua
UACO	Universidad Autónoma de Coahuila
UAEM	Universidad Autónoma de Estado de México
UAG	Universidad Autónoma de Guadalajara
UAM	Universidad Autónoma Metropolitana
UANL	Universidad Autónoma de Nuevo León
UAP	Universidad Autónoma de Puebla
UASLP	Universidad Autónoma de San Luis Potosí
UASIN	Universidad Autónoma de Sinaloa
UAT	Universidad Autónoma de Tamaulipas
UDLA	Universidad de las Américas-Puebla.
UG	Universidad de Guadalajara
UGUAN	Universidad de Guanajuato
UNAM	Universidad Nacional Autónoma de México
UV	Universidad Veracruzana

FIGURES

Higher Education Policy and the Achievements of the University System since 1929

In 1929 Mexican leaders took the first major step toward "institutionalizing" the Revolution of 1910 by consolidating competing political factions into the first official party of the Revolution—the PNR (Partido Nacional Revolucionario). The PNR united Mexico's diverse regional interests into a manageable political field and cleared the way for the energetic pursuit of economic and social goals. Institutionalization thus had two essential objectives: to forestall the rebellions of regional strongmen, which had fueled a decade of fighting after 1910 and a period of political instability to 1929, and to channel the economic and social aspirations sparked by the Revolution.

As part of its initiative to institutionalize the Revolution, the government formally incorporated the university system[1] into its development plans. Policymakers saw the university system as central to the process of institutionalization: as necessary for political stabilization, for economic development, and for social change. The aims of the government for the university have been intertwined since 1929 in public policy and the popular imagination. Together, they constitute a demand that the university be responsive to government policy priorities, to Mexican presidents' plans for economic and social development.

The Mexican university system was expected not only to respond to government development strategy but also to the needs of the

[1]I refer throughout to all public and private universities.

1

economy for professional expertise. The careers that university students chose and the sorts of jobs they found were intricately related to the economic development that unfolded after 1929. Both the structure and the function of the university system were shaped by economic realities; the most important of these influences was the evolving employment outlook for professionals.

Universities were expected to respond to social as well as economic demands. Mexicans from many different walks of life came to see university education as a way to take part in, and benefit from, the economic development promised by leaders. Pablo González Casanova, a sociologist and former rector of the Universidad Nacional Autónoma de México (UNAM), expressed this hope in 1962: "In today's Mexico which is being industrialized and urbanized there is permanent social mobility. The peasants of yesterday are today's workers, and the workers' children can be professionals."[2] University education became both a real conduit of upward mobility and an important symbol of social mobility and status.

The evolution of the university system in Mexico has never been studied in the context of these three interrelated demands—policy, economic, and social. Most important, the number of graduates of the university system and their fields of study have never been carefully considered in the light of the developing market for professional and technical skills.

To address this major gap in the literature on the Mexican university, the present volume develops original statistical data for the study of the relationship between university graduates and professional employment in Mexico in the years since 1929. The volume makes possible further research by providing comprehensive data on the two topics and presents a brief analysis of twentieth-century Mexican development based on this new information.

---

[2]Pablo González Casanova, "México: El ciclo de una revolución agraria," *Cuadernos Americanos*, 120, no. 1 (January-February, 1962). Compare González's later comments on social mobility in *Democracia en México* (México, D.F.: Ediciones Era, 1965).

Past Approaches to the Mexican University

Writers on Mexico's university system have traditionally treated the university as a hermetic institution with a structure and dynamic independent of outside economic and social change. They rely on traditional institutional sources and perspectives to describe institutional evolution. (The study of the development of various professional schools within universities forms a variant of this institutional current.) The institutional approach details the formal development of the Mexican higher education system, but does not explore why different forms and functions of the university developed over time.

Institutional approaches inhibit the study of the university system in its economic and social context in two important ways. First, the most important immediate product of university education—professional-level graduates—does not figure in institutional histories of the Mexican university. It is ironic that the decisions of professional students about career opportunities are lost in the institutional approach; after all, universities are the institutional expression of individual choices. Second, larger economic and social trends are perceived to unfold outside the university. This analytical isolation of the university system makes it impossible to assess the impact of economic and social factors on individual students as they make decisions about their professional careers.[3]

[3]For institutional studies, see Rosalío Wences Reza, *La universidad en la historia de México* (México, D. F.: Editorial Línea, 1984); Valdemar Rodríguez, "National University of Mexico: Rebirth and Role of the Universitarios (1910-1957)," Ph. D. Diss., University of Texas at Austin, 1958; Jaime Castrejón Diez and Marisol Pérez Lizaur, *Historia de las universidades estatales*, 2 vols. (México, D. F.: SEP, 1976); and Fernando Solana et al., *Historia de la educación pública en México* (México, D. F.: SEP, 1984). Martha Robles, *Educación y sociedad en la historia de México* (México, D. F.: Siglo XXI Editores, 1977), attempts to mate the institutional history of the university with an analysis of revolutionary ideology. A few works relate institutional developments to the educational projects of presidential administrations: see George Sánchez, *Mexico: A Revolution by Education* (New York: Viking Press, 1936); and Victoria Lerner, *La educación socialista* (México, D. F.: El Colegio de México, 1979). *Historia de las profesiones en México* (México, D. F.: El Colegio de México, 1982) focuses on the development of professional schools. For innovative departures within the institutional current, see Richard G. King, Alfonso Rangel Guerra, David Kline, and Noel F. McGinn, *Nueve universidades mexicanas: Un análisis de su crecimiento y desarrollo* (México, D.F.: ANUIES, 1972); Thomas N. Osborn, *Higher Education in Mexico: History, Growth, and Problems in a Dichotomized Industry* (El Paso:

In a major noninstitutional current of scholarship on the Mexican university, observers have focused on sociological and political aspects of university education. These authors concern themselves primarily with the function of the university in maintaining and re-inforcing social and political structures. The work of Roderic A. Camp proceeds furthest in the direction of relating data on the pro-fessional backgrounds of a select, elite group of university graduates (those who later attain political power) to the shifting develop-ment strategies of Mexican presidential coalitions.

Because the sociological-political current is primarily concerned with elite political actors, university education is addressed princi-pally as a common background of elites, as one of their defining characteristics.[4] Herein lies the limitation of this body of literature for the study of the university system as a whole in the broad context of Mexican society: university-trained elites are not repre-

Texas Western Press, 1976); Daniel C. Levy, *Higher Education and the State in Latin America: Private Challenges to Public Dominance* (Chicago: University of Chicago Press, 1986); Patricia de Leonardo R., *La educación superior privada en México: Bosquejo histórico* (México, D.F.: Editorial Línea, 1983); Oscar Hinojosa, "La universidad privada escala posiciones como proveedora de funcionarios," *Proceso*, March 31, 1986, 6-11; and Patricia de Leonardo Ramírez, "Los cuadros de la derecha," *El Cotidiano*, 24 (July-August, 1988), 89-94. On the professions, see Peter S. Cleaves, *Professions and the State: The Mexican Case* (Tucson: University of Arizona Press, 1987).

[4]See Peter H. Smith, *Labyrinths of Power: Political Recruitment in Twentieth-Century Mexico* (Princeton: Princeton University Press, 1979); Roderic A. Camp, *Mexico's Leaders: Their Education and Recruitment* (Tucson: University of Arizona Press, 1980); idem, "The Middle-Level Technocrat in Mexico," *Journal of Developing Areas*, 6, no. 4 (July, 1972), 571-582; and idem, "The Political Technocrat in Mexico and the Survival of the Political System," *Latin American Research Review*, 20, no. 1 (1985), 97-118. See also Rodolfo Figueroa's *Prioridades nacionales y reclutamiento de funcionarios públi-cos* (México, D. F.: El Colegio de México, 1981); Larissa Lomnitz, Leticia Mayer, and Martha W. Rees, "Recruiting Technical Elites: Mexico's Veterinarians," *Human Organization*, 42, no. 1 (Spring, 1983), 23-29; Donald Mabry, *The Mexican University and the State: Student Conflicts, 1910-1971* (College Station: Texas A & M Press, 1982); Daniel C. Levy, *University and Government in Mexico: Autonomy in an Authoritarian System* (New York: Praeger, 1980); Gilberto Guevara Niebla, ed., *Las luchas estudiantiles en México*, 2 vols. (México, D. F.: Editorial Línea, 1983); Salvador Martínez Della Rocca, *Estado y universidad en México 1920-1968: Historia de los movimientos estudiantiles en la UNAM* (México, D. F.: Joan Boldó i Climent Editores, 1986); Fernando Jiménez Mier y Terán, *El autoritarismo en el gobierno de la UNAM* (México, D. F.: Foro Universitario, 1982); and Jesús Silva Herzog, *Una historia de la Universidad de México y sus problemas* (México, D. F.: Siglo XXI Editores, 1986).

sentative of Mexican university students in general—for one thing, elites do not study the same professional fields as the majority of Mexican students.[5]

Economic and social forces underlying the historical roles of the Mexican university have only rarely made their way into the two dominant currents of writing on Mexican universities described above. For this reason I base my work on the small body of research that touches upon economic and social aspects of the development of the Mexican university. Although the number of such studies is small, they have been among the most influential in guiding this study.

An important starting point for data collection and development here was provided by the literature on human capital.[6] Human capital theory developed in the 1950s to explain the role of education in making labor more productive in the developed world. The theory posited that expenditure for education could be seen as investment in human capital rather than as consumption and held that education was a key ingredient in increasing productivity, in spurring economic growth, and in creating an egalitarian distribution of wealth.[7]

In Mexico, the idea that investment in human capital would lead to both increased national productivity and individual well-being had a direct impact not only on political rhetoric and discourse but also on public policy. The theory of human capital became the guiding light of educational policy in Mexico during the 1960s and 1970s as quantitative expansion at all levels of education,

[5]See David E. Lorey, "Professional Expertise and Mexican Modernization: Sources, Methods, and Preliminary Findings," in *Statistical Abstract of Latin America*, vol. 26, pp. 890-912.

[6]For a bibliography of the debate from its inception, see Mark Blaug, *The Economics of Education: An Annotated Bibliography* (Oxford: Pergamon Press, 1978). For an excellent review of the debate over human capital and more recent approaches to the study of the link between education and economic change, see Martin Carnoy, Henry Levin, et al., *Economía política del financiamiento educativo en países en vías de desarrollo* (México, D. F.: Ediciones Gérnika, 1986). In English, see Nigel Brooke, John Oxenham, and Angela Little, *Qualifications and Employment in Mexico* (Sussex: University of Sussex, 1978).

[7]For the classic statements of human capital theory, see Theodore Schultz, *The Economic Value of Education* (New York: Columbia University Press, 1963); and G. S. Becker, *Human Capital: A Theoretical and Empirical Analysis, with Special Reference to Education* (Princeton: Princeton University Press, 1964).

but particularly at the university level, was sought as a way to promote the rapid development of the Mexican economy.[8] Application of human capital ideas to the Mexican case spawned a large literature on higher education and "manpower" in Mexico throughout the 1960s.[9]

The early literature on human capital was answered in the 1970s by a counter literature which questioned several major tenets of human capital theory. The most penetrating critics suggested that productivity is not related to educational attainment as much as to the productivity inherent in jobs created by an economy. The education process, rather than training a worker with specific skills necessary for raising productivity, makes job applicants "trainable" by shaping their attitudes and their aptitude, providing a "fit" among workers, jobs, and firms. Worker "trainability" is determined by employers only partly on the basis of specific technical qualifications gained through education, since bringing a worker up to the level of productivity of a job is in large part a function of the personal characteristics of the worker. Desirable characteristics of workers, frequently attitudinal rather than manual or cognitive in nature, reduce the cost of training and turnover to employers and principally in this manner lead to higher profits.[10]

Much of the literature that followed from the work of the early human capital theorists showed that increased access to higher education and stepped-up production of professionally skilled graduates will not cause economic development. Rather, analysts have reached a broad consensus that the structure and function of higher education systems are shaped by the process of economic development itself. Other academic disciplines, notably sociology, share

[8]See, for example, Leopoldo Solís M., *Controversias sobre el crecimiento y la distribución* (México, D. F.: Fondo de Cultura Económica, 1972), pp. 203-204 and passim.

[9]Charles Nash Myers, *Education and National Development* (Princeton: Industrial Relations Section, Princeton University, 1965). Myers's volume is typical of the genre in most respects, but stands out for its analysis of regional differences in human resource development. See also Myers's article on estimating demand for health professionals: "Proyección de la demanda de médicos en México: 1965-1980," *Revista de Educación Superior*, 1, no. 3 (1972), 77-103.

[10]For the classic formulation of this critique, see K. Arrow, *Higher Education as a Filter* (Stanford: Stanford University Press, 1972). The debate has settled at a middle ground. See discussion in Carnoy et al., *Economía política*, pp. 25-36.

this view, seeing education primarily as reactive or reflective rather than causal. A new literature emerged in the 1970s to relate this fundamental change in perspective on the economic impacts of higher education to the Mexican experience.[11]

A second point of departure for this study was a small group of studies on the changing structures of class and occupation in Mexico. These studies form an essential backdrop for data development and analysis of the evolution of the Mexican university system. Work on social stratification shows that the Mexican middle class, which includes both professionals and technicians trained at the university level, has grown relative to both upper and lower classes since the beginning of the twentieth century. Both income and occupation, which are generally the basis for definitions of "class" in the literature, show strong statistical correlation with educational background. This correlation makes the consideration of the social class of university students a key unstudied aspect of the relationship between the university and historical economic development in Mexico.[12]

Studies of Mexico's changing occupational structure tend to focus on the economic sector of occupation, that is, activity in the primary

[11]In a series of articles published beginning in the 1970s, the Mexican education expert Carlos Muñoz Izquierdo applied the newer economics-of-education theories to different quantitative data sets with very enlightening results. See the following articles for more detailed development of Muñoz's arguments: Carlos Muñoz Izquierdo and José Lobo, "Expansión escolar, mercado de trabajo, y distribución del ingreso en México: Un análisis longitudinal, 1960-1970," *Revista del Centro de Estudios Educativos*, 4, no.1 (1978); and Carlos Muñoz Izquierdo, José Lobo, Alberto Hernández, and Pedro G. Rodríguez, "Educación y mercado de trabajo," *Revista del Centro de Estudios Educativos*, 8, no. 2 (1978). Also see Víctor Manuel Gómez Campo, "Relaciones entre educación y estructura económica: Dos grandes marcos de interpretación," *Revista de Educación Superior*, NS 41 (January-March, 1982), 5-43.

[12]Aída Mostkoff and Stephanie Granato, "Quantifying Mexico's Class Structure," in James W. Wilkie, ed., *Society and Economy in Mexico* (Los Angeles: UCLA Latin American Center Publications, 1990), synthesize the findings of two generations of scholars concerned with describing the evolution of class structure in twentieth-century Mexico. For approaches that focus on income distribution, see Gloria González Salazar, *Subocupación y estructura de clases sociales en México* (México, D. F.: UNAM, 1972); Pedro Aspe and Paul E. Sigmund, eds., *The Political Economy of Income Distribution in Mexico* (New York: Holmes and Meier Publishers, 1984); Wouter van Ginneken, *Socioeconomic Groups and Income Distribution in Mexico* (New York: St. Martin's Press, 1980); and Leopoldo Solís, *La realidad económica mexicana: Retrovisión y perspectivas* (México, D.F.: Siglo XXI, 1987).

(agricultural), secondary (industrial), or tertiary (service) sectors. It is clear that there has been a long-term decline in agricultural occupations, while employment in both industry and services has expanded rapidly since the beginning of the century and especially since 1940. But very few scholars have examined the evolution of occupational level in Mexico, that is, historical shifts in the numbers and shares of professionals and technicians, for example, within and among economic sectors.[13]

A third point of departure for data gathering and analysis in the present study is a body of literature treating economic and social aspects of higher education in Mexico. Scholars working within this literature make use of limited sets of quantitative data on university output, which makes their work distinct from the research discussed so far. Studies of university output have linked professional education with the job market. A small amount of very suggestive research using quantitative data has been carried out on specific professional fields.[14] But while these contributions introduce a

[13]The most sophisticated analyses are Donald B. Keesing, "Structural Change Early in Development: Mexico's Changing Industrial and Occupational Structure from 1895 to 1950," *Journal of Economic History*, 29, no. 4 (December, 1969), 716-738; idem, "Employment and Lack of Employment in Mexico, 1900-70," in James W. Wilkie and Kenneth Ruddle, eds., *Quantitative Latin American Studies: Methods and Findings* (Los Angeles: UCLA Latin American Center Publications, 1977), pp. 3-22; and Peter Gregory, *The Myth of Market Failure: Employment and the Labor Market in Mexico* (Baltimore: Johns Hopkins University Press, 1986). See also Clark Reynolds, *The Mexican Economy: Twentieth-Century Structure and Growth* (New Haven and London: Yale University Press, 1970); and Claudio Stern and Joseph A. Kahl, "Stratification since the Revolution," in Joseph A. Kahl, ed., *Comparative Perspectives on Stratification: Mexico, Great Britain, and Japan* (Boston: Little, Brown and Company, 1968), pp. 5-30.

[14]Víctor Urquidi and Adrián Lajous Vargas, for example, attempted to analyze the higher educational gains of Mexico during the López Mateos administration (1958–1964) in their *Educación superior, ciencia y tecnología en el desarrollo económico de México* (México, D. F.: El Colegio de México, 1967). Other attempts to gauge needs and supply of professionals are SEP-DGP, *Análisis del mercado nacional de profesionistas y técnicos: Oferta 1967-1978, demanda 1967-1978, y proyecciones a 1990* (México, D. F.: SEP, 1982); and Paul W. Strassman, *Technological Change and Economic Development: The Manufacturing Experience in Mexico and Puerto Rico* (Ithaca, NY: Cornell University Press, 1968). Clark W. Reynolds and Blanca M. de Petricioli examine the training received by economists in *The Teaching of Economics in Mexico* (New York: Education and World Affairs, 1967). Russell Davis's study *Science, Engineering, and Technical Education in Mexico* (New York: Education and World Affairs, 1967) uses data sets from several different sources to outline problems in engineering education at the university level.

new problematic, the short-term nature of their data limits the depth and the historical reach of analysis. The task at hand in the present volume is to develop data that facilitate the study of the economic and social roles of the university system over the long term. A great deal of work has been done on the institutional evolution of the Mexican university system and the major trends are now established. Analysts have clarified the Mexican university's role in political socialization. Historical analysis of quantitative data will make it possible to look beyond institutional and political aspects to the linkages among the university, economic development, and social change in the 60-year period from 1929 to 1989.

The Policy Context since 1929

Mexican presidential coalitions since 1929 have shown many more similarities than differences in their attitudes toward higher education. Historically, the Mexican government has been primarily concerned with stimulating the development of professional expertise to advance economic goals. At the same time, leaders have found it necessary to respond through higher education policy to the social demand for mobility and status attained through professional careers. Underlying large swings in the ideological debate over the purposes of higher education, these two aims for the university system have informed a stable project of the Mexican government.

The greatest element of continuity in government higher education policy has been the emphasis on the production of professional expertise to meet the demands of a changing economy. Professional expertise has been seen as central to development, both to the process of economic growth and to the important role of the university in creating an economically active population with modern values and attitudes.

A second element of continuity in government attitudes toward the university has been a rhetorical linking of professional expertise with the goal of social mobility—professional careers, and thus university education, have been championed as a medium of social ascension. This linkage has provided a way to relate government aims with revolutionary rhetoric emphasizing the university's role in social mobility for the children of workers and peasants. The presidents generally considered most socially "revolutionary"— Lázaro Cárdenas (1934-40) and Luis Echeverría (1970-76)—overtly attempted to facilitate the upward rise of working-class Mexicans through the higher education system. Both presidents encouraged the development of lower-level technical programs, shorter in duration and thus lower in opportunity cost, for students from working-class backgrounds.[15]

Mexican leaders have thus hoped that the university would accomplish two goals at the same time: contribute to creating a developed economy and contribute to raising the standard of living of the Mexican people. It has been assumed that, as economic development progresses, an important form of social mobility will be movement into professional-level employment.

These two continuities have undergirded the higher education policies of presidential administrations from 1929 to the present. A brief, analytical chronology of higher education policy since 1929 serves to underline these continuities, as well as to point out certain ironies in their historical manifestations.

The Cárdenas administration of the 1930s has often been noted for its drive to "socialize" the impact of the education system at all levels, in line with Vicente Lombardo Toledano's urging.[16] Yet it is clear that Cárdenas saw the university as primarily "responsible for providing the technical skills and professional services that would support national production." In the six-year plan for his administration (1933), Cárdenas planned to give higher-technical education preference over the liberal professions. The final purpose of this shift in emphasis was to better "the material conditions of life of the Mexican people."[17]

Cárdenas's curious blend of humanistic and utilitarian aims for higher education was clear in his sponsorship of the Instituto Politécnico Nacional (IPN). The IPN would accept more students from the working classes than the Universidad Nacional Autónoma de México (UNAM) and would thus serve both to produce needed professionals and to open up professional careers to less-favored Mexicans. The IPN was brought under the umbrella of government

[15]Technical professions also provide a greater number of "lateral exits," that is, an engineering student can leave the university at pre-degree levels with skills that will enable him or her to find work.

[16]For discussion of the links between engineering and technical education and the social revolutionary aims of the Cárdenas administration, see Francisco Arce Gurza, "El inicio de una nueva era, 1910-1945" in *Historia de las profesiones*, pp. 257-260.

[17]Robles, *Educación y sociedad*, p. 159.

policy by Cárdenas in the late 1930s.[18]

Some of Cárdenas's economic policies presented major challenges for university policy. The crisis surrounding the expropriation of foreign-owned oil industry in 1938, for example, provided a dramatic stimulus to development of professional expertise in the late 1930s and 1940s. The difficulties of technical adjustment following the expropriation startled Mexicans and underlined for policymakers the importance of the university's utilitarian function. Mexicans realized the enormity of their dependence on foreign expertise and the historical inability of Mexico's higher education system to produce professionals capable of managing the exploitation of the country's resources. At the time of the expropriation, the country's sole politechnical institute had only been functioning for two years. Mexico was barely able to muster the domestic expertise necessary to keep the oil industry running. Mexican technicians, hurriedly rounded up after the expropriation, reconstructed daily activities in the oil fields from worker recollections and proceeded from there to reconstruct one of Mexico's most important industries.

In the 1940s and early 1950s—during the administrations of Manuel Avila Camacho (1941-46), Miguel Alemán (1947-52), and Adolfo Ruiz Cortines (1953-58)—government economic development aims and higher education policy were successfully integrated for the purpose of promoting "economic revolution." The programs of these administrations, especially those of Alemán and Ruiz Cortines, created new needs for professionals, particularly technical and administrative personnel for the public sector.

Both public- and private-sector demands for university graduates were stimulated by the public projects of the stepped-up economic revolution under Alemán and Ruiz Cortines: roads, dams, airfields, bridges, highways, ports, public buildings, and electrical and irrigation works. Agricultural policies favoring medium and large producers stimulated the need for professionals to mechanize production; diversify crops; introduce fertilizers, insecticides, better seed, crop rotation techniques; as well as to manage rural credit and investment. The presidents responded to the greatly increased demand for professionals to plan and manage these projects by building the giant new university campus (the Ciudad Universitaria) in the

[18]The IPN was seen also as a counterweight to the "reactionary" UNAM of liberal professions, which put up a great deal of opposition to Cárdenas's program of socialist education.

south of the capital, by supporting the development of regional universities, and by sending civil servants abroad to acquire advanced training.[19]

One scholar calls this era of integration the "Long Peace," for political conflicts between the university and the state reached an all-time low in quantity and intensity. "Rather than a bastion of conservatism and reaction out of which came guerrilla-like attacks on cherished government programs, UNAM . . . became a partner in the Revolution."[20] It is interesting to note that the attitude of UNAM had not changed; rather policy had become more conservative, emphasizing rapid economic change and particularly industrialization over social change.

Two aspects of the integration of government economic development policy and higher education policy are especially noteworthy. First, UNAM was reorganized under the "Caso" law of 1944 as a decentralized state agency. That such a limitation of traditional university autonomy was possible indicates a basic harmony between university and government goals. Second, university graduates were brought into government in large numbers. President Alemán in particular gave many university graduates high government positions. Alemán's support for the construction of the Ciudad Universitaria in the south of Mexico City helped win over the students to the government's aims.

As the period of relative harmony between the university and the state ended in the late 1950s, Adolfo López Mateos assumed the presidency in 1958 with a call for university reform and stepped-up social programs. The end of the period of relative peace between the university and the state was not characterized by a monolithic relationship between two ideologically opposed sides. Student political agitation became a problem for the government ". . . sometimes because of its pro-Communist, pro-Castro, anti-American appeals, other times because of its anti-communist, pro-Catholic Church, and anti-'atheistic' education appeals."[21] The ambiguity of

[19]See Frank Brandenburg, *The Making of Modern Mexico* (Englewood Cliffs: Prentice-Hall, 1964), pp. 104, 108.

[20]Mabry, *Student Conflicts*, pp. 189-213. Silva Herzog terms the 1948-66 period the "Paz Cuasi Octaviana" in his *Una historia de la Universidad*. Daniel Levy, in his *Autonomy in an Authoritarian System*, writes that the conventional image of chronically bad relations between university and state in the 1940-66 period is grossly false.

[21]Brandenburg, *The Making of Modern Mexico*, p. 114.

student pressure on the system was important because, as I suggest in the following chapter, that pressure was due in good part to the changing employment opportunities for professionals provided by the Mexican economy.

From the beginning of the López Mateos administration into the 1980s, the main theme of government higher education policy has been "reform." Each six-year presidential administration has emphasized reform of a university system seemingly beyond the control of government policy and out of touch with economic and social needs. The rhetoric of reform has not led to a fundamental restructuring of the higher education system, however.

The main problem affecting the university's role in economic development has been seen by Mexican leaders since the late 1950s as the "massification," or the rapidly increasing student population of university campuses, caused by the dramatic growth of university enrollment.[22] By 1958, the demand for higher education created during the period of economic boom and integration during the 1940s and 1950s had outstripped university capacity; strains on the system had become pronounced and were attributed by most observers to overcrowded campuses. The pressures of massification, frequently seen as a problem of the 1970s and 1980s, then, had come to a head as early as the late 1950s. These pressures grew during the 1960s and forced their attention on the world with the violent clashes between Mexican students and soldiers in 1968.

As demand for places in the university system grew, students claimed that universities should open their doors wider and allow all applicants a place. They condemned the use of academic records or test scores to exclude them on the basis of their secondary school preparation or tested aptitude for university-level study. Critics of the open-door policy contended that an open university would damage the quality of the university's product. Generally, students won the continuation of open enrollment procedures, low fees, and low admission standards.[23]

The increasing number of conflicts between students and the government—between "university" and "state"—resulting from the pres-

[22]For a scholarly expression of this perception, see Robert E. Quirk, *Mexico* (Englewood Cliffs: Prentice-Hall, 1971), p. 121.

[23]For an analysis of the role of the Left in forcing open-door admission policies and lax achievement standards at Mexican universities, see Olac Fuentes Molinar, "Universidad y democracia: La mirada hacia la izquierda," *Cuadernos Políticos* , 53 (January/April, 1981), 4-18.

sures of massification and the debates arising out of them, and particularly the crises of 1958 and 1966-68, provided the main stimulus for programs of reform under López Mateos in the 1960s and under Echeverría in the 1970s.[24] The emphasis on reform has taken various guises since 1958.

López Mateos, who entered office during a period of student strikes and violence, introduced an eleven-year plan for development of the education system soon after taking office. He increased expenditure on all levels of education over his three predecessors to its highest level since the 1930s (from 10.6 percent of government expenditure under Cárdenas to an average of 11.5 percent during his administration). Planning and increased budgetary outlays were manifestations of the belief that the problems of the education system stemmed in the first instance from growth in enrollment.

President Díaz Ordaz, who entered office in 1964, further emphasized planning and expansion as the route to reform. More so than López Mateos, Díaz Ordaz supported the economic importance of university education, speaking of the ". . . necessity of Mexico to achieve high rates of intellectual investment in the formation of technicians, researchers, experts in administration . . . to foment . . . education for economic development."[25] With the government repression of student-led protests in 1968, most of the positive attitudes produced by the reform efforts of López Mateos and Díaz Ordaz disappeared.

President Echeverría, who had played a key role in the 1968 repression of the student movement, tried to resolve tensions between the university and the government in two main ways. First, Echeverría promised a political opening for university-educated intellectuals and professionals—and he did give some posts to highly educated friends and important intellectuals.[26] He also expanded

[24]For a narrative account of these student-state conflicts, see Mabry, *Student Conflicts*. For a more concise review, see Arthur Liebman, Kenneth N. Walker, and Myron Glazer, *Latin American University Students: A Six Nation Study* (Cambridge, MA: Harvard University Press, 1972), pp. 179-200.

[25]Quoted in Raúl Domínguez, *El proyecto universitario del rector Barros Sierra (estudio histórico)* (México, D. F.: Centro de Estudios sobre la Universidad, 1986), p. 118.

[26]Echeverría also greatly expanded press freedom (until 1976), giving intellectuals a greater voice, and released many political prisoners jailed during the railway strike of 1958 and the student unrest of 1968. In a direct move to curry favor with students and their sympathizers, Echeverría intervened on the side of students in a dispute at the Universidad

the grants program of CONACYT (Consejo Nacional de Ciencia y Tecnología), grants that allowed advanced Mexican students to study in the United States and Europe. Second, Echeverría supported the creation of new public institutions of higher education in an attempt to reduce the political power and influence of UNAM and IPN. The Universidad Autónoma Metropolitana (UAM) campuses, established in 1973, have concentrated on applied sciences, thus making up for a perceived deficiency in UNAM's production and placing UAM in direct competition with IPN. The creation of UAM considerably reduced the pressures of massification on the two public university giants in the capital during the 1970s.

At the same time, Echeverría did not seek to change the basic structure of the higher education system. Although his creation of a political opening had the effect of alleviating the tension remaining from 1968, Echeverría supported an open-door enrollment policy, increasing pressure on an already strained physical plant. His basic higher education policy, in fact, was one of greatly increasing public expenditure in the hope of creating enough jobs to satisfy aspirants to professional positions.[27]

Echeverría continued to emphasize the twin goals of professional training for economic advancement and university education as a form of social mobility:

> The contribution of education to development is obvious. It shows itself in the formation of qualified individuals, in the ability of a people to absorb and produce technological innovation and raise the level of productivity on the job. . . . Education also has direct effects on socio-economic mobility.[28]

Under Echeverría, technical schooling was given a boost in order to provide social mobility and to reduce pressure at the university level. In 1970, when Echeverría took office, there were 70 technical junior secondary schools in Mexico; by 1975 there were 581.[29] But the increase in opportunities at the secondary level would later, in fact, lead to increased pressure on the universities: graduates of secondary programs were not content to be technicians. Echeverría's at-

Autónoma de Nuevo León (June of 1970).

[27]In this connection, see "El progreso del país requiere que todos los técnicos tengan trabajo: Echeverría," *El Día,* July 23, 1971.

[28]Luis Echeverría quoted in Brooke, Oxenham, and Little, *Qualifications and Employment in Mexico,* p. 9.

[29]Brooke, Oxenham, and Little, *Qualifications and Employment in Mexico,* p. 10.

tempts in various fields to lay the basis for a "university of the masses" served to expand the system to massive proportions.

José López Portillo (1977-82), who presided over the oil boom of the late 1970s and early 1980s, did not have to use educational policy as a major policy tool to solve social and political problems. Whereas Echeverría had used educational reforms to patch up holes in the political fabric after the crisis of 1968, López Portillo was able to strengthen political alliances by forging agreements with the private sector—with the Alliance for Production and with a short period of austerity after Echeverría's spendthrift last years. After a year of austerity (1977), major oil finds were announced and revenue from petroleum exports flooded the treasury. The consequent hiring boom in both public and private sectors made the mismatch between the university system and society appear a less than immediate concern. The faith in a seemingly bottomless oil resource (and a ceilingless world price level for oil) led Mexican leaders to base the major economic development plan of the early 1980s—the Global Development Plan—squarely upon oil financing. University reform did not seem as urgent in the early 1980s as it had at the beginning of the 1970s.

The theme of university reform returned with the economic crisis of the 1980s. The universities themselves began an unprecedented process of self-criticism, with the major public universities releasing such documents as "The Strengths and Weaknesses of the UNAM," "Programs and Goals of the IPN, 1986-88," and the "Plan for Institutional Development" of the UAM system. In 1986, ANUIES, the national university association, introduced its ideas of necessary reforms in an "Integral Plan for the Development of Higher Education" (known by its Spanish acronym PROIDES).

Shortly after taking office, President de la Madrid introduced a policy to modernize higher education which had as its centerpiece the geographical decentralization of university opportunities, with costs shifted to the states. The university would be streamlined to match the new, "modernized" Mexican economy that would emerge with privatization and freer trade. The de la Madrid administration claimed that decentralization of opportunities would benefit both the professionals and the regional economies of the provinces, which had historically suffered from a lack of local higher educational opportunities. But the aim to decentralize higher educational costs ignored the fact that the states did not have the financial resources to fund a geographical substitution of higher-educational opportunities.[30]

As he attempted to reshape industrial production to make Mexico competitive in the world economy, de la Madrid reinforced the idea of the economic utility of university education. The universities were to be reformed because a Mexican economy truly competitive in the world market would need a great number of highly qualified professionals. This reform was developed in part by de la Madrid's secretary of planning, Carlos Salinas de Gortari, the architect of the legal basis for dismantling the state's involvement in the economy.

Salinas, who succeeded de la Madrid as president in 1988, carried forward the privatization and internationalization of the Mexican economy in an effort to restart sustained economic growth, seeking to open the traditionally closed economy. As he moved to free the economy from the state, from corruption, and from inefficiency, he took the same actions for the university system. Salinas stimulated private universities by various measures, including bringing large numbers of privately educated professionals into his administration. For the public universities, he established an informal system of incentives and penalties. Universities that supported government initiatives by tailoring their programs to government needs and orientations were rewarded with budgetary allocations that kept up with inflation; universities that encouraged advanced research in the right fields were granted special salary supports for active researchers.

Under Salinas, ideas for dramatic changes at the public universities never before openly discussed emerged into the policy arena— limiting the size of the student body, raising fees, seeking nongovernment sources of funding, and establishing closer ties with the needs of the business community. Many of these ideas resulted from close consultations with foreign education experts. In the potentially most far reaching move, Salinas's team suggested changes to Article 3 of the Constitution of 1917, which had guided education policy for over seventy years, to provide a legal framework for reform of the entire education system.

[30]On de la Madrid's educational policies, see Daniel Morales-Gómez and Carlos Alberto Torres, *The State, Corporatist Politics, and Educational Policy Making in Mexico* (New York: Praeger, 1990), pp. 70-74.

Trends in University Graduates, Egresados, and Degrees Registered since 1929

Quantitative data on the university system's primary function— producing graduates—provide a window both on the policymaking environment and on the economic development that informed that environment. Trends in the data allow us to establish the university system's response to the priorities of policymakers, the needs of the economy, and demands for social mobility.

This study introduces three basic data series on the output of Mexican universities. The development of professional and technical expertise by Mexican universities is measured by the number of persons who have:

1. received a licentiate degree,[31]
2. completed coursework for a licentiate degree but left the university without completing the required thesis or project for the degree (a person at this stage is called an *egresado*), or
3. registered a licentiate degree with the Mexican government.[32]

These three categories of university-trained persons (partially university-trained persons in the case of egresados) are used here as indicators of overall production of professional-level and technician-level skills by Mexican universities. The three series overlap in some years, making cross-checking possible and providing a way to assess the character and accuracy of each indicator.

The three series developed here reveal two important aspects of educating professionally skilled persons for economic development in Mexico. First, they reveal the number of professionals produced in a given year in specific areas of professional expertise. Second and more significant, the indicators represent evidence of career decisions made by students—decisions based on government rhetoric about the shape of the Revolution and actual employment opportunities created by the unfolding economic development process. This second aspect of the significance of the data used here makes necessary the incorporation of a six-year time lag (the lag between the time a student makes a career choice and his or her appearance as a

---

[31]The Mexican licentiate degree is roughly comparable to the Bachelor of Arts or Bachelor of Science degree in the United States, but more vocationally oriented.

[32]For further definition and discussion of these three indicators, see Chapter Three.

statistic) for analysis of long-term trends in the data.

Data on the degrees granted by Mexican universities allow us to analyze the 70-year period from 1900 to 1971. For the period from 1900 to 1927 data are aggregate thus making it impossible to discern year-to-year changes among career fields. In 1928, the data begin on a yearly basis and in 1940 the data become more detailed, allowing for more accurate analysis of shifts between fields.

The evidence of the first indicator of long-term trends in professional education (Table 1)[33] can be summarized as follows. The absolute number of professionals educated in the Revolution's early period was not striking. The number of professionals graduating from Mexican universities averaged approximately 300 per year between 1901 and 1927. But with the consolidation of political peace and the rebuilding of the economy in the late 1920s, the professional fields expanded quantitatively at a rapid rate. By 1940, the number of graduating university students had grown to more than three times the average for the years between 1901 and 1927.

Between 1928 and 1940, the basic pattern of field concentrations in degrees granted continued without radical change. Health, law, and engineering continued to account for almost nine-tenths of all university graduates. The only notable change in the period was seen in degrees for secondary-school and university teaching, which grew from a low average of 1.3 percent between 1930 and 1934 to an average of 8.1 percent between 1935 and 1939. The similarity in field concentrations to earlier patterns implies that little structural change in the Mexican economy occurred during the late 1920s or early 1930s.

Both the pace of quantitative growth in the number of professionals educated at Mexican universities and the relationship among professional fields changed dramatically around 1940. From an average of 570 between 1928 and 1934 and 977 under Cárdenas, the number of degrees granted yearly to graduating students climbed to 1,599 under Avila Camacho, to 2,176 under Alemán, to 3,405 under Ruiz Cortines, to 4,143 under López Mateos, and to 8,326 under Díaz Ordaz.

The quantitative expansion of degrees granted by Mexican universities after 1940 suggests that the universities responded to a sharply increased demand for professionals after the beginning of

[33]The statistical tables referred to in parentheses are found in Chapter Four below.

Mexico's industrial revolution. High growth rates through the end of the Second World War suggest that the number of graduating students increased rapidly as the Mexican economy expanded from the late 1930s through the mid-1940s.

After 1940 the dominance of the historically most important professional groups was sharply curtailed with the rise of business and the increasing importance of engineering. Health fell steadily from a high of almost 60 percent of all degrees in 1929 to a low of 21.4 percent in 1971. Law, which maintained a high average of almost 30 percent until 1940, saw its share decrease to less than half that share thereafter. While it is commonly thought that the legal profession remains the dominant profession in Mexico, it is clear from these data that law was never as important as medicine, and that as early as the 1950s law had fallen behind both medicine and engineering in importance. By 1971, business too overtook law in importance.

Of particular interest in the three decades after 1940 is the sudden quantitative takeoff of degrees granted in the business field after 1940. The yearly rate of growth of business was 13.0 percent for the period between 1940 and 1971, significantly higher than the 8.4 percent annual growth in all other fields. From under 6 percent of all degrees in 1941, business grew to 20.0 percent in 1971.[34]

The data imply that the process of economic development in Mexico underwent a major shift in orientation in the years just before 1940, and in response professional career fields shifted dramatically from the pattern established in the late nineteenth century. The mid-1960s saw the beginning of another very rapid overall quantitative expansion of the number of degrees granted and also of significant shifts among professional career fields. A significant shift in economic and social development left its mark in the data during the mid-1960s and can be dated roughly (taking into account a six-year time lag) to the late 1950s.

The series on university egresados (Tables 2 and 3) shows that in the two decades between 1967 and 1989, there was a dramatic quantitative expansion in the number of egresados as large numbers of students left Mexican universities having completed all coursework. The total number of egresados of all professional fields in-

[34]Compound rates of change calculated with the following formula: annual rate equals antilog of $(\log(P_n/P_0)/n)$, minus 1, where P_0 equals the original population and P_n equals the population after n years.

creased nine times during this short period. The data reveal two important trends in the period between 1967 and 1986. Egresados were leaving Mexican universities in large numbers although the rate at which they left decreased over the course of the period, from a high rate of 105.3 percent under Echeverría to a low of 22.4 percent under de la Madrid. At the same time, there was a remarkable stability in the relative importance of the numerically most significant fields—business, engineering, and health.

Summarizing the evidence on egresados, we can say that after 1970, in contrast to the earlier period between 1940 and 1970, the Mexican economy underwent no fundamental shifts in makeup or direction that in turn would stimulate shifts in the fields of professional study at Mexican universities. Field concentrations maintained the pattern set after the late 1950s. One key conclusion that can be derived from the egresados data is that the reaction on the part of universities to the student movement and repression of 1968, Mexico's most important post-1940 political crisis, was reflected in quantitative changes in enrollment and graduation rather than in relative shifts among professional fields.

Data on degrees registered (Tables 4 and 5) show that between 1970 and 1985, registrations of professional degrees grew particularly fast in three professional fields: health, engineering, and business. Law underwent a notable decline, from a high of 14.2 percent of all degrees registered in 1970 to a low at the end of the period of 6.3 percent.[35]

The data on degrees registered make clear the importance of public-sector employment in stimulating professional study in specific areas, for registration of a degree is necessary for employment in the public sector. The rapid quantitative expansion of degrees registered in the 1970s in good part reflects the rapid increase in public-sector hiring in that period. Engineering and health dominate the professional fields represented, and they are the two fields most in demand by government agencies involved in the provision of health care, public construction works, publicly owned or financed economic infrastructure, and parastatal industrial ventures. As shown above, the health and engineering professions are not as prominent in the other two data series.

Two trends span the entire period for which data have been de-

[35]See Chapter Three of this study for notes on the adoption of an appropriate time lag for Mexico.

veloped here. First there is the rapid rise to prominence of new fields such as business and engineering. Second, and simultaneous with this striking upward trend for new career areas, is the steady long-term decline of the traditionally most important career area in Mexico: law. Legal experts and health professionals together dominated Mexico's professional profile from the late nineteenth century to the late 1930s. By the mid-1980s, law claimed less than half of the share it held before 1940 and had fallen to fourth place behind business, engineering, and health in terms of relative importance.[36]

The key point of change within the course of these two trends came in the late 1930s. The nature of shifts among career fields appears to reflect shifts in the orientation of the course of economic development at that time, as business professionals and engineers rose to prominence afterward.[37]

Data on the number of professionally skilled Mexicans in the general population (Table 7) indicate that Mexican universities succeeded in producing professionals at a rate greater than the rate of population growth after 1929. Although dipping down to around the level of population growth in the late 1940s and 1950s, the overall growth rate far exceeded population growth over the period. This is a great accomplishment indeed given the extremely high rate of growth of the Mexican population in the years between 1940 and 1970.

Gaps between the different indicators of the development of professional expertise suggest a very significant trend (Tables 8 and 9): professional-level graduates have been outnumbered by technician-level degree-holders since the mid-1950s. Additionally, a ratio of at least two egresados for every degree registered has existed since the 1970s. These data imply that the Mexican economy has been creating relatively more positions at the lower technician level than at the upper professional level since at least the 1950s.

[36]Table 6 summarizes the long-term growth trends for all three indicators.

[37]Tables 10-18 in Chapter Four present data on professionals organized into social and economic areas of impact and detailed data on the engineering field. On the correlation between government policy priorities and professional fields, see Lorey, *The University System and Economic Development,* Chapter Three. On engineering, see Lorey, "The Development of Engineering Expertise for Economic and Social Modernization in Mexico since 1929," in James W. Wilkie, ed., *Society and Economy in Mexico,* pp. 71-102.

The identification of this trend provokes crucial questions about the structure of Mexican economic growth and the function of higher education in Mexico after 1929, topics to be examined at length in the following chapter.

Conclusions

Original time-series data on the number of graduates of Mexican universities and their fields of study reveal the basic quantitative dimensions of professional training in Mexico after 1929. The university system expanded rapidly to produce large numbers of graduates and egresados as Mexico entered a period of sustained economic growth by the 1940s that lasted well into the 1970s. The 1970s and 1980s saw dramatic leaps in the number of professionals leaving the university system and entering the job market.

At the same time that universities rapidly increased their output, there were important shifts in the field concentrations of graduates which reflected the changing policy emphases of Mexican presidential administrations. If the demand of Mexican leaders for professional expertise has been met to a significant degree, what of the demand expressed by the economy for professional skills? What sorts of professionals has the Mexican economy needed since 1929? And what has been the university's response to this demand?

The University System and Economic Development: Graduates and Employment

The Mexican university system has been accused by many observers of being unable to educate the professionals that the Mexican economy needs—both in specific fields and at different levels of expertise. The common perception has been that Mexican universities produce too many graduates of "traditional" fields (too many lawyers and not enough engineers and scientists) and too few graduates of high quality.[1] By the 1960s, such criticisms had become cen-

[1]See, for example, Frank Brandenburg, *The Making of Modern Mexico* (Englewood Cliffs: Prentice-Hall, 1964), pp. 240-241; Donald B. Keesing, "Structural Change Early in Development: Mexico's Changing Industrial and Occupational Structure from 1895 to 1950," *Journal of Economic History*, 29, no. 4 (December, 1969), 716-738; Peter Gregory, *The Myth of Market Failure: Employment and the Labor Market in Mexico* (Baltimore: Johns Hopkins University Press, 1986); José Angel Pescador Osuna, "El balance de la educación superior en el sexenio 1976-1982," in UAP, *Perspectivas de la educación superior en México* (Puebla: UAP, 1984), pp. 41-87; Howard F. Cline, *Mexico: Revolution to Evolution, 1940-1960* (New York: Oxford University Press, 1963), p. 204; Pablo Latapí, *Análisis de un sexenio de educación en México, 1970-1976* (México, D.F.: Editorial Nueva Imagen, 1980), pp. 207-208; María Esther Ibarra, "Decide la SEP que se encojan las universidades," *Proceso*, September 29, 1986, p. 19; Noel F. McGinn and Susan L. Street, *Higher Education Policies in Mexico* (Austin: Institute of Latin American Studies, University of Texas at Austin, 1980), p. 1. The Mexican press is full of articles claiming alternately that the university produces "too many" and "too few" professionals in certain fields: see, for example, Deirdre Fretz, "Wanted: Engineers," *Mexico Journal*, November 13, 1989, pp. 25-26; Isabel Llinas Zárate, "La universidad ha cumplido con creces después de la revolución: Luis E. Todd," *Unomásuno*, January 28, 1990, p. 2; "México necesita 300 mil profesionistas por año, para asegurar su crecimiento," *Ocho Columnas*

tral to perceptions of a "university crisis"; by the 1970s, voices in both public and private sectors were calling for closer cooperation between the universities and the economy.[2]

In this chapter I suggest that the logic of this standard view is flawed. Contrary to the generally accepted wisdom, the equation works the other way around: the Mexican economy has been unable to provide enough professional-level jobs for university graduates since at least the late 1950s. Because it cannot shape the job market for professionals, the university system has had to adapt itself to a historical reality of increasingly scarce opportunities for graduates in relative terms.

Issues of supply and demand are approached here by examining available data on the Mexican economy's expressed need for university graduates and trends in the university system's production of graduates in specifc fields and at specific levels of expertise. The evolution of Mexico's occupational structure in the twentieth century provides clues to the nature of the relationship between the university system and the economy and sheds light on how this relationship has changed over time.

Mexico's Changing Occupational Structure

It is surprising that few scholars have concerned themselves with the occupations of Mexicans in the twentieth century. Few underlying structures of every day life are more important in social and political terms than how people are employed, at which levels and within which economic sectors. What have been the most important historical changes in what Mexicans do for their livings, and what do these changes imply about Mexican economic development in the twentieth century?

While shifts of the Mexican labor force among economic sectors have been much studied, and we know that there has been a long-term trend from employment in agriculture to employment in indus-

(Guadalajara, Jalisco), October 15, 1989; "Mexican Higher Education Degrees," translation of article from *La Jornada,* October 6, 1989, in *U.S.-Mexico Report* 8, no. 11 (November, 1989), p. 12; and Mario García Sordo, "Desempleados o subempleados, más de 90 mil agrónomos," *El Financiero,* October 5, 1988, p. 39.

[2]See, for example, "El sector educativo debe preparar cuadros técnicos acorde con las necesidades del país: CANACINTRA," *Unomásuno,* June 26, 1987, p. 14.

try and services,[3] little is known about historical changes in the hierarchy of occupations. Data developed for this study from the Mexican census are presented here in condensed graphic form to give an at-a-glance view of basic twentieth-century trends in Mexican occupational structure.[4] While data in the statistical tables provide comprehensive coverage for the period from 1900 to 1980, the focus here is on the period from 1950 through 1980, for which data are both more reliable and easier to arrange into comparable sets.

Figure 1 shows that in the period between 1950 and 1980 the percentage of professionals and technicians in Mexican economically active population (EAP) grew from 2.5 percent to 7.4 percent.

Figure 1.   Professionals, Technicians, and Managers in Economically Active Population, 1950-80

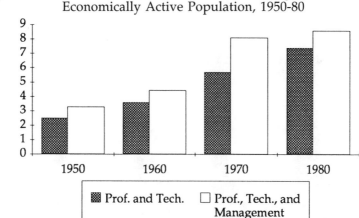

SOURCE: Table 22.

Combining the percentage of persons in the management of public- and private-sector enterprises with professionals and technicians, we get a rough figure for all professionals in EAP of 3.3 in 1950, 4.5 in 1960, 8.1 in 1970, and 8.6 in 1980. Whichever of these

[3]See Table 19. Considerable study has also been devoted to questions of unemployment and underemployment in Mexico. See Donald B. Keesing, "Employment and Lack of Employment in Mexico, 1900-70," in James W. Wilkie and Kenneth Ruddle, eds., *Quantitative Latin American Studies* (Los Angeles: UCLA Latin American Center Publications, 1977), pp. 3-21; and Gregory, *The Myth of Market Failure.*
[4]For 1980, I refer to the estimated totals in Table 22. For notes on the interpretation of census data on occupational level, see Chapter Three below.

measures we take as most accurate, the share of all professionals in Mexican society doubled in the course of the 30-year period in question.

There are two ways to disaggregate the data to examine more closely professionals and the sectors of their activity. Figure 2 presents data on the percentage distribution of professionals among different economic sectors. (The primary economic sector includes agriculture, livestock, and forestry; the secondary sector includes mining, industry, construction, and electricity; the tertiary sector includes transportation, commerce, services, and government.) It is no surprise that professionals are located overwhelmingly in service occupations. It is noteworthy, however, that, as more professionals entered industry, the share of professionals in services declined in the thirty years between 1950 and 1980, from 81.2 in 1950, to 68.6 in 1960, to 72.2 in 1970, to 63.9 in 1980.

Figure 2.   Professionals and Technicians in Services and
              Manufacturing, 1950-80
              (Percent of All Professionals and Technicians)

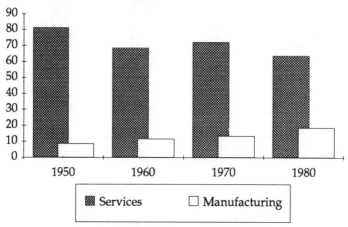

SOURCE: Table 22.

Data on the percentage share of professionals of all EAP within two key economic sectors are presented in Figure 3. While the percentage of professionals in all sectors grew steadily from 2.5 percent in 1950 to 7.4 percent in 1980 (as noted above), professionals in ser-

vices remained almost level as a share of all EAP in services between 1950 and 1970, at an average below 20 percent, and then
jumped to 25.9 percent in 1980. The growth of the share of professionals and technicians in the manufacturing sector grew rapidly
over the same period, from less than 2 percent of all EAP in 1950 to
more than 9 percent in 1980.[5]

Figure 3.   Professionals in All Economic Sectors, in Manufacturing,
             and in Services, 1950-80
             (Percent of Economically Active Population in Each Sector)

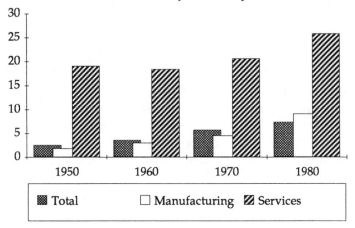

SOURCE: Table 23.

The Demand of the Mexican Economy for University Graduates

The simplest way to measure the relationship between changing
demand for professionals in the Mexican economy and university
production of professionals is to compare data on the sectoral distribution of professionals and technicians within the economically active population (EAP) with data on university graduates.[6] If
Mexican universities respond sluggishly and inefficiently to changes
in employment opportunities for graduates, then there should be an
obvious lack of adjustment between changes in professional employ-

[5]For data on professionals employed in the public sector (by field), see
Table 29.
[6]The comparison can be made too simply. See Latapí, *Análisis de un
sexenio*, pp. 207-208.

ment in EAP and shifts in career-field concentrations. On the other hand, if the universities' education of professionals has historically followed the lead of the economy, then EAP and university output should match relatively closely over time.

Professionals can be organized into primary, secondary, and tertiary economic sectors by using sample professions as indicators of the different sectors (Table 24). The primary economic sector (agriculture) is represented in the tables by agricultural engineering; the secondary sector (mining, industry, construction, and electricity) is represented by engineering fields other than agricultural engineering; the tertiary sector (transportation, commerce, services, and government) is represented by business, health, economics, and law. [7]

Comparison of the data on EAP by economic sector (Table 24) and university education (Tables 25 and 26) reveals a strikingly close fit between the evolution of professional EAP and the general career areas of professionals. Data on both professional employment and university output, for example, show that there has been a long-term decline in the share of professionals employed in the tertiary, or services, sector. While the share of professionals employed in this sector declined from 81.2 percent in 1950 to 63.9 percent in 1980 (as noted above), university graduates in sample fields in the services sector fell from 91.5 percent of degrees granted in 1950 to 81.4 percent of egresados and 72.7 percent of degrees registered in 1980. Data on university graduates confirm that this decline in relative importance of the services sector was due principally to a rise in the percentage of professionals educated and employed in the secondary, or industrial, sector. Training of professionals for the primary sector and professional employment in that sector show a rise from 1950 to 1960 and a gradual decline thereafter.

These data shed light on demand and supply for general areas of professional expertise: What about demand for university graduates in specific professional fields? A straightforward way to gauge demand for specific professional skills is to examine the employment of professionals with that skill. Detailed data on occupational structure in the 1950 and 1980 censuses allow comparison between employment of professionals in basic professional fields and university graduates and egresados (graduates in 1950, egresados in 1980) in those fields.

[7]For a detailed breakdown of professionals included in the three sectors, see Chapter Four below.

A comparison of data on employment and data on the fields of study of university graduates (Table 27) shows that the fit between fields such as engineering, health, law, and teaching was close in 1950 and remained close in 1980. The data actually indicate a closing of the gap by 1980: the university system has apparently become increasingly in tune with employment opportunities in the Mexican economy over time. This comparison bears out the conclusions drawn from the above comparison of EAP and university graduates in three broad economic sectors.

The close fit between these two data sets is extremely significant. It indicates a long-term confluence between the demand expressed by the Mexican economy for professionals to fill certain occupational niches in the economy and university production of professionals in the needed fields. The implicit cooperation between the university system and the employers of professionals has not grown worse in the period from 1950 to 1980. The data suggest that signals about the field distribution of job opportunities are available to students and are relatively accurate. (Until recently few Mexican universities have had career counseling programs.) The economy's demand appears to be clear, and students career choices appear to be in line with that demand.[8] This conclusion contrasts sharply with dominant conceptions of the university-economy nexus and of a university crisis.

The Demand for Technicians versus Professionals

In addition to its demand for general areas and specific fields of professional expertise, the economy expresses needs for different *levels* of expertise. The major division to be considered here is that between professionals and technicians, both of which groups are increasingly trained at the university level in Mexico. In this study, I employ two definitions of professionals and technicians, one based on function in the workplace, the other based on the structure of the Mexican education system.

In the context of the workplace, a professional is a person equipped with both general knowledge and the ability to apply this knowledge to change the production or management environment by increasing productivity, introducing innovations, or spreading attitudes and techniques. A technician's main function in the

[8]Data on the state of Nuevo León allow us to consider the relationship on a regional level (Table 28).

workplace, in contrast, is to apply specific techniques learned through the educational process. With regard to the university, "professionals" are graduates with a licentiate or higher degree. (See below, however, where I suggest that over time a growing portion of degree-holders have found it necessary to work as technicians.) "Technicians" are graduates of upper secondary, non-college preparatory courses, those students who leave the university system by way of a "lateral exit" or "short course" of study, and the portion of egresados of university careers that never achieves the licentiate degree.[9]

The difference between professionals and technicians is not to be confused with differences in economic sector of employment: sector is not the same as occupational level.[10] Intersectoral shifts in EAP are highly misleading if used to gauge historical shifts in the level of occupations of the work force. A close examination of census categories shows that a very large proportion of workers in communications, commerce, and industry, for example, have always been self-employed mule-drivers, shopkeepers, and artisans.[11] These are clearly not "professionals" by the definitions employed here. (The most difficult category to analyze is services. Clearly, many service occupations are not "modern sector" jobs but rather domestic workers of various types, as well as sellers of Kleenex and Chiclets on street corners. Shifts from occupations in agriculture to jobs in services and industry—the so-called modern sectors—do not necessarily indicate rapid growth of professional occupational niches.)

What has been the relationship *between* employed professionals and technicians over time? This relationship is of the first importance because the ratio between the two groups, and how that ratio

[9]For further discussion of these working definitions, see Chapter Three below.

[10]Many analysts equate sectoral distribution and occupational structure: see, for example, A. J. Jaffe, *People, Jobs, and Economic Development: A Case History of Puerto Rico Supplemented by Recent Mexican Experiences* (Glencoe, Il: The Free Press of Glencoe Illinois, 1959), p. 109 and passim; and Jorge A. Padua, "Movilidad social y universidad," in Gilberto Guevara Niebla, *La crisis de la educación superior en México* (México, D.F.: Nueva Imagen, 1981), pp. 131-132.

[11]For an early analysis, see Frank Tannenbaum, *Mexico: The Struggle for Peace and Bread* (Englewood Cliffs: Prentice-Hall, 1950), pp. 195-196 (analysis of 1940 census data). For an analysis of shifts in the services sector and what they mean, see Gregory, *The Myth of Market Failure*, Appendix to Chapter One.

has evolved over time, reveals a great deal about the nature of economic development in Mexico since 1929. The history of the developed economies is characterized in general by the creation over time of large numbers of positions at the professional level in both absolute and relative terms.[12]

While both professionals and technicians have made up an increasing part of Mexico's economically active population since 1950 (as indicated in the data discussed above), census data for 1950 and 1980 reveal that the two levels have not grown at the same rate. The data imply that Mexican economic development has created a differentially greater demand for technicians compared to professionals over time (Table 30). While positions for professionals grew 417.8 percent between 1950 and 1980, those for technicians grew 1,055.3 percent, annual rates of 5.6 and 8.5 percent.[13]

The Mexican economy has thus developed in a way that has led to limited job creation at a very important level of the occupational ladder. And the absorption of professionals is, if anything, overestimated in the census data because the data reflect to some extent the supply of professionals as well as demand.[14] That is, because the census is based on informants' responses, some university graduates will call themselves professional even though they are not working as professionals.

We can compare the rates of growth for employment positions for professionals and technicians in the census data with the rates

[12]Ideally, of course, numerous technicians should be educated to support each professional. But the ratio in Mexico by 1980 seems unusually large. The ratio in the United States in 1985 was 1.5 technicians for each professional, whereas that for Mexico (as determined above) was almost twice that at 2.7 to 1 in 1980. See *Statistical Abstract of the United States, 1987*, pp. 385-386. For a brief sketch of the U.S. case, see the discussion of John K. Folger and Charles B. Nam, "Education of the American Population," in Ivar Berg, *Education and Jobs: The Great Training Robbery* (Boston: Beacon Press, 1971), pp. 66-68.

[13]Compound rates of change calculated with the following formula: annual rate equals antilog of $(\log(P_n/P_0)/n)$, minus 1, where P_0 equals the original population and P_n equals the population after n year. The census data do not allow for calculation of implicit annual growth rates of professional and technician EAP by decade.

[14]It is probably impossible to ascertain the extent of overlap in the case of Mexico given available data. It is not easy to ascertain even in the case of the United States, with the availability of rich statistical resources. See Folger and Nam, "Education of the American Population," in Berg, *Education and Jobs*, pp. 66-67.

of production of professionals at Mexican universities (Table 31). Between 1950 and 1960, the number of degrees granted in all professional fields grew 75.1 percent; between 1960 and 1970, the number of degrees granted grew 232.1 percent. Between 1970 and 1980 the number of egresados grew 267.9 percent, while degrees registered grew 149.1 percent.

The growth rate of degrees granted was matched fairly closely by the growth rate of professionals until 1960. Between 1950 and 1980 the annual growth rate of professional EAP was 5.6 percent compared to 5.8 percent for degrees granted between 1950 and 1960. Between 1960 and 1970, however, the number of degrees granted grew at an annual rate of 12.4 percent. The annual rate of growth of degrees granted for the entire period from 1950 to 1970 was 9.0 percent.

By the 1960s, the universities were clearly producing graduates at a rate well above the rate of job creation for professionals in the Mexican economy. The number of degrees registered grew at an annual rate of 11.0 percent between 1975 and 1980, very close to the growth experienced by degrees granted in the 1960s.[15] The growth rate of egresados, in contrast, was significantly higher than that of either degrees granted or degrees registered and thus seems to reflect the higher growth of positions for technicians. While the number of positions for technicians in EAP grew at an annual rate of 8.5 percent between 1950 and 1980, egresados grew at an average annual rate of 13.9 percent between 1967 and 1980.

The data thus indicate that employment for technicians grew much more rapidly than for professionals after 1950. The growth rates of technicians and professionals in EAP were mirrored in the growth rates of egresados and degrees granted and registered. It seems clear that the major difference between university egresados and university degree holders in the job market is that egresados are more likely than graduates with degrees to be employed at the technician level.

Analysis of various data sets on professionals and technicians points to four general conclusions. First, the ability of the Mexican economy to absorb university graduates at the professional level has not grown as fast as the number of university students entering pro-

---

[15]It is necessary to restrict consideration to the 1975-80 period for registrations because changes in regulations caused a major surge in degrees registered between 1974 and 1975.

fessional courses of study. Second, the demand for technicians has grown at a much faster rate than that for professionals. Third, the universities have produced both professionals and technicians at rates significantly greater than the rate of job creation. Fourth, the mismatch between demand and output and the differentially greater demand for technicians than for professionals appears to have been particularly marked since the late 1950s.

The data allow us to sketch the long-term trends. Until the late 1950s, the expanding industrial and commercial sectors, and the growing state apparatus, absorbed the bulk of the universities' production of professionals relatively easily. The perception of observers in the late 1950s that there was a shortage of engineers, business managers, highly skilled workers, and scientists was generally correct.[16] Demand for engineers and business managers was especially high as government policy focused economic development efforts on industrialization and the modernization of commercial networks. The fact that many persons working at the technician and lower occupational levels were promoted to professional positions implies a vacuum at the professional level during this period.[17]

Government employment of professionals accounted for a large part of the professional employment boom from the time of the institutionalization of the Revolution in 1929 forward. Professional employment in the public sector received its first real boost with the rise of the active state in the late 1920s and in the 1930s under Cárdenas. The expansion of state employment benefited a broad cross section of Mexican society, but particularly the professionally trained offspring of the growing middle sectors. The infrastructure projects of the early years of Mexico's economic revolution—land distribution, banking, transportation, and irrigation and the establishment of myriad government agencies and enterprises—required a great many skilled persons for management and direction. The public sector needed professionals with experience in "modern production engineering, in the careful computation of costs and returns, in market analysis, in the scientific appraisal of alternative opportu-

[16]See Brandenburg, *The Making of Modern Mexico*, pp. 232-233; and Clark Reynolds, *The Mexican Economy: Twentieth-Century Structure and Growth* (New Haven and London: Yale University Press, 1970), pp. 236-238.

[17]See William P. Glade, "Revolution and Economic Development: A Mexican Reprise," in William P. Glade and Charles W. Anderson, *The Political Economy of Mexico* (Madison: University of Wisconsin Press, 1963), pp. 87-88.

nities."[18] The demand for professionals for public-sector banking services was an important stimulus to professional education, for example, as the government established a string of credit institutions to finance economic development between 1935 and 1957.

Since the late 1950s, there has been a decline in the ability of the economy to produce jobs for professionals at the rate that students have been leaving the universities. This decline in professional hiring relative to the supply of university graduates and egresados is seen both in the census data and in data on the number of university graduates. Increasing numbers of university graduates and egresados had to find work not as professionals but as technicians. By the 1970s, the reduced ability of the economy to produce professional jobs led to overt government concern under President Echeverría. Echeverría attempted to stimulate the direct creation of employment at the professional level in the private sector and at the same time greatly expanded public-sector job opportunities for university graduates.[19]

The post-1950 trend of increasingly depressed demand for professionals as compared to technicians is related to three main characteristics of the historical development of the Mexican economy that shaped professional employment in the public and private sectors. These three factors, and others of less importance, worked in concert to influence major changes in the university system's functioning after the late 1950s.

First, employment opportunities for professionals were restricted by historically high levels of protection of Mexican industry. Protection of manufacturing concerns had its roots in the Porfiriato; protection under the Institutionalized Revolution began in earnest in the late 1930s and increased rapidly and steadily until the mid-1980s. Mexican industries received a wide range of protective covers, particularly overvalued exchange rates from the early 1940s through 1954, quantitative control of imports thereafter, and generous tax breaks and implicit subsidies throughout. The employment-

[18]Glade, "Revolution and Economic Development," pp. 45-47.

[19]This basic trend in the employment opportunities for professionals is partially related to the general inability by the 1960s of the Mexican economy to create jobs at the rate of population growth. Unemployment at all levels rose, although it is difficult to ascertain rates of unemployment by occupation owing to the nature of census and other official data. See Robert E. Looney, *Mexico's Economy: A Policy Analysis with Forecasts to 1990* (Boulder: Westview Press, 1978), p. 61.

creating effects of the dynamic economic growth after 1940, growth which was engendered by such protective policies, were much diminished by the 1970s, a fact reflected in Echeverría's stopgap attempts to slow decreasing employment at the professional level.

Protection from domestic and international competition allowed Mexican industry to produce goods with outmoded equipment, minimal investment for research and development, and limited innovation: protection limited the need for new technology and associated professional knowledge.[20] Limited spending for research and development restricted job creation in a key area of professional employment. The use of outmoded technology, and the reliance for economic growth during the 1940s and 1950s on increased utilization of installed capacity idle up to the late 1930s, greatly reduced both the number of professionals needed by the economy and the level of professional training at the universities. Most of the technology used in industrial plants in the 1980s continued to be obsolete or lag behind state-of-the-art innovations.[21]

A second factor that restricted employment opportunities for professionals was the importation of capital goods and thus technology for industrial expansion. Importation of professional expertise embodied in foreign-made machines constricted employment opportunities for Mexican professionals. For technology in industry is not an independent, abstract body of knowledge held by professionals but rather a function of machines and their development. Capital-goods industries have a much greater relative need for professional-level employees than other manufacturing firms.

The reliance of Mexican industry on imported capital goods meant historically that the primary stimulus to professional education took place in the countries that produced advanced capital goods for domestic use and for export. Because a capital-goods industry developed haltingly in Mexico, it should not be surprising that Mexican universities have not educated the large numbers of graduate-level experts in science and technology associated with advanced, competitive economies. They have not been needed by the

---

[20]Frank Tannenbaum early recognized this relationship in Mexico. See his *Mexico*, p. 198.

[21]"La investigación tecnológica, en crisis," *Unomásuno*, January 29, 1990, p. 3, claims that 92 percent of Mexican businesses, both public and private, possess obsolete machinery.

Mexican productive apparatus.[22]

Such impacts of the protection of industry and dependency on imported capital goods on professional employment are apparent, to give just one example, in the case of the textile industry of Mexico, particularly the cotton textile industry concentrated in the states of Puebla and Veracruz. Because of protection from competing imports and oligopolistic access to the domestic market, the Mexican textile industry was able to operate profitably with pre-Revolutionary equipment imported from Europe and little innovation in production or management up through the 1960s.[23] Protection, along with other factors, meant that a strong incentive to reinvestment in research and development or in physical plant did not exist.[24] Because of these factors, textile manufacturing in Mexico did not lead to the development of a textile machine industry which would in turn have provided demand for machine-tool and specialty-steel industries.[25] (The concomitant sluggish growth of the textile engineering field, to be expected in such a situation, can be seen in Tables 14-18.)

A third factor which increasingly limited the employment of professionals after the late 1950s was the pattern of government employment of university graduates. Public-sector employment of pro-

[22]The author of "La investigación tecnológica, en crisis," *Unomásuno*, January 29, 1990, p. 3, claims that ten times as much is invested to import capital goods than is invested in research in Mexico. Little scholarly work has been done on the relationship between the production of capital goods and demands for professional expertise in Mexico; the best study for Latin America is that of Nathaniel H. Leff, *The Brazilian Capital Goods Industry, 1929-1964* (Cambridge, MA: Harvard University Press, 1968), especially pp. 41-87. For an interesting analysis of the relationship between technological development and economic growth in Mexico, see Centro de Investigación para el Desarrollo, A. C. (CIDAC), *Tecnología e industria en el futuro de México: Posibles vinculaciones estratégicas* (México, D. F.: Editorial Diana, 1989). See also Anne Lorentzen, *Capital Goods and Technological Development in Mexico* (Copenhagen: Centre for Development Research, 1986), especially pp. 13, 14.

[23]Protection of the textile industry has a long history in Mexico. For its development during the early years after Independence, see Robert A. Potash, *Mexican Government and Industrial Development in the Early Republic: The Banco de Avío* (Amherst: University of Massachusetts Press, 1983).

[24]Lack of investment and reinvestment was also due to lack of investor confidence during the violent phase of the Revolution and during the depressed 1925-32 period. Lack of new investment or reinvestment was common in many industries besides textile manufacturing. See Stephen H. Haber, *Industry and Underdevelopment: The Industrialization of Mexico, 1890-1940* (Stanford: Stanford University Press, 1989).

[25]Haber, *The Industrialization of Mexico*, p. 193.

fessionals has always shaped general demand for university graduates and university training in Mexico, as shown above. And much of the increase in Mexico's professional and technician EAP since the late 1930s occurred in state or parastatal agencies and firms, the number of which mushroomed after the 1950s. In both centralized and decentralized sectors, the government has acted since the late 1950s as a sponge for absorbing professionals produced by the universities but not needed in the private sector, and perhaps not really needed in the public sector. Over time, the government has grown into the largest employer of university graduates and egresados. The state's importance as a first employer of professionals who later find employment in the private sector is also very great.

The rapid expansion of the public sector since the 1930s was driven in part by the need to create jobs for professionals from middle-sector backgrounds. The growth of public-sector hiring of professionals reached a peak in the late 1970s and early 1980s; public-sector employment exploded by 82 percent between 1975 and 1983. By 1983, public-sector employees accounted for 20.4 percent of all Mexican employees.[26] Many state industries and agencies had limited real needs for the skills of highly trained professionals. Increasing state employment produced the illusion of rapidly growing professional cadres, when, in fact, the level of skills really needed was significantly lower than appearances suggested. Demand for professional degrees increased while the need for high-level professional skills probably stagnated. This mismatch is reflected in the differential demand for professionals and technicians since the late 1950s already discussed.

The absorption of large numbers of professionals into the workplace from the late 1930s through the 1950s did not indicate the beginning of indefinitely expanding employment opportunities for professionals. This earlier phase of employment expansion was itself illusory in good part. Increases in production and employment were due principally to increased utilization of idle capacity.[27] Because there was little change in the nature of the machinery used and little increase in expenditure for research and development, the em-

[26]See Instituto Nacional de Estadística, Geografía e Informática (INEGI), *Participación del sector público en el producto interno bruto de México, 1975-1983* (México, D. F.: Secretaría de Programación y Presupuesto (SPP), 1984), p. 5.

[27]Clark Reynolds, *The Mexican Economy*, passim; and Jaffe, *People, Jobs, and Economic Development*, p. 269.

ployment of professionals underwent no dramatic qualitative change.[28]

Limited real demand for professionals reflects the uncompetitive, inefficient nature of Mexican industry and its reliance on the Mexican government for protection and on foreign capital-goods producers for technological innovation.[29] It is thus the historical pattern of economic development that has limited demand for professionals, not any absolute lack of professionals, or relative lack of professionals in specific fields, that has limited economic development.[30]

Analysts of the Mexican economy have tended to confuse growing employment in "modern" sectors of the economy since 1940 with a "modern" occupational profile. Although the modern sectors of Mexico's economy may have expanded, that expansion was characterized by the continuation of rather traditional needs for professional skills. This continuity implies that the Mexican economy, although highly developed in some aspects, has not achieved a self-sustained development characterized by innovation and competitiveness. It was possible to develop in key ways—the economy has clearly grown, become more diversified, and changed structurally—without creating an independent capital-goods and research and development infrastructure. And without the development of a self-sustaining capital-goods industry and domestic research and development networks, opportunities for professionals were severely limited.[31]

[28]For a recent review of these issues, see *The Economist*, January 4, 1992, pp. 15-18.

[29]The reasons why a self-sustaining and competitive Mexican industry did not develop can be traced to the dynamic of the first wave of industrialization in Mexico, 1890-1940. Stephen Haber suggests that constraints such as a low rates of capacity utilization, low productivity of labor, and difficulties in mobilizing capital led to a manufacturing sector that could not export competitively, needed a great deal of protection, and relied heavily upon imported capital goods. See Haber, *The Industrialization of Mexico*.

[30]It is all too common to assert the opposite without evidence from the historical record: see, for example, José de Jesús Guardarrama H., "México necesita multiplicar 20 veces su número de ingenieros antes de 25 años," *El Financiero*, April 19, 1988, p. 53 (Guadarrama reports on comments of Daniel Reséndiz, director of UNAM's engineering faculty).

[31]It is this relationship between Mexico's economic development and opportunities for professionals that makes untenable most arguments that a brain drain of professionals has slowed Mexico's development. (For a typical statement of this argument, see Matt Moffett, "Brain Drain Slows Mexico's

While it is clear that the proportion of professional and technician labor increased in the Mexican economy between 1950 and 1980, then, this general trend obscures the differential growth of technicians within the group. While GDP grew rapidly during the 1960s (7.0 percent per year) and 1970s (6.6 percent a year), employment for professionals did not increase at a similar rate. Economic, social, and political stresses have arisen from this aspect of Mexico's economic development that were not foreseen by optimistic observers of the "Mexican Miracle." And in looking back, analysts have inaccurately attributed these stresses to the internal faults of the university system rather than to the pattern of Mexico's economic development.

Impacts of Changing Demand for Professionals and Technicians

How did historically changing demand for professionals and technicians affect Mexican universities? The university system's most significant response (discussed above) was to produce a small number of graduates to fill the need for the most highly qualified professionals and a much larger number of egresados to fill the need for technicians. The government's emphasis on increasing enrollment capacities at public universities in the 1940s and 1950s thus paid off in an ironic way: it made possible the university system's twin roles of training professionals and technicians.

Two other important impacts of the economy's evolving demand are seen in changes in the quality of professional education and the deconcentration of the university system. By producing very different sorts of graduates, public and private universities acted together in responding to the economy's demand for university graduates and egresados. A "system" of public and private universities evolved after the 1940s as the two types of institutions came to feed different labor markets.

Data on the deconcentration of the university system are pre-

Development: Researchers, Professionals, Skilled Workers Are Lured Abroad," *Wall Street Journal*, May 5, 1989, p. A10.) Ironically, it is Mexico's historical economic development, with its restricted opportunities for betterment at the professional level, that has caused the flight of professionals toward opportunities abroad. See David Lorey, "Mexican Professional Education in the United States and the Myth of 'Brain Drain'," *Ensayos* (Revista del Departamento de Relaciones Internacionales, Universidad de las Américas-Puebla), 4, no. 9 (1988), 56-59.

sented in Tables 41-48. (In the following discussion I use the term
"deconcentration" rather than decentralization to emphasize the
declining importance of the historically largest and oldest institutions as opposed to trends in geographical location or financial status of universities.) During the period until 1938, UNAM and IPN
dominated all aspects of professional training—they were the
largest institutions of higher education and at the same time they
were closely associated with government plans for development.
After the late 1950s, the preeminence of these two institutions was
greatly eroded.

Data on the share held by the 14 most important public and private universities in the period give a sense of rapidly advancing
diversity and deconcentration of the whole system (Table 45; see
also Tables 41-48). The trend toward increasing diversity and deconcentration away from the largest and oldest institutions was the
case with both public and private universities. The data also reveal that there was a noticeable shift at the end of the 1950s away
from public institutions and toward private universities and provincial public universities.[32]

A secular leveling-off of quality at Mexican universities was the
second most important result of the changing demand of the economy
and was closely related to deconcentration (Tables 32-40). Data
series developed here from existing statistical sources rely on three
ways to gauge quality at the university level: (1) per-student expenditure on higher education; (2) teacher-student ratios; and (3) ratios of full-time faculty to teaching staff hired on an hourly basis.
These three indicators form a very useful, if imperfect, gauge of
quality.[33]

The data indicate that although a "crisis" in quality has not
occurred in Mexican higher education, there was a leveling-off of increases in quality in the 1940s and a gradual decline in quality after
the late 1950s, with significant upturns in the late 1970s and early

[32]Because of these trends, it is no longer desirable to focus analysis on
UNAM, viewing it as a microcosm of the Mexican university system or of
the experience of Mexican university students.

[33]For a discussion of quality at Latin American universities and its
measurement, see Arthur Liebman, Kenneth N. Walker, and Myron
Glazer, *Latin American University Students: A Six Nation Study* (Cambridge,
MA: Harvard University Press, 1972), pp. 68-78. The authors emphasize the
importance of teachers and the quality of instruction received by students
(pp. 74-78).

1980s. Changes in quality thus mirror the timing of changes in the Mexican economy and in its demand for professionals and technicians. It cannot be concluded that growth in student enrollment caused low quality in education received by Mexican public university students, as is often asserted. The overcrowding which is often blamed for declines in quality is a matter of financial support in Mexico, not the sign of a student population which is "too large" in any objective sense.[34]

Within the general trends of changes in quality, important differences exist between public and private universities, with private institutions attaining a higher level of quality before the 1980s (Table 40). These differences are determined primarily by two main factors: (1) the demand of private-sector and certain public-sector employers for the highest quality professionals that could not be met by the public university system alone, and (2) the tighter market for professionals compared to that for technicians.

The demand in the private sector, and at the highest level of the public sector, for high-quality professionals grew faster than quality at the public universities after the late 1950s (expenditure and teaching staff did not keep pace with growing enrollment). Private universities expanded rapidly to fill the gap. At the same time, public and private institutions came to satisfy the needs for different levels of expertise. Graduates of private universities increasingly filled the need for top-level professionals in Mexico while the public universities, particularly the public universities of the provinces, produced large numbers of graduates and egresados who found work primarily as technicians. Quality declined at many public institutions, then, in response to the economy's demand for different levels of skills. Public and private universities came to be driven by qualitatively different labor markets but functioned relatively efficiently together to meet the economy's needs.

The deconcentration of the Mexican university system and important changes in quality after the 1950s coincided with the shift in the economy's demand for professionals and technicians toward a relatively greater demand for technicians. Public and private universities played different but complementary roles in the process of deconcentration. The development of the regional public universities served to partially relieve the tremendous pressure on the public

---

[34]See Olac Fuentes Molinar, "Universidad y democracia: La mirada hacia la izquierda," *Cuadernos Políticos*, 53 (January-April, 1981), 4-18.

university giants in the Federal District by keeping a good part of increased demand for higher educational opportunities confined to the provinces. Private universities concentrated their resources on producing high-quality graduates for top-level professional jobs.

The University System and Social Mobility

After the 1950s, social demand came into ever greater conflict with the reality of Mexico's historical economic development (Tables 49-54; contrast Tables 21, 22, 30, 31, 51, 53, and 54). Eventually, as the process of economic development created a progressively smaller relative number of jobs at the professional level, the university's ability to provide social mobility was limited by the relatively reduced opportunities for professionals.

While universities did have a positive effect on social mobility until at least 1960 through their role in preparing students for professional occupations, after that time university production of egresados and graduates outpaced economic development. Large and increasing numbers of university graduates had to find work not as professionals but as technicians after the 1950s. My data show that the number of university graduates has exceeded the number of economic and social places for professionals by a factor of more than two.

The university system evolved to meet the challenge of changing demand for professionals, adapting to the social circumstances brought by economic development after the late 1950s. As the possibility of social mobility decreased, public universities opened their doors to entrants from working-class backgrounds (Tables 55-57).[35]

After the late 1950s, the public university system adopted the function of providing social status rather than social mobility to many university students. While public universities took over the task of providing social status to students of humble backgrounds, private universities came to focus on the reinforcement of middle- and upper-class status through the provision of high-level professionals to both the public and the private sector. It is the opening at the bottom and the function of providing social status that have determined the historical inability of the public university to keep up with the quality demands of the economy. The government subsidy to the public university system has been spent on supporting

[35]Data on women professionals in Mexico presented in Tables 58-64.

huge entering classes and providing the maximum number of university places for the first few years of university education.

The adaptation of providing social status in place of significant upward social mobility, as a hedge against decreasing chances of mobility, assured the survival of the myth of social mobility by way of university education. Different roles for public and private universities—with public and private universities linked to different labor markets—proved functionally useful in Mexico because of the importance of the social role of the public universities to the rhetoric of the Mexican Revolution. The response of the university system was entirely in line with the universities' responsibilities under the implicit political pact of 1929 and completely consistent with the reality of changing opportunities for professional-level university graduates.

University Politics

The historical adaptation of the Mexican university system to a changing economic reality is central to the political history of the university. It has been commented that the large numbers of entering students who do not find professional employment are not casualties of the education system as much as successes for the political system.[36] At the same time, it is widely believed that the government has historically supported open doors at the universities because the university seemed to offer an escape valve for unemployable youth. Such a scheme would appear to have backfired; students' dissatisfaction with the university's ability to provide employment has led to broad student involvement in extra-university political issues.

The political activity of Mexican university students must be interpreted in the light of the historical limitations facing them in their professional careers, the same limitations that have forced the shift from emphasis on social mobility to emphasis on social status at the universities. Students clearly benefit from the system in some important ways: the universities provide status to an important number of university students (even if in lieu of a ticket to professional employment); the reformist and radical creeds propagated at the public universities represent an important psychological benefit because they teach students to externalize blame for limited

[36]See Peter S. Cleaves, *Las profesiones y el estado: El caso de México* (México. D. F.: El Colegio de México, 1985), p. 109.

employment opportunities. But in the long view, university students, unable to find professional-level work, are the victims of the historical pattern of Mexico's economic development. The university cannot change this situation even with thoroughgoing internal reforms: the determining factors are beyond the control of university administrators or students.

The relationship between economic development and social mobility outlined above lies at the root of post-1958 political debates involving the university in Mexico. Political conflicts in which university students have played major roles have had their most profound roots in dissatisfaction with scarce opportunities for professional employment. Public employment could hold off the student-led middle-class explosion of 1968 for some time, but not indefinitely, given the nature of Mexico's economic development. Nor could greatly increased government hiring of professionals in the 1970s solve the basic mismatch between jobs and graduates. The virtual orgy of public-sector hiring of professionals that followed the discovery of oil in the late 1970s became a bust after 1982.

The historically declining relative number of opportunities for professionals is a key factor in understanding the students' activism and their broad support within the middle classes in the late 1960s. Discontent with the implications of historical economic development among professionals, and within the middle class from which most came, was widespread and profound. The inherent tension between the number of opportunities and the number of university entrants and graduates was a nationwide phenomenon. The disturbances of 1968 were not isolated in Mexico City but spread across the nation.

Increasingly scarce jobs for professionals would tend to shift the focus of university politics toward issues involving the provision of social status. And since at least 1958, political struggles have revolved around issues of entrance and advancement at the universities. Higher qualitative norms and more restrictive admission policies, while perhaps improving the quality of professional expertise produced by the universities, also make higher education less accessible to poorer aspirants. And indeed, almost all university conflicts in Mexico since the late 1950s have been rooted ultimately in disputes over admissions and degree criteria.[37] The unrest of 1966 was

[37]Scholars have not seen the connection I suggest here, but many have noted the fact. See, for example, Donald J. Mabry, *The Mexican University*

triggered by debate over changes in the structure of examinations, remedial courses, and discipline procedures.[38] Student protests in the winter of 1986-87 were likewise triggered by the resolve of UNAM's administration to raise academic standards. Even the 1968 social reform movement, which spread far beyond the original protest of university students over the violation of university autonomy to become a watershed in Mexican political history, can be seen as having a substantial part of its roots in student objections to attempts to raise academic standards a few years earlier.[39] Recognition of this pattern follows logically from a careful analysis of the various data sets presented here.

The idea that the politics of the Mexican university follow some internal dynamic conditioned principally by intrauniversity political struggles over autonomy or democracy must be revised. The timing of university politics suggests that while the mismatch between professional opportunities and university graduates developed before the 1950s, it was at the end of that decade that it became difficult to manage social tensions arising from the mismatch within the political framework established in 1929.

The drastic reduction of government employment of professionals in the late 1980s meant that pressures within the system would continue to build: with the thrust to privatize parastatal economic enterprises, the state planned to transfer 35 percent of the work force to the private sector which undoubtedly would cut waste by reducing superfluous labor.[40] While the university can be said to have responded with flexibility to the challenge of social demand, the overall situation remained grave as UNAM, for example, could only make room for half of all applicants by the late 1980s. In August of 1988, 500,000 students who had been denied entrance to IPN marched through Mexico City.[41] The mismatch between the number of seekers, the number of university places, and the number of

and the State: Student Conflicts, 1910-1971 (College Station: Texas A&M Press, 1982); and Daniel C. Levy, University and Government in Mexico: Autonomy in an Authoritarian System (New York: Praeger, 1980).

[38]Liebman, Walker, and Glazer, Latin American University Students, p. 180.

[39]For a discussion of the conflicting interpretations of this broadly based social-protest movement, see Sergio Zermeño, México: Una democracia utópica. El movimiento estudiantil del 68 (México, D. F.: Siglo XXI, 1985).

[40]See María Amparo Casar, "La reestructuración de la participación del estado en la industria nacional," El Cotidiano, 23 (1988), pp. 28-38.

[41]Unomásuno, August 5, 1988.

professional-level posts has grown dramatically since it first emerged, largely unrealized, in the late 1950s.

Conclusions

The data developed here reveal a complex relationship between the Mexican university system and the process of economic development after 1929. On the whole, the data indicate that the university system produced graduates and egresados in general areas and specific fields of study that corresponded to the economy's needs for expertise. The same basic correspondence is apparent between the levels of expertise needed by the economy and different levels of university training. Over time, the economy exerted a greater relative demand for technicians than for professionals. In response, universities began to produce ever larger numbers of egresados, a large percentage of whom would not continue on to the degree stage but would fill technician-level job slots.

But while we see a basic confluence of the demands of economic development and the role played by the university, we see also an increasing social strain expressed at the professional level. The economy did not provide upward mobility into professional strata as fast as university enrollment grew. As a result, the university system stepped up its output of egresados and developed increasingly distinct public and private components in order to allocate ever larger numbers of aspirants between available professional and technician positions.

The social and political implications of these changes for the future are profound. If economic recovery after the crisis of the 1980s continues to produce disappointing rates of social mobility, political pressure within Mexico will continue to mount. And while political pressure may lead to reforms of the university, institutional reforms cannot resolve the fundamental stresses to which the university system has been subjected.

CHAPTER THREE

Sources and Methods

Developing and analyzing quantitative data for historical analysis provide a way to critique assumptions about quantitative aspects of the past. Mexican and U.S. scholars and observers have posited a rapid decline in the quality of Mexican higher education since the late 1950s, for example. But what do these observers mean by quality? That is, how do they measure quality? Is quality measurable? This study presents the quantitative data that are available for gauging the quality of university education in Mexico. The data suggest that the evolution of quality at Mexican universities has been much more complex than previously imagined, that there are great differences in quality between public and private institutions, and that differences in quality are related to the changing economic and social functions of the university.

Quantitative data are intrinsically no more or less accurate than notarial records, personal papers, newspaper accounts, or other archival sources. In basing a study on any of these types of primary sources, the historian must make judgments about accuracy based on what he or she knows of the period and the person or institution that produced the records. Quantitative data are much more important than other sources for policymaking, however, because policymakers rely heavily on statistics, accurate or not, and statistical reality often becomes as important as reality itself in the decision-making process.[1]

Statistics on higher education in Mexico must be treated with a great deal of care. Data on various aspects of the structure and func-

[1]See my caveats concerning the use of historical statistics in David E. Lorey, *United States-Mexico Border Statistics since 1900* (Los Angeles: UCLA Latin American Center Publications, 1990), Preface.

tion of the university have been produced by many different institutions and agencies in the period since 1929. The categories used in
sources are sometimes misleading or unclear; the rationale behind
categorization in one source is frequently very different from that in
another. Each institution or agency that produces data on the university does so for certain reasons particular to its own form and
function. Statistics from different sources generally vary widely in
coverage and quality.[2]

While every attempt has been made in this study to carefully
construct and fairly interpret the statistical series, the reader is re-
minded that the series are approximations of reality and should be
taken as such. The data developed here are accurate and consistent
given the original source materials, but the numbers should not be
thought of as inherently "exact" or "correct." Throughout the analysis of the statistics, I have made a point of focusing on long-term
trends rather than on a specific datum for a given year.

Definitions

The most important difference between Mexican and North
American universities is the inclusion of upper secondary students as
part of university programs in Mexico. Statistics on the Mexican
university generally include the numbers of secondary-school students studying in dependent preparatory schools.[3] The UNAM, for
example, is fed by fourteen "incorporated" preparatory schools.

The inclusion of these students in the "university" reflects the
historic character of Mexican university education as essentially
professional in nature. Students study in order to practice a certain
career; they begin their professional training in secondary school
and continue it at the university. In this respect, Mexican students
are similar to their counterparts in most European universities.
Students of dependent secondary schools in Mexico have historically
been able to enter the large public universities' professional schools
automatically, regardless of grade averages or aptitude-test scores.

Data developed for this study do not incorporate trends in the
education of upper secondary students in order to focus attention on

2For an example of the limited usefulness of statistics on education in
Mexico in general, see COPLAMAR, *Necesidades esenciales en México*
(México, D.F.: Siglo XXI, 1982), Vol. 2 (La Educación).

3See, for example, Frank Brandenburg's university enrollment statistics
for 1925-61 in *The Making of Modern Mexico* (Englewood Cliffs: Prentice-Hall,
1964), p. 81.

the professional level of university education in Mexico. Not only does this focus enhance analysis, but it also reflects a long-term trend in Mexico to make the two levels more distinct, particularly in private-sector education. Further, the data on secondary education in Mexico, particularly data that provide information on the fields of study of students, are inconsistent and unreliable.

"Professionals" are usually defined in sociological or sociopolitical terms that reflect their historical development as a prominent feature of modern Mexican society. Thus Peter Cleaves, in his study of the relationship between professional groups and the Mexican state, sees the professions as privileged occupations with a certain mystique. Cleaves views professionals as expressions of the bureaucratic state apparatus that has developed in Mexico and analyzes them primarily as representatives of organized professional pressure groups. Roderic Camp sees professional training in Mexico primarily as a political process, as the most important step in the political apprenticeship and recruitment of political elites in Mexico.[4]

Another set of definitions of professionals builds from the function of professionals in the workplace in Mexico. Charles Myers, for example, divided employment of professionals into three strata: professional, sub-professional, and technician.[5] Likewise, the Banco de México, in its 1955-57 study of employment in Mexico, divided occupations at the sub-management level into professionals, sub-professionals, and "prácticos," this last definition being approximately equivalent to Myers's technician.[6]

While accepting these various definitions, I add to them definitions that are based on the output of Mexico's higher education system and that aid in the development of time-series data. My defi-

[4]See Peter S. Cleaves, *Professions and the State: The Mexican Case* (Tucson: University of Arizona Press, 1987); Roderic A. Camp, *Mexico's Leaders: Their Education and Recruitment* (Tucson: University of Arizona Press, 1980); and Peter H. Smith, *Labyrinths of Power: Political Recruitment in Twentieth-Century Mexico* (Princeton: Princeton University Press, 1979).

[5]Charles Nash Myers, *Education and National Development* (Princeton: Industrial Relations Section, Princeton University, 1965).

[6]Banco de México, Departamento de Investigaciones Industriales, *El empleo de personal técnico en la industria de transformación* (México, D. F.: Banco de México, 1959). A few observers equate professionals and technicians: see Sanford Mosk, *Industrial Revolution in Mexico* (Berkeley and Los Angeles: University of California Press, 1950), p. 268; and Larissa Lomnitz, Leticia Mayer, and Martha W. Rees, "Recruiting Technical Elites: Mexico's Veterinarians," *Human Organization*, 42, no. 1 (Spring, 1983), 23.

nitions also reflect the single most basic occupational division among employed university graduates and egresados, that between professionals and technicians. Thus, "professionals" are university graduates with a licentiate or higher degree.[7] (Over time, however, a growing portion of degree holders found work as technicians; see Chapter Two above.) "Technicians" are graduates of upper secondary, non-college preparatory courses, those students who leave the university system by way of a "lateral exit" or "short course" of study, and those egresados who never achieve the licentiate degree.

These definitions fit the reality of Mexico's university system, in which the production of professional skills through university education is directly linked to employment. This linkage is borne out, among other factors, by the terminology employed in the university system: a student studies not a major, but a "career"; the first university degree is not a Bachelor of Arts, but rather a "license" (*licenciatura*) to practice in the career area studied; the student must register this degree with the Dirección General de Profesiones to receive the official permit (*cédula*) to practice his or her career.[8] The definitions used in this study also conform to the categories of the Mexican census. According to the census definition, a professional is a person who receives professional training at the university level and who executes responsibilities related to his or her professional training.

The basic assumption underlying the distinction between professionals and technicians is that a completed university education of high quality differs significantly in type and level of skills from a secondary, "short course," or incomplete university education. A professional is a person equipped with both general knowledge and the

[7]The licentiate degree should not be confused with the bachelor's degree (B.A.) in the United States: the licentiate degree represents a much greater degree of specialization and is better compared with European first-professional degrees. See Marcel de Grandpré, *Glossaire international: Thèmes d'usage courant en matière de certificats d'études secondaires et de diplômes et l'enseignement supérieur dans quarante-cinq pays* (New York: UNESCO, 1969) for information on cross-national comparisons of degrees.

[8]The professional orientation of the Mexican university has had a great impact on student views of the purposes of higher education. In one survey, 87 percent of Mexican students identified the main function of the university as that of preparing the student for professional life: see Arthur Liebman, Kenneth N. Walker, and Myron Glazer, *Latin American University Students: A Six Nation Study* (Cambridge, MA: Harvard University Press, 1972), p. 65.

ability to apply this knowledge to change the production or management environment by increasing productivity, introducing innovations, or spreading attitudes and techniques. A technician's main function in the workplace, in contrast, is to apply specific techniques learned through the educational process. The work of a technician is generally overseen by a professional or forms a part of the work of a professional higher-up.[9] Theories of segmented labor markets propose two main segments of the labor market, primary and secondary. Within the primary labor market, theorists see two levels: independent and dependent. These two latter categories correspond closely to my "professional" and "technician" categories.

This differentiation between professionals and technicians fits the evidence of studies on employers' expectations of employees in Mexico, even if there have been important shifts over time. Brooke, Oxenham, and Little, for example, note that:

> Professional jobs are accessible only to *pasantes* [egresados] and full university or polytechnic graduates. They are the most prestigious and best paid. In the sample, few people who had not completed their university course, and to a lesser extent, their thesis so as to obtain the full degree or title, could hope to reach the topmost ranks. . . . The subprofessional jobs are open to the range of educational level between complete junior secondary, secondary or its equivalent, and a university degree.

The data series discussed in detail in the following section have been developed around these definitions. The series on the number of degrees granted has been adjusted to represent the licentiate level from 1928 to 1971. The data on degrees registered represents holders of university degrees at the licentiate level. The egresados indicator includes a great number of persons who will not finish university work for the licentiate degree and who will enter the job market as technicians. The percentage of egresados which goes on to achieve the degree is considered professional, that which does not, technician; arriving at the ratio of professional to technician egresados is discussed below.

---

[9]This basis for distinguishing between professionals and technicians is used by other analysts of education in Latin America and the United States. See, for example, Ivar Berg, *Education and Jobs: The Great Training Robbery* (Boston: Beacon Press, 1971), pp. 57-58.

Mexican Archives and Enrollment Statistics

Mexican archives hold little information of use for examining long-term trends in the social economy of the Mexican university system after 1929. Mexico's Archivo General de la Nación, for example, offers collections of petitions by professionals asking that their titles be confirmed or reinstated, not a useful sample for this study. Archival documents pertaining to professionals tend to display a bias toward central Mexico and Mexico City in particular. In general, the Mexican archives do not contain information on professionals or universities that can be quantified and constructed into long-term series to examine historical change. While there is much micro-level detail, little information is available on the national picture—and yet the nation as a whole is the necessary level for analysis of the most important questions about university education and the economy in Mexico.

The most important sources for the study of the university system are the offices of government agencies that deal in one way or another with the higher education system. Frequently, these agencies publish samples of the information they collect. These data can be reworked, disaggregated, and employed in historical analysis.[10] Discussion of sources of this type as used in the present study follows a few notes on enrollment data.

The majority of the scholarly work on higher education in Mexico that attempts to quantify aspects of historical change in the university system relies on enrollment statistics.[11] Enrollment data are easily found and are generally consistent over long periods of time (although differences among series from different sources can be

[10]On the use of government agencies as archives for quantitative history of twentieth-century Mexico, see Jeffrey Bortz, "The Development of Quantitative History in Mexico since 1940: Socioeconomic Change, Income Distribution, and Wages," in *Statistical Abstract of Latin America*, vol. 27, pp. 1107-1127.

[11]For example, see Daniel C. Levy, *University and Government in Mexico: Autonomy in an Authoritarian System* (New York: Praeger, 1980), *Higher Education and the State in Latin America: Private Challenges to Public Dominance* (Chicago: University of Chicago Press, 1986), passim, and Levy's defense of his preference for enrollment data in *Higher Education*, pp. 335-337; Thomas N. Osborn, *Higher Education in Mexico: History, Growth, and Problems in a Dichotomized Industry* (El Paso: Texas Western Press, 1976); José Angel Pescador Osuna, "El balance de la educación superior en el sexenio 1976-1982," in UAP, *Perspectivas de la educación superior en México* (Puebla: UAP, 1984); and Gilberto Guevara Niebla, *La rosa de los cambios: Breve historia de la UNAM* (México, D.F.: Cal y Arena, 1990).

great).

The three major indicators I develop for this study are superior to data on enrollment in several important ways. First, differential dropout rates among professional fields mean that the field distribution of students studying is in many cases very different from that of students who actually leave the system, either as egresados or graduates with degrees. This difference is particularly great between first-year students and graduating students and thus can be used to show how expectations for employment opportunities change during the course of professional study.[12] The difference can sometimes be as great as 10 percent between fields of study.

Second, dropout rates at public universities are much higher than those at private universities, and thus the importance of the public university system is overrepresented in enrollment data. While the efficiency rate (graduates divided by entrants) at UNAM or IPN is 35-40 percent, for example, that at the Universidad de las Américas, a small private school in the state of Puebla, is 70-80 percent. As noted above, graduates of private universities may also be relatively more important for other reasons. Thus there is a double devaluation of the real role of the private university in the Mexican system inherent in the use of enrollment figures for public and private universities.

Third, enrollment statistics are frequently inflated at public universities, which gives a false impression of the relative importance of public and private institutions as producers of employable graduates. Public universities in Mexico, like most public universities in the world, are allotted varying amounts of state subsidy depending on the number of students enrolled. The usual procedure is to add a certain percentage of students who are in the "active archive" of students to those who are actually taking courses. In other words, students who have the right to take classes, although they may not actually enroll, are included in enrollment totals.[13]

Fourth, enrollment data do not present an accurate portrayal of the availability of professionals and perceived employment opportunities at a given time. If only 26 percent of engineering students

[12]See *Statistical Abstract of Latin America*, vol. 25, Tables 910 and 911; UNESCO, *Statistical Yearbook*; and Víctor Urquidi and Adrián Lajous Vargas, *Educación superior, ciencia y tecnología en el desarrollo económico de México* (México, D. F.: El Colegio de México, 1967), pp. 39, 46.

[13]See Frank Brandenburg's discussion of university enrollment statistics in *The Making of Modern Mexico*, pp. 180-181.

who entered UNAM in 1973 actually earned degrees,[14] for example, studies that attempt to measure supply and demand for human resources using undeflated enrollment figures may be off by almost 75 percent. Enrollment statistics, then, are not a good gauge of available professional expertise.

Enrollment figures are most useful for simply quantifying the growth in the general student population. They do not allow us to interpret the relationship between growing student populations and changes in the economy, in society, and in the higher education system. Enrollment data show most clearly the increasing demand over time for higher educational opportunities and the dominant historical response of the university: to continue to open its doors to all, or most, aspirants. To explain this response in broad historical context more complex data must be consulted.

Data on University Graduates and Egresados

In providing detailed coverage of shifts in the development of various professional areas, this study develops data on the university system that can be disaggregated to reflect the career choices of Mexican students and the historical production by the university of particular areas of professional expertise. I have constructed three main statistical time series to track the numbers of persons who were granted a university degree; persons who completed coursework but left the university without completing the required thesis or project for the degree (egresados); and persons who registered a professional-level degree with the Mexican government.[15]

[14]Graciela Garza, *La titulación en la UNAM* (México, D.F.: UNAM, Centro de Estudios sobre la Universidad, 1986).

[15]The value of these and other data (including enrollment) as indicators of trends in Mexican professional education is discussed briefly in Levy, *Higher Education*, and Charles Nash Myers, *Education and National Development*. While there is reason to believe that some data published by the Mexican government are willfully manipulated to show a desired reality (e.g., election statistics), it is not very likely that such manipulation has substantially affected my data series. The data used in this study come from many decentralized sources all over Mexico and concern aspects of economic and social development not generally deemed threatening to the government. It is unlikely that any one person could have modified the basic trends in the series, as many persons have been involved in collecting and reproducing the statistics over the years since 1929. The problem of willful manipulation of data is relevant in the case of enrollment data, which, as noted above, are routinely inflated at public universities for the purpose of laying claim to larger government subsidies.

The longest consistent series of data—that for "professional degrees granted"[16]—was derived from the *Anuario estadístico* and *Compendio estadístico* of Mexico's Dirección General de Estadística (DGE) and runs from 1900 to 1971.[17] The number of degrees granted in the various professional fields by all Mexican universities included in these compilations gives a good indication of the career choices of university entrants and the availability of professional expertise for the period.[18] The series on degrees granted has certain limitations. Categories used by the DGE did not change greatly over the period from 1900 to 1971, and thus the categories do not adequately reflect historical shifts among student concentrations in the professional fields. Further, until 1964, data from these publications combined degrees from university and higher-secondary levels of education. Since 1971, statistics on professional degrees have not been published in the *Anuario*. Many of the manuscripts for the older series were destroyed and data cannot be comprehensively checked for accuracy.

I have reorganized and recategorized these data to make the series consistent over time and to represent degrees granted at the university level only.[19] The "commerce" category in the original data sources, for example, included degrees granted at both university and upper-secondary levels in the original data. Secondary-level degrees in commerce are not at all like degrees in business administration, generally recognizing the acquisition of secretarial skills such as typing and the taking of dictation. I have estimated

[16]"Títulos expedidos" or "títulos otorgados." The former term refers to the number of degrees actually handed out to university graduates, the latter to the number of persons who passed the final exam or requirement for the degree and may or may not have picked up the physical degree. The numerical difference between the two indicators is not large and data found under the two rubrics have been averaged in the construction of the statistical series for this study.

[17]The data are for the period 1900-27 and yearly from 1928 to 1971; trends in the pre-1928 period are not discernible.

[18]Francisco García Sancho and Leoncio Hernández, *Educación superior, ciencia y tecnología en México, 1945-1975: Un diagnóstico de la educación superior y de la investigación científica y tecnológica en México* (México, D.F.: SEP, 1977), compiled data on professional theses filed at UNAM and IPN for the 1945-75 period. Their data are not comprehensive, are generally very highly aggregated, and are not presented on a yearly basis.

[19]The inclusion of the data on secondary-level degrees can greatly affect analysis. See, for example, Howard F. Cline, *Mexico: Revolution to Evolution, 1940-1960* (New York: Oxford University Press, 1963), p. 204.

data for 1940-63 using the ratio of upper- to lower-level degrees in the 1964-71 period. No obvious trend is apparent in this period and thus I deflate the given data series by a constant factor of 95.8 percent.[20]

The second longest series I develop here to gauge historical trends in professional skills is derived from data on egresados of professional fields provided in the statistical yearbooks, other periodic publications, and unpublished data of ANUIES (Asociación Nacional de Universidades e Institutos de Educación Superior).[21] I have restructured this series to produce consistent data for the 1967-89 period.[22]

An egresado has finished all the necessary coursework and has only to complete the final requirement—a project involving practical application of professional skills, a thesis, or an exam—to earn the degree. The series on egresados provides information on a large group of persons leaving universities, ranging from a number of relatively highly skilled persons qualified for high-level employment in the professional fields to relatively untrained persons who will accept work as technicians. The egresados series includes very detailed categories of professional fields, thereby avoiding the underrepresentation of new fields apparent in the data on degrees.[23]

The data on egresados are plagued by lack of consistent reporting, particularly in the early years of ANUIES activity. The 1972-75 period is especially difficult—the number of universities included for this period by ANUIES is lower than in other years, and there is little indication of how more comprehensive coverage would have affected the data. I have made numerous estimates and

[20]I have adjusted a few other career fields in the series in a similar fashion, using the ratios among fields of the late 1960s to make estimates for earlier periods.

[21]Until 1991 Asociación Nacional de Universidades e Institutos de Enseñanza Superior.

[22]The data compiled by ANUIES became increasingly comprehensive over time as more universities became members of the association and the association began gathering more complete statistics. Member universities, when they alone appear in earlier data sets, are considered representative of all Mexican universities. ANUIES is an independent body established in 1945 which serves as a consulting organization to both the government and the university sector.

[23]The number of egresados has grown roughly at the same rate as the number of entering university students—thus this indicator also gives an idea of the explosion in university enrollment without the disadvantages associated with the use of enrollment statistics.

adjustments to correct for these shortcomings in the original sources.[24] The series on egresados is also complicated by the fact that those egresados who will complete a thesis project and receive a licentiate degree are hidden among egresados who will not. We have no reliable data on how the ratio between these two groups of egresados has changed over time, leaving any adjustment of the data to make them comparable with data on degree-holders risky. Some rough estimates are made below.

I have supplemented these two series, drawn for the most part from published materials, with a third series constructed with unpublished data on degrees registered in the Dirección General de Profesiones (DGP) for the period from 1970 to 1985. Once a degree has been granted, it is required by the 1945 Law of Professions that it be registered with the DGP before employment may begin. When the degree is registered the degree-holder receives a cédula, a license giving him or her the legal right to practice the profession. The number of degrees registered represents a percentage of professionals practicing their profession or expecting employment. In practice, registration may or may not be necessary for employment. Since professionals in certain fields for which there is high demand can and do practice their professions without registration, data on registrations also give an indication of differential demands for the various professions.[25]

The data on degrees registered with the DGP also have their problematic aspects. By nature, the data from this source are not comprehensive since they do not include degrees held by persons who did not register them. Changes in official policy on the regis-

[24]It should be noted that most ANUIES data on egresados are based on the number of students in their final year of study, and thus are estimates of the number of students who actually complete coursework and become egresados. The dropout rate during the final year is very low, however, so the series is only slightly inflated.

[25]Certain professionals, notably those in health and teaching fields, will almost always register their degrees: these groups frequently work directly for government agencies in which proof of registration is required and checked. The registration process was changed in 1973 and after that year persons with degrees in almost all professional fields were required to register their degrees with the DGP. Most categories other than health and teaching see large jumps in 1974 that are due to this change. The Law of Professions does not require certain professionals to register their degrees. The most important such group of professionals is accountants and certain other business professionals who do not need the cédula to practice the profession.

tration of degrees in 1974 also shaped the series. I have made small adjustments in order to make data from this source consistent over time. The series is presented in round numbers so as to give no illusion of exactness in yearly data.

These three series represent three different methods for tracking university production of professionals and technicians over time. The numbers of degrees granted and degrees registered yield conservative estimates of professional availability, while the number of egresados yields a more liberal gauge. The DGE has generally opted for the most restrictive measures and began using degrees registered instead of degrees granted in the *Anuario estadístico* after 1971.[26] ANUIES, on the other hand, has increasingly employed the more open-ended definition of professional training represented by egresados. Although ANUIES included data on degrees granted together with those for egresados in 1967-71, more recent publications provide data only for egresados.[27]

In addition to their role in indicating available professional and technician skills, these three indicators reflect the career choices and thus the employment expectations of college students. Because there is almost no formal career counseling in Mexican universities, these indicators represent a direct link between career choices made by students and government strategy for economic development (as expressed in both government rhetoric and expenditure), job opportunities in the Mexican economy, and the perceived social needs of students and their families. Choices reflected in these data also reveal trends within Mexico's occupational structure after 1929.[28]

[26]Data on degrees registered for the periods 1945-75 and 1945-76 were provided by the DGP for the DGE's *Anuario estadístico* of 1975 and 1976. But these data are not consistent, the totals given for the second period being less than those for the first period. The DGP has updated its files since the publication of these volumes; data used here are derived directly from unpublished DGP manuscript data.

[27]ANUIES administrators entering in the mid-1970s decided to make the statistical yearbook a compilation of only the most "basic" data on higher education: number of institutions, number of teachers, first-year enrollment, total enrollment, and egresados. Egresados can easily be presented as the result of a year's academic cycle. Data on degrees granted, on the other hand, represent students from many different student generations and thus are not as useful for accurate calculation of such things as the efficiency rate of the system, for which the data are used by analysts and policymakers.

[28]See Alfonso Rangel Guerra, *Systems of Higher Education: Mexico* (New

That career choices and occupational changes are reflected in the data is complicated by the fact that students decide what they will study long before they appear as egresados, degrees granted, or degrees registered in statistical sources. The time-lag adjustment used to take this factor into account is discussed below.

Relationships among the Statistical Series

Numerical relationships among the three indicators can be calculated where data exist for overlapping years. The data show, for example, that for every two engineering egresados in 1970, one person received a professional degree in an engineering field. For 1980, the absolute data on egresados and on degrees registered with the DGP show a ratio of 2.4 engineering egresados to 1 engineering degree registered. Analysis of one of the two years in which all three series overlap shows a ratio of 2.7 egresados to 1.3 degrees granted to 1 degree registered in 1970. There are large differences in these ratios from field to field and from year to year: business fields show a ratio of 6.4 to 1.7 to 1 in 1970 while engineering specialties show a ratio of 2.3 to 1 to 1 in the same year.[29]

While use of these ratios in historical analysis is complicated by several factors, it is possible to perceive some significant change in the ratios of egresados to degrees granted and degrees registered over time. If we consider that a person registering a degree in 1971 probably received the degree in 1970 and finished coursework (reached egresado status) in 1967 or 1968, the data indicate a ratio of 1.5 egresados to 1 degree granted to 1 degree registered in the late 1960s and early 1970s.[30] At this time, then, roughly two-thirds of all egresados went on to finish the degree.[31] For the 1980s we lack

York: International Council for Educational Development, 1978), p. 20.

[29]Richard G. King, Alfonso Rangel Guerra, David Kline, and Noel F. McGinn, *Nueve universidades mexicanas: Un análisis de su crecimiento y desarrollo* (México, D.F.: ANUIES, 1972), suggest a ratio of two egresados to one degree granted (p. 110).

[30]Data for a single year do not represent a single generation of university students. Rather, each indicator represents a cluster of students from different entering classes at different stages of the career. Because a degree can be registered at any time, the data from the DGP also include many registrations of degrees earned long before the date of registration. The registration process became more strictly controlled after 1970, and particularly after 1973, and so there are quantitative bulges in 1971 and 1974.

[31]Donald J. Mabry, *The Mexican University and the State: Student Conflicts, 1910-1971* (College Station: Texas A & M Press, 1982), claims that 30.7 percent of egresados achieved the degree. Graciela Garza's data sug-

consistent data and must rely on informed estimates. The director of statistics at ANUIES estimated in 1988 that in the late 1980s 10 percent of entering students reached the egresado stage, while 3 percent earned the licentiate degree.[32] This estimate provides a ratio of 3.3 egresados for every person receiving a degree. By this rough measure, only slightly more than one quarter of egresados eventually received the licentiate degree by the late 1980s.

Although such ratios give an idea of the relationships among the three categories at different points in time and over time for a very restricted period, use of the ratios to extrapolate either forward or backward in time is most likely to be misleading. It is very difficult to determine with accuracy how many persons from a given entering class reach the egresado stage, earn the licentiate degree, and then register the degree with the DGP. That these ratios seem to have changed over time further complicates the picture. It is also clear that the ratios differ from institution to institution, between public and private schools, and among the various professional fields.[33] For all these reasons, attention must be focused on the implications of the relationships among the different data sets and historical changes in these relationships rather than on absolute data.

The ratio between egresados who become professionals and those who find employment as technicians is particularly important to the themes developed in this study; the most important occupational distinction I make is between professionals and technicians. Egresados who do not finish their studies represent an intermediate level of professional training, somewhere between a graduate of a secondary school program and the university graduate with the licentiate degree. In most professional fields, egresados fill the de-

gest that only about 40 percent of students entering UNAM in the 1970s finished the degree. In 1988, UNAM officials estimated that only 30 percent of entering students achieved the degree. UNAM is probably not representative of all Mexican universities in this regard and data for UNAM thus represent a somewhat lower than average figure. See also Milena Covo, "Apuntes para el análisis de la trayectoria de una generación universitaria," in CEE, *Educación y realidad socioeconómica* (México, D. F.: Centro de Estudios Educativos, 1979), who estimates that in 1954/55 there were more degrees granted than egresados, 1.3 to 1, but that by 1973/74 this ratio had slipped to .6 degrees granted to 1 egresado.

[32]Interview with Lic. Jesús Barrón of ANUIES, June, 1988.

[33]See Salvador Malo, Jonathan Garst, and Graciela Garza, *El egresado del posgrado de la UNAM* (México, D.F.: UNAM, 1981).

mand for technicians while degree-holders or persons with graduate education hold the more demanding and more rewarding positions. Blanca Petricioli and Clark Reynolds point out in regard to the training of Mexican economists, for example, that egresados frequently make up the pool of secretaries, clerks, compilers of data, and other auxiliary workers for both private firms and government agencies. Degree recipients, in contrast, are the source of the Mexican system's professional economists.[34]

The ratio derived above from the relationship among the three indicators in 1970 provides a rough estimate of the percentage of egresados who go on to achieve the licentiate degree—the number of degrees granted in 1970 was about two-thirds that of egresados in 1968. This share probably does not include all egresados who eventually achieve the professional degree, but represents the elite of that group—those students who achieve the degree within two years or less from time of completion of coursework and have the best chances of finding high-level employment in their field. Most of the remaining third probably did not finish work for the degree. Some egresados, of course, quickly find their way to professional-level employment because of personal or family contacts, aptitude, or other reasons, but there is most likely an equal share of professional-level egresados who slide down the employment ladder. Because it is apparent that the ratio between egresados and degree-holders has changed over time, the two-thirds estimate here will be an underestimate for years prior to 1970 and an overestimate in later years.[35]

Because the nature of the relationships among the three indicators is useful in revealing shifts in supply and demand for professionals, it is important to explain why differences exist among the three indicators—why all egresados do not continue on to complete the degree. The following explanations are those that conform most closely with data on the relationships between the series over time

[34]Clark W. Reynolds and Blanca M. de Petricioli, *The Teaching of Economics in Mexico,* Occasional Report 1 (New York: Education and World Affairs, 1967).

[35]As noted earlier, there is also a great difference among institutions. At UNAM, for example, about 56 percent of egresados received the degree. See *Unomásuno,* June 11, 1988, p. 3, which quotes a study by UNAM's Dirección General de Planeación and a paper given by Rafael Vidal Uribe y Pío Alcántara, "Trayectoría escolar en el nivel licenciatura."

and those most commonly expressed by professionals themselves:[36]

1.   Students find employment while still in school.[37] This employment is generally at the technician level (as defined above). Students frequently intend to finish their university work. As to registration, if a working student does eventually achieve the degree, he or she may have no reason to register it with the DGP, as he or she is already employed.

2.   Students find work upon completion of coursework (egresado stage) and do not fulfill all the requirements for the degree. For some students the cost (in time and money) of producing the frequently 100-page plus thesis is prohibitive.[38]

3.   It can be difficult and time-consuming to register the degree. The registration process can take longer than a year, and while the university usually handles some part of the process, students are frequently responsible for initiating it or seeing it through to completion.[39]

All of these factors suggest that students are able to develop a marketable skill without achieving the formal degree, generally if they are willing to accept work at the technician level. Students do not necessarily need the formal degree, nor do they always need to register the degree, if they achieve it, in order to find employment. The growing practice of hiring in Mexico based on job-entry exami-

[36]Information from interviews and from questionnaires on professional career patterns.

[37]Compare ECLA, *Education, Human Resources, and Development in Latin America* (New York: United Nations, 1968), and Pablo Latapí, *Análisis de un sexenio de educación en Mexico, 1970-1976* (México, D.F.: Editorial Nueva Imagen, 1980).

[38]There is a great diversity among universities in requirements for the degree. Many of the newer public schools founded in the 1970s, as well as many private schools, make finishing coursework and receiving the degree practically simultaneous. Frequently, the thesis, the required period of social service, and/or the final examination are incorporated into the period of coursework. This integration of requirements was often adopted with the explicit aim of narrowing the difference between egresados and degree-holders; it was felt that degree requirements were too difficult and were keeping many students from their career objectives.

[39]For the graduate level, Malo, Garst, and Garza, in *El egresado de posgrado,* found that the three most important motives given by graduate egresados of UNAM for not finishing degree work were: not enough time to finish (42.1 percent of responses), process for presenting professional exam or project too complicated (8.1 percent), degree not necessary for work (7.4 percent), other reasons (30.3 percent).

nations, in both public and private sectors, makes a degree increasingly less important in obtaining certain kinds of work.[40] And because public university education is essentially free, secondary-school graduates are implicitly encouraged to continue their job search as college students if they do not find employment upon leaving secondary school. All students who leave the university at the egresado stage have not necessarily found work, however. Rather, the extra time spent completing the thesis or preparing for the professional exam for the degree is not perceived as making a great difference in one's ability to find employment at the desired level. The ability to discontinue studies at the egresado level has often been seen as an advantage to students, particularly to students from lower socioeconomic strata receiving technical training at the university level: ". . . students acquire remunerative abilities which serve them in the case that they are obliged to interrupt the course of study before its conclusion."[41]

Estimating a Time-Lag Factor

It takes several years to educate a professional specialist in a given field: the university system cannot respond overnight to changes in government strategy or in the economy. Decisions made by students based on government spending and employment opportunities in the economy will only become apparent in data series years after those decisions were made. The time lag developed and employed here is an estimate that takes into account the difference between data on degrees granted, egresados, and degrees registered, differences in time lags in various professional fields, and differences among universities.[42]

The appropriate time lag is best chosen by consulting data on average enrollment-to-graduation time in professional fields. It has

[40]For a discussion of the growing importance of such exams, see Peter S. Cleaves, *Las profesiones y el estado: El caso de México* (México: El Colegio de México, 1985), pp. 122-130.

[41]Francisco Arce Gurza, "El inicio de una nueva era, 1910-1945," in *Historia de las profesiones en México* (México, D.F.: El Colegio de México, 1982), p. 257. See also pp. 259-260 for discussion of how this advantage (to the student) of engineering education was incorporated into a stepped degree structure in certain specialties.

[42]In *Paradox* I adjust the data for a six-year time lag in order to compare statistics on government expenditure and professional occupation with data on university graduates and egresados. See the discussion in Chapter Three of that study and Table 12 here.

been shown that the average professional career at UNAM—from time of matriculation to time of award of degree—lasted an average of 7.8 years (with an average standard deviation of 3.2 years) in the period 1955-71. There is a great degree of difference among professional fields in this respect, varying from a high of 9.2 years in economics to 5.7 years in dentistry.[43] Data for 1980 for the Universidad Autónoma de Nuevo León (UANL) suggest a seven-year difference from time of enrollment to achievement of degree. As in enrollment-to-graduation data for UNAM, differences among professional fields are notable at UANL. Sciences have a high lag time of 4.5 years between egresado and degree levels, compared to an average period of 3.2 years for all fields.[44]

The six-year time lag adopted in this study takes into account several other factors. Some factors would tend to suggest a slightly longer time lag. Students must make some choice of general field orientation, for example, before entering one of three different preparatory tracks (sciences, social and administrative sciences, humanities) and this would tend to lengthen time from choice of career to employment. It is fairly difficult in the Mexican system to change careers outside a fairly narrow range upon entering the university, although it has become easier over time. The development of a common body of coursework (a *tronco común*) in the first year of university study at many universities has apparently made changes between fields more common in the first two years of study.[45] One key factor suggests a shorter time lag in settling upon a national average. It is clear that matriculation to degree time is shorter at private universities and for many public universities other than UNAM. Licentiate engineering studies at the Universidad de las Américas-Puebla last 4 to 4.5 years, about half that of the large public institutions. And some public universities, such as the

[43]Garza, *La titulación en la UNAM*.

[44]Programa de Seguimiento de Egresados UANL, *Estudio sobre el egresado al titularse en la Universidad Autónoma de Nuevo León 1980/81* (Monterrey: UANL, n.d.[1981]), p. 46.

[45]At the most traditionally structured universities in Mexico (UNAM, UANL, UAEM, UACH, etc.), it remains difficult to switch between faculties and thus career fields. At some of the newer institutions, on the other hand, it is much easier. Many institutions of higher education have adopted three-stage degree programs. All students take a group of core courses upon entering the institution, usually for a year. They then take a group of core courses in their major area. Finally, students take a series of specialty courses.

Universidad Autónoma Metropolitana (UAM), appear to have shorter matriculation-to-degree times than does UNAM. Because newer public universities in the provinces and in the Federal District have been producing an increasing share of egresados since the late 1950s, I have settled on a shorter rather than a longer time lag.

A six-year time lag facilitates comparison among the three basic data series developed here. Because matriculation-to-degree time has lengthened over time, particularly at public universities, the six-year time lag averages out the effect of the change from degrees-granted data to egresados data. In the 1950s and 1960s students frequently achieved the degree in the time it took to reach the egresado stage in the 1980s. Because I shift from degrees granted to egresados between 1967 and 1970, I have applied the six-year lag uniformly across the time series where I have applied it.

It takes approximately six years for the effects of individual student decisions based on government spending or economic changes to appear in data on the professional fields. A six-year lag makes it possible to gauge the power of government policy to stimulate specific professional fields and specialties. With the time lag taken into consideration, the data reveal the number and relative importance of individual decisions about future employment and other career factors. Among its advantages, the time-lag approach allows discussion of professional field development in the 1920s and 1930s, for which data are available only in highly aggregate form.[46] On the other end of the time period, the time lag limits analysis to six years before the year of the most recent data.

Data on the Employment of Professionals and Technicians

Data on the occupational structure of Mexico have been developed here to shed light on two key segments of the work force: professionals and technicians. The meaning of these two terms in this study has been discussed above. Analysis of census data on professionals and technicians is based on a broad definition for the two categories: professionals include persons tallied as "professionals," "upper-level public officials," "private sector managers," and secondary and college-level teachers in the census; technicians include

---

[46]Other factors—including the lingering prestige of some professions—are discussed in UNESCO, *Higher Education: International Trends, 1960-70* (New York: UNESCO, 1975).

the "technicians" category of the census, as well as upper-level office employees and primary school teachers.[47] To achieve a broad representation of persons with professional and technician-level training here, many of the statistical tables on professionals and technicians in the Mexican work force present data on professionals and technicians (disaggregated where possible), upper-level managers and public officials, and office workers.

The early censuses of the twentieth century offer a set of interrelated challenges to the researcher interested in occupational change. While there was no functional occupational breakdown until the census of 1950, the censuses of 1895, 1900, 1910, 1921, 1930, and 1940 each contain some information on professionals. Each census uses the occupational breakdown determined primarily by sector of economic activity. But along with the usual divisions of agriculture and commerce, there are categories for "public administration" and "liberal professions." These two categories can be taken as indicators of growth in professional and technician occupations.

Only one calculation was made here in order to make the early census data comparable with census data after 1950. For the five censuses prior to the census of 1950 and the introduction of the current definitions of occupational categories, only 3 percent of "domestic workers" (an estimate of those who were paid based on the percentage of domestic workers paid in 1940) were included in total EAP.

The most difficult challenge in developing data on occupations in Mexico is the incorporation of data on occupations and economic sector from the 1980 census. For the development of overall data on occupational structure in 1980 the most serious problem is that 16.9 percent of census respondents could not be classified by principal occupation. Because the census questionnaire asked the principal occu-

---

[47]See the definitions in the census of 1980 in Secretaría de Programación y Presupuesto (SPP), *X Censo: Resumen general* (México, D. F.: SPP, 1980), vol. 1, p. 918. The census categories for "professionals" and "technicians" are not comprehensive: secondary and university-level teachers are placed in a separate category, artists and writers in another. Although secondary teachers were trained outside the university system until the 1980s, they are clearly an important group of professionally skilled persons. The census categories of "higher public-sector functionaries" and "higher private-sector functionaries" are mostly made up of persons with university education. The relevant census question (number 16 in the 1980 census) asks simply "What was your occupation in your principal job last week or the last time you were employed?"

pation performed in the week previous to the administration of the census, many persons who either were not working during that week or who could claim more than one occupation were not classified by occupation.

Further, large numbers of census respondents could not be classified by economic sector of activity. Overall, 29.7 percent of EAP were not classified by economic sector. The number of professionals and technicians that census workers could not classify by sector was 394,752 or 25.0 percent of the total. Managers and public officials who could not be specified amounted to 34.4 percent of all managers and government officials; office workers who could not be fit into a sector of occupation were fully 52.9 percent of all office workers.

It is important to note that census data from 1980 do not indicate that large percentages of professionals and technicians were left out of the 1980 census, but rather that census workers tabulating from census manuscripts could not assign persons to economic sectors of activity. The most likely explanation for this problem is that many persons who had worked in more than one sector over the course of the year previous to the taking of the census were tabulated as "not specified."

Another problem with making the 1980 data comparable with data from earlier years is that more sectorial categories were added to census computations in 1980. Petroleum and government, which had been added as separate sectors in 1970, were retained in 1980; a communications sector was added. Expanding the services sector, the 1980 census presented data for workers in financial institutions and hotels.

Several steps were taken here to develop data for 1980 that would be comparable with 1950, 1960, and 1970 census data. First, sectoral categories were collapsed to make eight basic categories for the period from 1950 to 1980. For 1970, for example, "government" and "petroleum" sectors were included in "services" and "extractive" sectors respectively. Second, a new percentage of "not specified" was estimated for 1980 based on trends in the "not specified" category between 1950 and 1970. Third, the remaining percentage of "not specified" was distributed back into the sectoral categories following the relative percentage shares of those categories. No assumptions were made about the likelihood of over- or underrepresentation of some sectors in the original data, for there is little indication that professionals in one sector would be more or less likely to have been classified as "not specified." Finally, new estimated category totals and percentage shares were calculated (see Table 22). It should be noted that these manipulations do not affect the basic long-term trend in the data. Rather, they make comparison more accurate by replacing the raw 1980 data with data that more accurately reflect reality.

Statistical Series

Previous data sets on university education in Mexico have been plagued by extremely general categories for fields of professional study. Most commonly used data have been organized into large, aggregate groupings such as "social sciences" and "engineering and technical" professions. Some of these groupings, such as "philosophy and letters," have been retained from the names of university faculties established in colonial times. The "philosophy and letters" category includes careers that are now generally considered both social sciences, such as history and geography, and humanities, such as philosophy and literature.

The most problematic aggregate category is "social sciences" or, more commonly, "social and administrative sciences." The "social and administrative science" category in the ANUIES statistical yearbook, for example, groups the following fields under that single heading: business administration, anthropology and archaeology, public administration, communications, accounting, law, economics, geography, sports organization, psychology, international relations, tourism, social work, and several others. It does not include history. ANUIES presents the data in a way that allows for easy disaggregation by career and specialty, but the data are generally not disaggregated when used by analysts.

The use of such aggregate fields can greatly affect research and analysis. For example, the historical growth in the catch-all category of "social and administrative sciences," which has been due to dramatic growth in a few fields like accounting and business administration, is commonly assumed to be a sign of the continuing importance in Mexico of "traditional" careers, as opposed to "modern" careers like engineering and the sciences.[1] But clearly there is nothing particularly "traditional" about tourism or international relations, not to mention sports organization. Division into "traditional" and "modern" career fields has been avoided in this study and data on historical changes in fields of study are presented at a low level of aggregation. Organization in this fashion allows us to see, among many other things, that there has actually been a long-term decline in the importance of the so-called traditional fields and not an increase as many observers believe.

The basic organizing principle for the categories developed here is the employment of professionals: fields of study and specialties are placed in categories according to the area in which graduates of those areas will most probably work. Thus, veterinary doctors, sometimes included in the data with other medical professionals, are here grouped with agricultural engineers; actuaries, who are trained in mathematics, law, or engineering departments, have been placed in the business category, as they generally work for insurance firms.

Several professions present special problems. Economists, for example, while frequently working in business, also are important in industry and government.[2] For crossover fields such as economics, the data have not been combined with other groups by employment sector; economists have been placed in their own category.[3] Psychologists and social workers, who usually work in health care institutions, are here grouped separately from other health professionals such as doctors, dentists, optometrists, and licentiate-level nurses. Architects have been tabulated separately from engineers, with whom they are frequently grouped.

[1]See, for example, José Angel Pescador Osuna, "El balance de la educación superior en el sexenio 1976-1982," in UAP, *Perspectivas de la educación superior en México* (Puebla: UAP, 1984), pp. 41-87; Howard F. Cline, *Mexico: Revolution to Evolution, 1940-1960* (New York: Oxford University Press, 1963), p. 204; Arthur Liebman, Kenneth N. Walker, and Myron Glazer, *Latin American University Students: A Six Nation Study* (Cambridge, MA: Harvard University Press, 1972), pp. 49-50; and Pablo Latapí, *Análisis de un sexenio de educación en México, 1970-1976* (México, D.F.: Editorial Nueva Imagen, 1980), pp. 207-208.

[2]SEP, *Información profesional y subprofesional de México* (México, D. F.: SEP, 1958), p. 26.

[3]Some scholars combine economics with other fields. See, for example, Roderic A. Camp, "The Political Technocrat in Mexico and the Survival of the Political System," *Latin American Research Review,* 20, no. 1 (1985), 101, who combines economics with accounting.

All major data series are presented by calendar year. This form of presentation is most accurate for data on degrees granted, egresados, and degrees registered, the three basic series developed and analyzed in this study. In contrasting data on university expenditure and enrollment, which are generally tabulated on the basis of the academic year after 1970, with other data series, I use the later calendar year. For example, expenditure data for the academic year 1975-76 are compared with data on egresados for 1976. The decision to compare 1975-76 with 1976 instead of 1975 does not lead to any major changes in the interpretation of the series.

I have attempted to make the three historical times series consistent over time and consistent with one another as to field makeup. Notes as to specific inclusions and problems with consistency are included in the following field breakdown where explanation might be useful to the reader. Uppercase letters (e.g., "BUS") indicate an aggregate field, lower case letters (e.g., "Econ.") a field made up of a single degree.

Professional-Field Categories Used in the Tables

1. Field Breakdown by Indicator

Degrees Granted[4]

Business (BUS)
Accounting
Actuary
Business Administration
Commerce

---

[4]Basic field definitions for degrees granted are adopted from AE and CE; no indication is generally given in these sources as to changing specific makeup of these fields. For example, the DGE organized engineering fields into the "classic" engineering groupings: agricultural, chemical, civil, electrical, mechanical, extractive. Growth in newer engineering specialities is thus represented in the growth of the "other engineering specialty" category.

Engineering (ENG)

Agricultural Engineering
    Agricultural Engineering
    Veterinary Medicine

Chemical Engineering
    Chemical

Civil Engineering
    Civil Engineering

Electrical, Mechanical, and Mechanical-Electrical Engineering[5]
    Electrical
    Mechanical
    Mechanical-Electrical

Extractive Engineering
    Extractive
    Petroleum
    Mining
    Metallurgy

Other Engineering
    Other Engineering Specialities (Not Specified in Source)

Health Professions (HEALTH)[6]
Dentists
Medical Doctors

[5]Electrical, mechanical, and mechanical-electrical engineering are combined here for several reasons. Much older data on engineering degrees granted combine the three groups under one heading and separate fields cannot be disaggregated. This aggregation does not cause a large problem, however, because these three involve similar training and the fields are closely tied in modern practice in Mexico.

[6]Military and rural doctors are included. Specialists in homeopathic medicine, who work primarily with herbal cures, have also been included. Pharmaceutical chemists have been included.

Sciences (SCIENCE)
Chemistry
"Scientific Professions"

Teaching Professions (TEACH)
Secondary School Teachers
University Professors

Other
Diplomacy
Pharmaceutical Chemists
Psychology[7]
Various Other Professions[8]

Egresados[9]
Architecture and Design (Arch.)
Architecture
Architectural Engineering
Design

Business (BUS)
Accounting
Banking and Finances
Business Administration
Commercial Relations
Communications

[7]Psychology is tabulated separately only for the years 1964-71 in data sources and so is placed in the other category for all years. In the egresados and degrees-registered series, psychology and social work have their own category.

[8]The "other" category in sources apparently includes only secondary-level degrees and diplomas and so has not been included in my tabulations. After 1963, the "other" category becomes more specific, and I have included other university-level degrees when it was possible to discern differences in levels of degrees. Such degrees include licentiate degrees in social sciences, political science, public administration, tourism, optometry, and library sciences.

[9]An egresado has finished coursework for a degree but has yet to complete the written thesis or other requirements for the degree. Degree-program names vary from university to university; I have used the most common designations.

Customs
Industrial Relations
International Relations
Public Administration[10]
Public Relations
Sales and Marketing
Tourism

Engineering and Applied Sciences (ENG)

Agricultural Engineering
    Agricultural Chemistry with specialty in Bacteriology and
        Parasitology
    Agricultural Engineering (27 specialties)
    Agrochemistry
    Agroindustrial Engineering
    Forestry and Forest Development
    Fruticulture
    Rural Development
    Veterinary Medicine
    Zoological Engineering (3 specialties)

Chemical Engineering
    Administration
    Chemical
    Industrial Chemical
    Industrial Chemistry

Civil Engineering
    Civil (8 specialties)
    Construction
    Municipal

Computer Engineering
    Cibernetics and Computer Science
    Computers

[10]The public administration degree granted in business programs has
been included here; degrees granted as "Social Science and Public
Administration" or "Political Science and Public Administration" have been
placed in the social sciences category.

Computer Systems
Systems Administration

Earth Sciences
Earth-Science Engineering
Geophysical, Geographic, Geologic, and Geochemical
    Engineering

Electrical and Electronic Engineering
Communications and Electronics
Electrical (6 specialties)
Electronic

Extractive Engineering
Chemical—specialty in Metallurgy and Petroleum
Mining and Metallurgy
Petroleum

Industrial Engineering
Industrial (13 specialties)

Mechanical and Mechanical-Electrical Engineering
Electromechanical (4 specialties)
Mechanical (2 specialties)

Other Engineering
Aeronautic
Applied Chemistry
Biomedical
Ecological
Fishing
Food Sciences
Naval
Oceanic
Physical
Planning
Textile
Transport
Wood

Health Professions (HEALTH)
Bacteriologists, Parasitologists
Dentistry
Medical Doctors
Nursing
Optometrists
Pharmaceutical Chemists

Humanities and Arts (HUM)
Dramatic Art
Dance
History
Language
Letters
Music
Philosophy
Religion
Scenery

Psychology and Social Work (Psych./SW)
Psychology
Social Work

Sciences (SCIENCE)[11]
Atmospheric Sciences
Biochemistry
Biology
Chemistry
Geology
Marine Sciences
Mathematics
Physics

[11]The sciences category includes only professionals who have simple titles. Complex degree fields have been included in fields of similar occupational orientation. Industrial chemistry, for example, has been tabulated with chemical engineering.

Social Sciences (SS)
Anthropology and Archaeology
Archival and Bibliographical Studies
Geography
Latin American Studies
Political Science
Political Science and Public Administration
Sociology
Sports Organization

Teaching (TEACH)
Egresados of Normal Superior (Higher Teacher Training) courses at
    secondary level
Education
Pedagogy

Degrees Registered
Business (BUS)
Accounting
Business Administration
Commerce

Engineering (ENG)[12]

Agricultural Engineering
    Agronomist
    Veterinary Medicine

Chemical Engineering
    Chemical

Civil Engineering
    Civil

[12]The degrees registered category represents only the most numerous
specialties in each discipline, and thus is not comprehensive. For this reason, an index has been constructed in order to show the changing relative
importance and growth rates of the different engineering fields and for contrast with the two other series.

Electrical and Electronic Engineering
Communications and Electronics
Electrical

Extractive Engineering
Mining and Metallurgy
Petroleum

Industrial Engineering
Industrial

Mechanical
Mechanical

Mechanical-Electrical Engineering
Mechanical-Electrical

Health Professions
Dentistry
Medical Doctors
Nursing
Optometrists

Humanities and Arts
Language and Letters
Music
Philosophy
Visual Arts

Psychology and Social Work (Psych./SW)
Psychology
Social Work

Sciences (SCIENCE)
Biology
Mathematics
Physics

Social Sciences (SS)
Anthropology
History
Sociology

Teaching Professions (TEACH)
Egresados of Normal Superior (Higher Teacher Training) courses at
   secondary level
Education
Pedagogy

Other
All other degrees

2. Field Breakdown by Function

Social
HEALTH
TEACH

Economic
BUS
ENG

3. Field Breakdown by Economic Sector

Primary Sector—Agriculture
Ag./Vet.

Secondary Sector—Industry
ENG (Other than Ag./Vet.)

Tertiary Sector—Services
Arch.
BUS
SCI, SS, HUM[13]

   [13]Persons who work primarily in institutions of higher education are
here considered service professionals. These three fields are the most

Professional-Field Abbreviations

Arch.   Architecture

BUS   Business
Bus. Ad.   Business Administration
Acct.   Accounting

Econ.   Economics
Ed.   Education

ENG   Engineering
Ag.   Agricultural
Ag./Vet.   Agricultural Engineering and Veterinary Medicine
Biochem   Biochemical
Chem.   Chemical
Civil   Civil
Comp.   Computer Engineering
Earth   Earth-science fields
El.   Electric
El./Electronic   Electrical and Electronic
Extr.   Extractive Engineering[14]
Indust.   Industrial
Mech./El.   Mechanical and Electrical
Mech./
  Mech.-El.   Mechanical and Mechanical-Electrical
Mining   Mining and Metallurgy
Petrol.   Petroleum
Text.   Textile
Top./Hyd.   Topographic and Hydraulic
Vet.   Veterinary Medicine

HEALTH   Health Professions
Med.   Medicine
Dent.   Dentistry
Nurse   Nursing
Pharm.Chem.   Pharmaceutical Chemistry

purely academic fields that can be drawn from the data.

[14]Extractive is a field name used in many older data series. It generally means mining, metallurgical, and petroleum engineering.

Psych./SW   Psychology and Social Work

HUM   Humanities and Arts

SCI   Sciences

SS   Social Sciences

TEACH   Teaching Professions
NS   Normal Superior (Teacher Training for Secondary
             School)

T A B L E S

University Graduates, Egresados, and Degrees Registered
Table 1   Degrees Granted, Nine Fields, 1928-71

Table 2   University Egresados, Nine Fields, 1963-67

Table 3   University Egresados, Eleven Fields, 1967-89

Table 4   Degrees Registered, Six Fields, 1945-70

Table 5   Degrees Registered, Eleven Fields, 1970-85

Table 6   Percentage Change in Degrees Granted, Egresados, and
           Degrees Registered

Table 7   Degrees Granted, Egresados, and Degrees Registered per
           One Million Inhabitants, 1928-89

Table 8   Professional Degrees as Percentage of All Degrees, 1928-71

Table 9   Ratios of Degrees Granted, Egresados, Degrees Registered,
           and Enrollment

Table 10   Professionals in Sample Economic and Social Fields,
           1928-89

Table 11   Indexes of Professionals in Sample Economic and Social
           Fields, 1928-89

Table 12   Average Index and Percentage Distribution of
           Professionals in Sample Economic and Social Fields,
           1928-89

Table 13   Engineering Degrees Granted, Egresados, and Degrees
           Registered, 1929-89

Table 14   Engineering Degrees Granted, Nine Specialties, 1928-71

Symbols Used in Tables

~   Data not available

Zero or negligible

Abbreviations for Sources Used in Tables

AE   Dirección General de Estadística, *Anuario
                estadístico.*

ANUIES-AE   Asociación Nacional de Universidades e
                Institutos de Enseñanza Superior. *Anuario
                estadístico.*

ANUIES-ESM   Asociación Nacional de Universidades e
                Institutos de Enseñanza Superior. *La
                educación superior en México* (1967) and *La
                enseñanza superior en México* (1968-76).

CE   Dirección General de Estadística. *Compendio*
              estadístico.

Census   Mexican Decennial Census.

DGP   Dirección General de Profesiones, unpublished
              data.

EHM   Instituto de Estadística, Geografía, e
              Informática (INEGI). *Estadísticas históricas de*
              México. México, D. F.: INEGI, 1985.

FU   Attolini, José. *Las finanzas de la universidad a*
              través del tiempo. México, D. F.: Escuela
              Nacional de Economía, UNAM, 1951.

HEU   González Cosío, Arturo. *Historia estadística de la*
              universidad, 1910-1967. México, D.F.: UNAM,
              1968.

NAFINSA-EMC   Nacional Financiera, S.A. *La economía*
              mexicana en cifras.

OELM   *Obra educativa de López Mateos.* N.p.: n.p.
              [ANUIES], n.d. [1965].

PROIDES   ANUIES. *Programa integral para el desarrollo de*
              la educación superior. México, D. F., 1986.

QMCS   Mostkoff, Aída, and Stephanie Granato.
              "Quantifying Mexico's Class Structure." In
              James W. Wilkie, ed., *Society and Economy*
              in Mexico. Los Angeles: UCLA Latin
              American Center Publications, 1989.

SALA   *Statistical Abstract of Latin America.* Los Angeles:
              UCLA Latin American Center Publications.

SEP-EBSEN   SEP. *Estadística básica del sistema educativo*
              nacional, 1971-1972. México, D. F.: SEP, 1972.

SEP-EPM   SEP. *La educación pública en México 1964/1970.*
              México, D. F.: SEP, 1970.

SEP-ESM   SEP. *La educación superior en México.*

SEP-OE   SEP. *Obra educativa, 1970-1976.* México, D. F.:
              SEP, n.d. [1976].

UNAM-AE   UNAM. *Anuario estadístico.*

UNAM-CEAL   Dirección General de Administración,
              Departamento de Estadística. *Cuadernos*

	estadísticos año lectivo 1979-1980. México, D. F.: UNAM, n.d. [1980].
UNAM-CU	UNAM. *Primer censo universitario*. México, D. F.: UNAM, 1953.
UNAM-EAE	UNAM. Dirección General de Administración. *Estadísticas del aspecto escolar, 1970*. México, D.F.: UNAM, 1970.
UNAM-PP	UNAM. *Presupuesto por programas*. Various years.
UNESCO-SY	UNESCO. *Statistical Yearbook*.

Abbreviations for Mexican Universities Used in Tables

Anahuác	Universidad Anahuác
Ibero	Universidad Iberoamericana
IPN	Instituto Politécnico Nacional
ITAM	Instituto Tecnológico Autónomo de México
ITESM	Instituto Tecnológico y de Estudios Superiores de Monterrey
MICHSN	Universidad Michoacana de San Nicolás
UABC	Universidad Autónoma de Baja California
UACH	Universidad Autónoma de Chihuahua
UACO	Universidad Autónoma de Coahuila
UAEM	Universidad Autónoma de Estado de México
UAG	Universidad Autónoma de Guadalajara
UAM	Universidad Autónoma Metropolitana
UANL	Universidad Autónoma de Nuevo León
UAP	Universidad Autónoma de Puebla
UASLP	Universidad Autónoma de San Luis Potosí
UASIN	Universidad Autónoma de Sinaloa
UAT	Universidad Autónoma de Tamaulipas
UDLA	Universidad de las Américas-Puebla
UG	Universidad de Guadalajara
UGUAN	Universidad de Guanajuato
UNAM	Universidad Nacional Autónoma de México
UV	Universidad Veracruzana

TABLE 1. **Degrees Granted, Nine Fields,** [1] **1928-71**

PART I. **Absolute Data**

Year	Arch.	Econ.	HEALTH	TEACH	Law	BUS	ENG	SCIENCE	Other	Total
1928	4	0	238	6	144	0	134	9	0	535
1929	10	0	265	0	83	0	79	6	0	443
1930	6	0	249	0	138	0	117	15	0	525
1931	7	0	258	1	127	0	62	29	0	484
1932	4	0	282	15	156	0	98	27	0	582
1933	6	0	289	8	152	0	65	23	0	543
1934	8	0	422	21	285	0	92	52	0	880
1935	5	3	381	21	264	0	87	23	0	784
1936	18	1	409	86	298	0	124	11	0	947
1937	9	1	424	88	277	0	128	51	0	978
1938	9	3	430	82	296	0	200	5	0	1,025
1939	18	6	405	128	289	0	148	84	0	1,078
1940	22	3	428	74	286	0	148	88	0	1,049
1941	12	6	477	215	229	70	137	69	0	1,215
1942	12	6	538	269	257	80	140	97	0	1,399
1943	8	8	587	203	314	90	299	123	0	1,632
1944	12	17	657	304	270	100	277	97	0	1,734
1945	7	10	677	280	248	90	253	110	0	1,675
1946	16	13	748	250	293	100	350	171	0	1,941
1947	23	15	807	167	466	120	360	169	0	2,127
1948	23	10	774	294	255	120	323	151	0	1,950
1949	12	5	847	212	291	100	495	191	0	2,153

TABLE 1, PART I (Continued)

Year	Arch.	Econ.	HEALTH	TEACH	Law	BUS	ENG	SCIENCE	Other	Total
1950	15	9	865	291	238	130	256	97	0	1,901
1951	15	10	1,064	232	245	150	401	292	0	2,409
1952	21	16	1,011	253	316	160	461	277	0	2,515
1953	39	9	1,146	581	406	250	434	294	0	3,159
1954	55	5	1,152	299	341	290	544	242	0	2,928
1955	9	9	1,355	653	381	290	651	240	0	3,588
1956	8	11	996	644	366	280	480	98	0	2,883
1957	127	33	1,070	797	488	350	1,164	389	0	4,418
1958	138	19	1,072	217	523	360	894	229	0	3,452
1959	102	20	700	151	355	370	705	267	0	2,670
1960	113	32	795	169	588	380	1,013	239	0	3,329
1961	178	51	1,195	159	553	460	1,048	296	0	3,940
1962	211	23	1,365	141	502	480	1,349	164	0	4,235
1963	195	83	1,316	296	678	880	1,306	346	0	5,100
1964	248	174	1,391	728	755	532	1,507	111	137	5,583
1965	321	143	1,786	537	904	488	1,903	192	166	6,440
1966	441	134	1,851	705	789	734	1,894	203	230	6,981
1967	488	177	1,840	556	928	803	2,141	176	183	7,292
1968	320	314	2,480	578	1,121	925	2,633	381	342	9,094
1969	463	232	2,653	594	1,283	928	2,514	442	369	9,478
1970	522	281	2,305	776	1,440	1,386	2,965	360	636	10,671
1971	448	302	2,943	777	1,752	2,744	2,779	1,347	640	13,732

TABLE 1, PART II. Percentage Data

Year	Arch.	Econ.	HEALTH	TEACH	Law	BUS	ENG	SCIENCE	Other
1928	0.7	0.0	44.5	1.1	26.9	0.0	25.0	1.7	0.0
1929	2.3	0.0	59.8	0.0	18.7	0.0	17.8	1.4	0.0
1930	1.1	0.0	47.4	0.0	26.3	0.0	22.3	2.9	0.0
1931	1.4	0.0	53.3	0.2	26.2	0.0	12.8	6.0	0.0
1932	0.7	0.0	48.5	2.6	26.8	0.0	16.8	4.6	0.0
1933	1.1	0.0	53.2	1.5	28.0	0.0	12.0	4.2	0.0
1934	0.9	0.0	48.0	2.4	32.4	0.0	10.5	5.9	0.0
1935	0.6	0.4	48.6	2.7	33.7	0.0	11.1	2.9	0.0
1936	1.9	0.1	43.2	9.1	31.5	0.0	13.1	1.2	0.0
1937	0.9	0.1	43.4	9.0	28.3	0.0	13.1	5.2	0.0
1938	0.9	0.3	42.0	8.0	28.9	0.0	19.5	0.5	0.0
1939	1.7	0.6	37.6	11.9	26.8	0.0	13.7	7.8	0.0
1940	2.1	0.3	40.8	7.1	27.3	0.0	14.1	8.4	0.0
1941	1.0	0.5	39.3	17.7	18.8	5.8	11.3	5.7	0.0
1942	0.9	0.4	38.5	19.2	18.4	5.7	10.0	6.9	0.0
1943	0.5	0.5	36.0	12.4	19.2	5.5	18.3	7.5	0.0
1944	0.7	1.0	37.9	17.5	15.6	5.8	16.0	5.6	0.0
1945	0.4	0.6	40.4	16.7	14.8	5.4	15.1	6.6	0.0
1946	0.8	0.7	38.5	12.9	15.1	5.2	18.0	8.8	0.0
1947	1.1	0.7	37.9	7.9	21.9	5.6	16.9	7.9	0.0
1948	1.2	0.5	39.7	15.1	13.1	6.2	16.6	7.7	0.0
1949	0.6	0.2	39.3	9.8	13.5	4.6	23.0	8.9	0.0

TABLE 1, PART II (Continued)

Year	Arch.	Econ.	HEALTH	TEACH	Law	BUS	ENG	SCIENCE	Other
1950	0.8	0.5	45.5	15.3	12.5	6.8	13.5	5.1	0.0
1951	0.6	0.4	44.2	9.6	10.2	6.2	16.6	12.1	0.0
1952	0.8	0.6	40.2	10.1	12.6	6.4	18.3	11.0	0.0
1953	1.2	0.3	36.3	18.4	12.9	7.9	13.7	9.3	0.0
1954	1.9	0.2	39.3	10.2	11.6	9.9	18.6	8.3	0.0
1955	0.3	0.3	37.8	18.2	10.6	8.1	18.1	6.7	0.0
1956	0.3	0.4	34.5	22.3	12.7	9.7	16.6	3.4	0.0
1957	2.9	0.7	24.2	18.0	11.0	7.9	26.3	8.8	0.0
1958	4.0	0.6	31.1	6.3	15.2	10.4	25.9	6.6	0.0
1959	3.8	0.7	26.2	5.7	13.3	13.9	26.4	10.0	0.0
1960	3.4	1.0	23.9	5.1	17.7	11.4	30.4	7.2	0.0
1961	4.5	1.3	30.3	4.0	14.0	11.7	26.6	7.5	0.0
1962	5.0	0.5	32.2	3.3	11.9	11.3	31.9	3.9	0.0
1963	3.8	1.6	25.8	5.8	13.3	17.3	25.6	6.8	0.0
1964	4.4	3.1	24.9	13.0	13.5	9.5	27.0	2.0	2.5
1965	5.0	2.2	27.7	8.3	14.0	7.6	29.5	3.0	2.6
1966	6.3	1.9	26.5	10.1	11.3	10.5	27.1	2.9	3.3
1967	6.7	2.4	25.2	7.6	12.7	11.0	29.4	2.4	2.5
1968	3.5	3.5	27.3	6.4	12.3	10.2	29.0	4.2	3.8
1969	4.9	2.4	28.0	6.3	13.5	9.8	26.5	4.7	3.9
1970	4.9	2.6	21.6	7.3	13.5	13.0	27.8	3.4	6.0
1971	3.3	2.2	21.4	5.7	12.8	20.0	20.2	9.8	4.7

1. Business category estimated 1940-63. The numbers of business degrees in these years have been rounded to the nearest ten degrees.
SOURCE: Data were derived from AE and CE in various years and from SEP-EPM.

TABLE 2. University Egresados, Ten Fields, 1963-67

PART I. Absolute Data

Year	Arch.	BUS	Econ.	ENG	HEALTH	HUM	Law	SCI	SS	Other	Total[1]
1963	1,007	1,552	272	3,382	1,981	1,420	1,624	429	51	25	11,743
1964	1,087	1,941	390	3,400	2,218	1,780	1,728	453	62	50	13,109
1965	999	2,637	452	3,686	2,406	2,504	1,932	492	88	45	15,241
1966	1,060	3,148	543	4,365	2,909	2,841	2,358	575	120	68	17,987
1967	975	3,423	591	4,685	3,041	2,821	2,086	700	136	95	18,553

PART II. Percentage Data

Year	Arch.	BUS	Econ.	ENG	HEALTH	HUM	Law	SCI	SS	Other
1963	8.6	13.2	2.3	28.8	16.9	12.1	13.8	3.7	0.4	0.2
1964	8.3	14.8	3.0	25.9	16.9	13.6	13.2	3.5	0.5	0.4
1965	6.6	17.3	3.0	24.2	15.8	16.4	12.7	3.2	0.6	0.3
1966	5.9	17.5	3.0	24.3	16.2	15.8	13.1	3.2	0.7	0.4
1967	5.3	18.4	3.2	25.3	16.4	15.2	11.2	3.8	0.7	0.5

1. Cf. total in Table 3, from published data of ANUIES. I use the published totals in all calculations.

SOURCE: Adrián Lajous Vargas, "Aspectos regionales de la expansión de la educación superior en México, 1959-1967," *Demografía y Economía* 2:3 (1968), 422. See also Lajous Vargas's licentiate thesis, "Aspectos de la educación superior y el empleo de profesionistas en México, 1959-1967," UNAM, 1967.

TABLE 3.   University Egresados, Eleven Fields, 1967-89

PART I. Absolute Data

Year	Arch.	BUS	Econ.	ENG	HEALTH	HUM	Law	Psych./SW	SCI	SS	TEACH[1]	Total
1967	1,080	3,111	530	3,583	2,798	169	1,986	148	312	285	1,265	15,267
1968	862	3,416	677	4,495	3,014	385	1,936	248	697	364	888	16,982
1969	843	4,511	702	5,580	3,667	566	2,897	222	713	574	1,120	21,395
1970	1,010	5,384	736	6,647	3,608	259	2,820	326	454	283	1,068	22,595
1971	1,005	6,562	855	7,348	4,267	256	2,819	355	607	259	1,265	25,598
1972[a]	1,060	5,640	840	9,660	5,220	310	3,380	360	620	320	1,880	29,290
1973[a]	900	7,770	1,040	10,440	5,480	360	3,140	550	620	410	2,320	33,030
1974[a]	1,590	7,680	1,030	12,230	7,240	380	3,830	510	1,030	550	3,040	39,110
1975[a]	1,790	7,580	1,370	13,480	8,470	500	5,330	900	900	650	3,560	44,530
1976	2,043	12,142	1,663	13,828	10,547	350	5,192	684	853	874	4,373	52,549
1977	2,183	12,094	2,065	17,136	13,557	414	5,231	1,087	787	831	6,477	61,862
1978	2,905	10,709	2,290	16,605	15,269	492	6,038	1,917	1,324	891	8,393	66,833
1979	3,811	13,290	1,786	18,757	18,534	508	5,497	1,829	1,530	664	10,654	76,860
1980	2,556	13,819	1,722	20,798	18,051	622	6,154	2,545	1,586	783	14,167	82,803
1981	2,771	14,964	2,186	23,296	20,744	871	6,933	2,845	1,985	1,305	13,901	91,801
1982	3,189	17,812	2,158	25,538	20,872	829	6,516	3,705	2,175	1,514	16,496	100,804
1983	4,111	23,809	1,775	26,756	20,177	1,078	8,498	4,463	2,335	1,383	19,225	113,610
1984	4,583	25,061	1,817	28,150	18,740	1,235	8,572	4,599	2,705	1,547	18,207	115,216

TABLE 3, PART I (Continued)

Year	Arch.	BUS	Econ.	ENG	HEALTH	HUM	Law	Psych.	SW SCI	SS	TEACH[1]	Total
1985	4,182	28,101	1,859	27,135	17,205	1,168	9,516	4,339	2,873	2,025	21,697	120,100
1986	5,261	28,210	1,936	31,278	16,414	1,194	10,568	4,969	2,629	2,253	20,928	125,640
1987	5,792	32,844	2,335	33,817	17,272	1,526	11,478	5,184	2,949	2,244	17,451	132,892
1988	5,716	31,928	2,267	34,885	15,965	1,564	10,621	5,083	3,085	2,341	25,591	139,046
1989	5,857	34,990	2,111	32,694	14,789	1,426	11,465	4,372	3,191	2,280	27,265	140,440

PART II. Percentage Data

Year	Arch.	BUS	Econ.	ENG	HEALTH	HUM	Law	Psych.	SWSCI	SS	TEACH
1967	7.1	20.4	3.5	23.5	18.3	1.1	13.0	1.0	2.0	1.9	8.3
1968	5.1	20.1	4.0	26.5	17.7	2.3	11.4	1.5	4.1	2.1	5.2
1969	3.9	21.1	3.3	26.1	17.1	2.6	13.5	1.0	3.3	2.7	5.2
1970	4.5	23.8	3.3	29.4	16.0	1.1	12.5	1.4	2.0	1.3	4.7
1971	3.9	25.6	3.3	28.7	16.7	1.0	11.0	1.4	2.4	1.0	4.9
1972	3.6	19.3	2.9	33.0	17.8	1.1	11.5	1.2	2.1	1.1	6.4
1973	2.7	23.5	3.1	31.6	16.6	1.1	9.5	1.7	1.9	1.2	7.0
1974	4.1	19.6	2.6	31.3	18.5	1.0	9.8	1.3	2.6	1.4	7.8
1975	4.0	17.0	3.1	30.3	19.0	1.1	12.0	2.0	2.0	1.5	8.0
1976	3.9	23.1	3.2	26.3	20.1	0.7	9.9	1.3	1.6	1.7	8.3
1977	3.5	19.5	3.3	27.7	21.9	0.7	8.5	1.8	1.3	1.3	10.5
1978	4.3	16.0	3.4	24.8	22.8	0.7	9.0	2.9	2.0	1.3	12.6
1979	5.0	17.3	2.3	24.4	24.1	0.7	7.2	2.4	2.0	0.9	13.9

TABLE 3, PART II (Continued)

Year	Arch.	BUS	Econ.	ENG	HEALTH	HUM	Law	Psych./SWSCI		SS	TEACH
1980	3.1	16.7	2.1	25.1	21.8	0.8	7.4	3.1	1.9	0.9	17.1
1981	3.0	16.3	2.4	25.4	22.6	0.9	7.6	3.1	2.2	1.4	15.1
1982	3.2	17.7	2.1	25.3	20.7	0.8	6.5	3.7	2.2	1.5	16.4
1983	3.6	21.0	1.6	23.6	17.8	0.9	7.5	3.9	2.1	1.2	16.9
1984	4.0	21.8	1.6	24.4	16.3	1.1	7.4	4.0	2.3	1.3	15.8
1985	3.5	23.4	1.5	22.6	14.3	1.0	7.9	3.6	2.4	1.7	18.1
1986	4.2	22.5	1.5	24.9	13.1	1.0	8.4	4.0	2.1	1.8	16.7
1987	4.4	24.7	1.8	25.4	13.0	1.1	8.6	3.9	2.2	1.7	13.1
1988	4.1	23.0	1.6	25.1	11.5	1.1	7.6	3.7	2.2	1.7	18.4
1989	4.2	24.9	1.5	23.3	10.5	1.0	8.2	3.1	2.3	1.6	19.4

1. Secondary teaching only, 1967-84; for 1985-89 the data include all licentiate-level egresados of teaching fields.
a. Data for 1972-75 were partially estimated to adjust for incomplete coverage in source.

SOURCE: Data derived from ANUIES-AE and ANUIES-ESM, various years, and unpublished ANUIES data.

TABLE 4. **Degrees Registered, Six Fields, 1945-70**

(%)

Year	BUS	ENG	HEALTH	Law	SCI	TEACH
1945-70	5.3	31.2	30.9	13.0	1.7	1.1

SOURCE: DGP.

TABLE 5.   **Degrees Registered, Eleven Fields,**[1] **1970-85**

PART I. Absolute Data

Year	Arch.	BUS	Econ.	ENG	HEALTH	HUM	Law	Psych.	/SWSCI	SS	TEACH	Total
1970	510	840	190	2,920	2,330	0	1,180	0	90	170	100	8,330
1971	900	1,850	440	4,860	3,500	0	1,890	0	170	410	290	14,310
1972	510	1,690	280	3,280	2,900	0	1,460	0	110	260	260	10,750
1973	460	1,800	280	3,000	3,030	0	1,450	0	130	230	180	10,560
1974	710	3,970	380	4,640	4,750	190	1,700	150	300	540	250	17,580
1975	1,010	4,450	440	5,650	5,380	220	2,120	250	350	720	610	21,200
1976	1,140	4,230	400	7,120	5,680	260	2,010	280	390	730	3,620	25,860
1977	1,270	4,580	590	8,680	6,920	240	2,360	290	440	1,120	4,620	31,110
1978	1,500	4,990	630	9,080	9,350	320	2,920	350	480	1,080	1,710	32,410
1979	1,430	4,940	570	8,780	10,140	480	2,800	450	500	1,230	2,240	33,560
1980	1,160	4,460	670	8,580	12,060	290	2,800	750	520	2,090	2,260	35,640
1981	1,380	4,730	700	9,350	12,170	740	2,850	710	450	1,630	4,030	38,740
1982	1,490	4,400	1,030	10,470	13,650	890	2,870	1,170	540	3,270	3,720	43,500
1983	1,680	5,040	1,000	12,630	12,880	1,100	2,850	1,200	540	2,750	2,790	44,460
1984	2,190	7,670	1,040	13,630	13,710	1,800	3,550	1,350	670	3,730	1,700	51,040
1985	2,020	8,500	1,000	15,040	14,000	16,80	3,480	1,300	390	4,470	3,770	55,650

PART II. **Percentage Data**

Year	Arch.	BUS	Econ.	ENG	HEALTH	HUM	Law	Psych.	SWSCI	SS	TEACH
1970	6.1	10.1	2.3	35.1	28.0	0.0	14.2	0.0	1.1	2.0	1.2
1971	6.3	12.9	3.1	34.0	24.5	0.0	13.2	0.0	1.2	2.9	2.0
1972	4.7	15.7	2.6	30.5	27.0	0.0	13.6	0.0	1.0	2.4	2.4
1973	4.4	17.0	2.7	28.4	28.7	0.0	13.7	0.0	1.2	2.2	1.7
1974	4.0	22.6	2.2	26.4	27.0	1.1	9.7	0.9	1.7	3.1	1.4
1975	4.8	21.0	2.1	26.7	25.4	1.0	10.0	1.2	1.7	3.4	2.9
1976	4.4	16.4	1.5	27.5	22.0	1.0	7.8	1.1	1.5	2.8	14.0
1977	4.1	14.7	1.9	27.9	22.2	0.8	7.6	0.9	1.4	3.6	14.9
1978	4.6	15.4	1.9	28.0	28.8	1.0	9.0	1.1	1.5	3.3	5.3
1979	4.3	14.7	1.7	26.2	30.2	1.4	8.3	1.3	1.5	3.7	6.7
1980	3.3	12.5	1.9	24.1	33.8	0.8	7.9	2.1	1.5	5.9	6.3
1981	3.6	12.2	1.8	24.1	31.4	1.9	7.4	1.8	1.2	4.2	10.4
1982	3.4	10.1	2.4	24.1	31.4	2.0	6.6	2.7	1.2	7.5	8.6
1983	3.8	11.3	2.2	28.4	29.0	2.5	6.4	2.7	1.2	6.2	6.3
1984	4.3	15.0	2.0	26.7	26.9	3.5	7.0	2.6	1.3	7.3	3.3
1985	3.6	15.3	1.8	27.0	25.2	3.0	6.3	2.3	0.7	8.0	6.8

1. It was not required that humanities degrees be registered until 1974.

SOURCE: Data derived from unpublished manuscripts and tabulations at DGP.

TABLE 6. **Percentage Change in Degrees Granted, Egresados, and Degrees Registered**

PART I. **By Presidential Sexenio, 1929-89**
(Percentage Change by 6-year Period)

Sexenio	Degrees Granted	Egresados	Degrees Registered
1929-34	98.7	~	~
1935-40	33.8	~	~
1941-46	59.8	~	~
1947-52	18.2	~	~
1953-58	9.3	~	~
1959-64	109.1	~	~
1965-70	65.7	~	~
1971-76	~	105.3	80.7
1977-82	~	62.9	39.8
1983-89[a]	~	22.4	48.5

PART II. **Implicit Annual Percentage Change[1] by Decade, 1930-89**

Decade	Degrees Granted	Egresados	Degrees Registered
1930-40	7.2	~	~
1940-50	6.1	~	~
1950-60	5.8	~	~
1960-70[b]	12.4	9.8	~
1970-80[c]	~	13.9	10.7
1980-89	~	5.4	~

1. Compound rates of change calculated with the following formula: annual rate equals antilog of $(\log(P_n/P_0)/n)$, minus 1, where P_0 equals the original population and P_n equals the population after n years. A 100 percent change over ten years equals 7.18 percent change per year.

a. Partially estimated for degrees registered.
b. Egresados data are for 1963-70.
c. Degrees registered data are for 1971-80.

SOURCE: Calculated from Tables 1, 3, and 5.

TABLE 7. **Degrees Granted, Egresados, and Degrees Registered
per One Million Inhabitants, 1928-89**

Year	Degrees Granted	Egresados	Degrees Registered
1928	33		
1929	26		
1930	32		
1931	29		
1932	34		
1933	31		
1934	50		
1935	43		
1936	51		
1937	52		
1938	54		
1939	56		
1940	53		
1941	60		
1942	68		
1943	77		
1944	80		
1945	75		
1946	85		
1947	91		
1948	81		
1949	87		
1950	74		
1951	94		
1952	90		
1953	110		
1954	99		
1955	117		
1956	91		
1957	136		
1958	102		
1959	77		

TABLE 7 (Continued)

Year	Degrees Granted	Egresados	Degrees Registered
1960	92		
1961	106		
1962	110		
1963	128		
1964	139		
1965	156		
1966	167		
1967	168	334	
1968	191	359	
1969	201	437	
1970	218	446	164
1971	256	488	273
1972		540	198
1973		588	188
1974		673	303
1975		740	353
1976		843	415
1977		958	482
1978		1,021	495
1979		1,140	498
1980		1,194	514
1981		1,290	544
1982		1,381	596
1983		1,513	592
1984		1,500	665
1985		1,530	709
1986		1,579	
1987		1,637	
1988		1,681	
1989		1,667	

SOURCE: Calculated from Tables 1, 3, and 5 and population data from SALA.

TABLE 8. **Professional Degrees as Percentage of All Degrees, 1928-71**

Year	Percent	Year	Percent
1928	26.9	1960	19.6
1929	27.7	1961	19.9
1930	29.7	1962	17.9
1931	25.6	1963	13.1
1932	27.1	1964	16.8
1933	28.6	1965	19.3
1934	31.3	1966	19.5
1935	31.9	1967	16.5
1936	40.3	1968	22.0
1937	39.1	1969	20.1
1938	42.0	1970	17.3
1939	35.7	1971	23.2
1940	43.3		
1941	31.4		
1942	30.7		
1943	33.5		
1944	32.5		
1945	30.1		
1946	33.4		
1947	33.7		
1948	32.1		
1949	35.0		
1950	32.8		
1951	23.4		
1952	23.2		
1953	27.6		
1954	21.5		
1955	25.4		
1956	23.0		
1957	26.7		
1958	19.1		
1959	16.4		

SOURCE: Calculated from Table 1 and AE, CE, and SEP-ESM.

TABLE 9.   **Ratios of Degrees Granted, Egresados,
Degrees Registered, and Enrollment**

PART I. **Comparison of Egresados
and Degrees Registered, 1970-85**

Year	Egresados per Degree Registed
1970	2.7
1971	1.8
1972	2.5
1973	3.0
1974	2.0
1975	1.9
1976	2.0
1977	2.0
1978	2.1
1979	2.2
1980	2.3
1981	2.4
1982	2.3
1983	2.6
1984	2.3
1985	2.1

SOURCE: Calculated from Tables 3 and 5.

PART II. Indexes of Degrees Granted, Egresados, Degrees Registered, and Enrollment, 1928-89

Year	Index of Degrees Granted (1970=100)	Index of Egresados (1970=100)	Index of Registered Degrees (1971=100)	Index of Enrollment (1970=100)
1928	4.8			6.2
1929	4.0			5.5
1930	4.7			8.7
1931	4.4			7.8
1932	5.3			
1933	4.9			
1934	8.0			
1935	7.1			5.6
1936				
1937	8.8			
1938	9.3			
1939	9.8			
1940	9.5			
1941	11.0			
1942	12.7			
1943	14.8			
1944	15.7			
1945	15.2			
1946	17.6			
1947	19.2			
1948	17.6			
1949	19.5			8.4
1950	17.2			11.0
1951	21.8			6.5
1952	22.8			11.8
1953	28.6			10.6
1954	26.5			8.4
1955	32.5			17.2
1956	26.1			8.7
1957	40.0			17.5
1958	31.2			10.1
1959	24.2			9.2

TABLE 9, PART II (Continued)

Year	Index of Degrees Granted (1970=100)	Index of Egre-sados (1970=100)	Index of Registered Degrees (1971=100)	Index of Enroll-ment (1970=100)
1960	30.1			10.4
1961	35.6			30.6
1962	38.3			35.1
1963	46.1			35.8
1964	51.8			40.3
1965	60.3			51.9
1966	66.7			64.3
1967	69.6	66.6		72.7
1968	81.5	74.2		81.9
1969	89.0	84.2		90.7
1970	**100.0**	**100.0**	58.2	**100.0**
1971	121.3	114.3	**100.0**	116.5
1972		118.3	75.1	130.9
1973		140.6	73.8	148.5
1974		155.7	122.9	173.9
1975		175.7	148.1	200.2
1976		235.0	180.7	209.8
1977		276.0	217.4	224.5
1978		299.5	226.5	272.8
1979		328.1	234.5	312.9
1980		367.9	249.1	345.7
1981		407.5	270.7	371.3
1982		447.1	304.0	
1983		504.7	310.7	
1984		511.9	356.7	
1985		527.3	388.9	
1986		542.5		
1987		586.5		
1988		590.7		
1989		579.3		

SOURCE: Calculated from Tables 1, 3, and 5.

PART III. **Degrees Granted, Egresados, and Degrees Registered
per Enrolled Student, 1928-81**

	A. Enrolled Student per Degree Granted	B. Enrolled Student per Egresado	C. Enrolled Student per Degree Registered	Index of A. (1970= 100)	Index of B. (1970= 100)	Index of C. (1970= 100)
Year						
1928	31			124.0		
1929	34			136.0		
1930	45			180.0		
1931	44			176.0		
1935	19			76.0		
1949	11			44.0		
1950	16			64.0		
1951	7			28.0		
1952	13			52.0		
1953	9			36.0		
1954	8			32.0		
1955	13			52.0		
1956	8			32.0		
1957	11			44.0		
1958	8			32.0		
1959	9			36.0		
1960	8			32.0		
1961	21			84.0		
1962	22			88.0		
1963	19			76.0		
1964	19			76.0		
1965	21			84.0		
1966	24			96.0		
1967	26	13		104.0	108.3	
1968	25	13		100.0	108.3	
1969	25	13		100.0	108.3	
1970	**25**	**12**	**33**	**100.0**	**100.0**	**100.0**
1971	24	12	22	96.0	100.0	66.7
1972		13	33		108.3	100.0
1973		13	38		108.3	115.2
1974		13	27		108.3	81.8

TABLE 9, PART III (Continued)

Year	A. Enrolled Student per Degree Granted	B. Enrolled Student per Egre-sado	C. Enrolled Student per Degree Registered	Index of A. (1970= 100)	Index of B. (1970= 100)	Index of C. (1970= 100)
1975	14	26			116.7	78.8
1976	11	22			91.7	66.7
1977	10	20			83.3	60.6
1978	11	23			91.7	69.7
1979	11	25			91.7	75.8
1980	11	26			91.7	78.8
1981	11	26			91.7	78.8

SOURCE: Calculated from Tables 1,3, 5, and population data from SALA.

TABLE 10. **Professionals in Sample Economic[1] and Social[2] Fields, 1928-89**

PART I. **Absolute Data**

Year	Time-Lag[3] Year	Degrees Granted Economic	Social	Egresados Economic	Social	Degrees Registered Economic	Social
1928	1922	134	244				
1929	1923	79	265				
1930	1924	117	249				
1931	1925	62	259				
1932	1926	98	297				
1933	1927	65	297				
1934	1928	92	443				
1935	1929	87	402				
1936	1930	124	495				
1937	1931	128	512				
1938	1932	200	512				
1939	1933	148	533				
1940	1934	148	502				
1941	1935	207	692				
1942	1936	220	807				
1943	1937	389	790				
1944	1938	377	961				
1945	1939	343	957				
1946	1940	450	998				
1947	1941	480	974				
1948	1942	443	1,068				
1949	1943	595	1,059				
1950	1944	386	1,156				
1951	1945	551	1,296				
1952	1946	621	1,264				
1953	1947	684	1,727				
1954	1948	834	1,451				
1955	1949	941	2,008				
1956	1950	760	1,640				
1957	1951	1,514	1,867				
1958	1952	1,254	1,289				
1959	1953	1,075	851				

TABLE 10, PART I (Continued)

Year	Time-Lag[3] Year	Degrees Granted Economic	Social	Egresados Economic	Social	Degrees Registered Economic	Social
1960	1954	1,393	964				
1961	1955	1,508	1,354				
1962	1956	1,829	1,506				
1963	1957	2,186	1,612				
1964	1958	2,180	2,119				
1965	1959	2,615	2,323				
1966	1960	3,023	2,556				
1967	1961	3,342	2,396	6,694	4,063		
1968	1962	3,468	3,058	7,911	3,902		
1969	1963	3799	3,247	10,091	4,787		
1970	1964	4,734	3,081	12,031	4,676	3,760	2,430
1971	1965	5,201	3,720	13,910	5,532	6,710	3,790
1972	1966			15,300	7,100	4,970	3,160
1973	1967			18,210	7,800	4,800	3,210
1974	1968			19,910	10,280	8,610	5,000
1975	1969			21,060	12,030	10,100	5,990
1976	1970			28,747	14,920	11,350	9,300
1977	1971			30,851	20,034	13,260	11,540
1978	1972			31,507	23,662	14,070	11,060
1979	1973			36,586	29,188	13,720	12,380
1980	1974			40,575	32,218	13,040	14,320
1981	1975			43,114	34,645	14,080	16,200
1982	1976			44,947	37,368	14,870	17,370
1983	1977			55,087	39,402	17,670	15,670
1984	1978			58,878	36,947	21,300	15,410
1985	1979			62,986	38,902	23,540	17,770
1986	1980			60,904	37,342		
1987	1981			32,844	34,723		
1988	1982			35,511	41,556		
1989	1983			39,485	42,054		

PART II. Percentage Data

Year	Time-Lag[3] Year	Degrees Granted Economic	Social	Egresados Economic	Social	Degrees Registered Economic	Social
1928	1922	25.0	45.6				
1929	1923	17.8	59.8				
1930	1924	22.3	47.4				
1931	1925	12.8	53.5				
1932	1926	16.8	51.0				
1933	1927	12.0	54.7				
1934	1928	10.5	50.3				
1935	1929	11.1	51.3				
1936	1930	13.1	52.3				
1937	1931	13.1	52.4				
1938	1932	19.5	50.0				
1939	1933	13.7	49.4				
1940	1934	14.1	47.9				
1941	1935	17.0	57.0				
1942	1936	15.7	57.7				
1943	1937	23.8	48.4				
1944	1938	21.7	55.4				
1945	1939	20.5	57.1				
1946	1940	23.2	51.4				
1947	1941	22.6	45.8				
1948	1942	22.7	54.8				
1949	1943	27.6	49.2				
1950	1944	20.3	60.8				
1951	1945	22.9	53.8				
1952	1946	24.7	50.3				
1953	1947	21.7	54.7				
1954	1948	28.5	49.6				
1955	1949	26.2	56.0				
1956	1950	26.4	56.9				
1957	1951	34.3	42.3				
1958	1952	36.3	37.3				
1959	1953	40.3	31.9				

TABLE 10, PART II (Continued)

Year	Time-Lag[3] Year	Degrees Granted Economic	Social	Egresados Economic	Social	Degrees Registered Economic	Social
1960	1954	41.8	29.0				
1961	1955	38.3	34.4				
1962	1956	43.2	35.6				
1963	1957	42.9	31.6				
1964	1958	38.1	37.0				
1965	1959	39.2	34.9				
1966	1960	41.0	34.7				
1967	1961	43.5	31.2	43.8	26.6		
1968	1962	38.5	34.0	46.6	23.0		
1969	1963	38.6	33.0	47.2	22.4		
1970	1964	42.8	27.9	53.2	20.7	45.1	29.2
1971	1965	38.8	27.7	54.3	21.6	46.9	26.5
1972	1966			52.2	24.2	46.2	29.4
1973	1967			55.1	23.6	45.5	30.4
1974	1968			50.9	26.3	49.0	28.4
1975	1969			47.3	27.0	47.6	28.3
1976	1970			49.4	28.4	43.9	36.0
1977	1971			47.3	32.4	42.6	37.1
1978	1972			40.9	35.4	43.4	34.1
1979	1973			41.7	38.0	40.9	36.9
1980	1974			41.8	38.9	36.6	40.2
1981	1975			41.7	37.7	36.3	41.8
1982	1976			43.0	37.1	34.2	39.9
1983	1977			44.5	34.7	39.7	35.2
1984	1978			46.2	32.1	41.7	30.2
1985	1979			46.0	32.4	42.3	31.9
1986	1980			47.3	29.7		
1987	1981			50.2	26.1		
1988	1982			48.1	29.9		
1989	1983			48.2	29.9		

1. BUS and ENG categories.
2. HEALTH and TEACH categories.
3. Estimated year of career-field decision of university degree-holders or egresados.

SOURCE: Calculated from Tables 1, 3, and 5.

TABLE 11.   Indexes of Professionals in Sample Economic[1] and
Social[2] Fields, 1928-89

(1970=100)

Year	Time-Lag[3] Year	Degrees Granted		Egresados		Degrees Registered	
		Economic	Social	Economic	Social	Economic	Social
1928	1922	3	8				
1929	1923	2	9				
1930	1924	2	8				
1931	1925	1	8				
1932	1926	2	10				
1933	1927	1	10				
1934	1928	2	14				
1935	1929	2	13				
1936	1930	3	16				
1937	1931	3	17				
1938	1932	4	17				
1939	1933	3	17				
1940	1934	3	16				
1941	1935	4	22				
1942	1936	5	26				
1943	1937	8	26				
1944	1938	8	31				
1945	1939	7	31				
1946	1940	10	32				
1947	1941	10	32				
1948	1942	9	35				
1949	1943	13	34				
1950	1944	8	38				
1951	1945	12	42				
1952	1946	13	41				
1953	1947	14	56				
1954	1948	18	47				
1955	1949	20	65				
1956	1950	16	53				
1957	1951	32	61				
1958	1952	26	42				
1959	1953	23	28				

TABLE 11 (Continued)

Year	Time-Lag[3] Year	Degrees Granted Economic	Social	Egresados Economic	Social	Degrees Registered Economic	Social
1960	1954	29	31				
1961	1955	32	44				
1962	1956	39	49				
1963	1957	46	52				
1964	1958	46	69				
1965	1959	55	75				
1966	1960	64	83				
1967	1961	71	78	56	87		
1968	1962	73	99	66	83		
1969	1963	80	105	84	102		
1970	1964	100	100	100	100	100	100
1971	1965	110	121	116	118	178	156
1972	1966			127	152	132	130
1973	1967			151	167	128	132
1974	1968			165	220	229	206
1975	1969			175	257	269	247
1976	1970			239	319	302	383
1977	1971			256	428	353	475
1978	1972			262	506	374	455
1979	1973			304	624	365	509
1980	1974			337	689	347	589
1981	1975			358	741	374	667
1982	1976			374	799	395	715
1983	1977			458	843	470	645
1984	1978			489	790	566	634
1985	1979			524	832	626	731
1986	1980			506	799		
1987	1981			273	743		
1988	1982			295	889		
1989	1983			328	899		

1. BUS and ENG categories.
2. HEALTH and TEACH categories.
3. Estimated year of career-field decision of university graduates.

SOURCE: Calculated from Tables 1, 3, and 5 above.

TABLE 12. Average Index and Percentage Distribution of Professionals in Sample Economic[1] and Social[2] Fields, 1928-89

PART I. Yearly Data

Year	Time-Lag Year	Average Index of Absolute Data (1970=100) Economic	Social	Percentage Distribution Economic	Social
1928	1922	3	8	25.0	45.6
1929	1923	2	9	17.8	59.8
1930	1924	2	8	22.3	47.4
1931	1925	1	8	12.8	53.5
1932	1926	2	10	16.8	51.0
1933	1927	1	10	12.0	54.7
1934	1928	2	14	10.5	50.3
1935	1929	2	13	11.1	51.3
1936	1930	3	16	13.1	52.3
1937	1931	3	17	13.1	52.4
1938	1932	4	17	19.5	50.0
1939	1933	3	17	13.7	49.4
1940	1934	3	16	14.1	47.9
1941	1935	4	22	17.0	57.0
1942	1936	5	26	15.7	57.7
1943	1937	8	26	23.8	48.4
1944	1938	8	31	21.7	55.4
1945	1939	7	31	20.5	57.1
1946	1940	10	32	23.2	51.4
1947	1941	10	32	22.6	45.8
1948	1942	9	35	22.7	54.8
1949	1943	13	34	27.6	49.2
1950	1944	8	38	20.3	60.8
1951	1945	12	42	22.9	53.8
1952	1946	13	41	24.7	50.3
1953	1947	14	56	21.7	54.7
1954	1948	18	47	28.5	49.6

TABLE 12, PART I (Continued)

Year	Time-Lag Year	Average Index of Absolute Data (1970=100) Economic	Social	Percentage Distribution Economic	Social
1955	1949	20	65	26.2	56.0
1956	1950	16	53	26.4	56.9
1957	1951	32	61	34.3	42.3
1958	1952	26	42	36.3	37.3
1959	1953	23	28	40.3	31.9
1960	1954	29	31	41.8	29.0
1961	1955	32	44	38.3	34.4
1962	1956	39	49	43.2	35.6
1963	1957	46	52	42.9	31.6
1964	1958	46	69	38.1	37.0
1965	1959	55	75	39.2	34.9
1966	1960	64	83	41.0	34.7
1967	1961	63	82	43.7	28.9
1968	1962	70	91	42.6	28.5
1969	1963	82	104	42.9	27.7
1970	1964	100	100	47.1	25.9
1971	1965	134	132	46.7	25.3
1972	1966	130	141	49.2	26.8
1973	1967	140	149	50.3	27.0
1974	1968	197	213	49.9	27.4
1975	1969	222	252	47.5	27.6
1976	1970	270	351	46.7	32.2
1977	1971	305	452	44.9	34.7
1978	1972	318	481	42.1	34.8
1979	1973	335	567	41.3	37.4
1980	1974	342	639	39.2	39.5
1981	1975	366	704	39.0	39.8
1982	1976	384	757	38.6	38.5
1983	1977	464	744	42.1	35.0
1984	1978	528	712	44.0	31.1
1985	1979	575	781	44.1	32.2
1986	1980	253	399	47.3	29.7
1987	1981	273	743	50.2	26.1
1988	1982	295	889	48.1	29.9
1989	1983	328	899	48.2	29.9

PART II. Sexenial Data, Time-Lagged Six Years, 1923-82

Time-Lag Sexenio	Econ. Fields	Social Fields
1923-28	15.4	52.8
1929-34	14.1	50.6
1935-40	20.3	54.5
1941-46	23.5	52.5
1947-52	28.9	49.5
1953-58	40.8	33.3
1959-64	42.7	30.1
1965-70	48.4	27.7
1971-76	40.9	37.5
1977-82	46.0	30.7

1. BUS and ENG categories.
2. HEALTH and TEACH categories.
3. Estimated year of career-field decision of university degree recipients or egresados.

SOURCE: Calculated from Part I above.

PART III. Comparison of Federal Expenditure in Social and Economic Areas (Actual and Projected) with Univerity Graduates in Social and Economic Fields, 1929-34 to 1971-76

(% of Total Expenditure/% of University Graduates)

Sexenio	Areas of Actual Federal Expenditure		Fields of University Graduates	
	A Economic	B Social	C Economic	D Social
1929-34[1]	25.2	15.2	14.1	50.6
1935-40	37.6	18.3	20.3	54.5
1941-46	39.2	16.5	23.5	52.5
1947-52	51.9	13.3	28.9	49.5
1953-58	52.7	14.4	40.8	33.3
1959-64	39.0	19.2	42.7	30.1
1965-70	40.6	21.0	48.4	27.7
1971-76	44.7	23.5	40.9	37.5

TABLE 12, PART III (Continued)

Sexenio	Projected Federal Expenditure E Economic	F Social	University Graduates C Economic	D Social
1929-34[1]	25.5	15.1	14.1	50.6
1935-40	30.5	23.0	20.3	54.5
1941-46	30.7	23.5	23.5	52.5
1947-52	39.2	18.6	28.9	49.5
1953-58	43.8	20.4	40.8	33.3
1959-64	38.8	30.8	42.7	30.1
1965-70	38.1	37.4	48.4	27.7
1971-76	39.1	30.6	40.9	37.5

1. For university graduates, data reflect six-year time lag.

Correlation Matrix for Part III

	B	C	D	E	F
A	-.139	.540	-.305	.871*	.103
B		.510	-.457	.125	.833*
C			-.937**	.847*	.789*
D				-.718	-.713
E					.398

One-tailed significance: *—.01; **—.001.

SOURCE: Calculated from Part I above and James W. Wilkie, *La revolución mexicana: Gasto federal y cambio social* (México, D.F.: Fondo de Cultura Económica, 1978).

PART IV. Comparison of Federal Expenditure in Social and Economic Areas (in Pesos of 1950 per Capita) with Univerity Graduates in Social and Economic Fields (Degrees per Million Inhabitants), 1923-28 to 1959-64

	Degrees per Million Mexicans Fields		Actual Expenditure (Pesos of 1950 per Capita) Areas		Projected Expenditure (Pesos of 1950 per Capita) Areas		Percentage Change					
	G	H	I	J	K	L	M (G)[1]	N (H)	N (I)	P (J)	Q (K)	R (L)
Sexenios	Economic	Social	Economic	Social	Economic	Social	~	~	~	~	~	~
1923-28	5.0	17.5	14.6	6.4	14.2	7.6						
1929-34	7.3	26.0	14.6	8.8	15.7	8.9	46.7	48.5	0.5	37.9	10.3	16.9
1935-40	15.3	40.3	30.9	15.0	19.3	14.6	108.7	54.8	111.2	69.8	22.9	64.5
1941-46	20.3	44.9	40.4	17.0	21.7	16.6	32.4	11.4	30.7	13.3	12.4	13.7
1947-52	31.8	53.7	76.1	19.5	41.3	19.6	56.7	19.7	88.4	14.7	90.3	18.1
1953-58	44.2	36.4	95.3	26.0	51.9	24.2	39.1	-32.3	25.2	33.3	25.7	23.5
1959-64	74.6	59.4	95.2	47.0	56.5	45.2	68.8	63.3	-0.1	80.8	8.9	86.8

1. Percentage change from period to period in columns G through L is represented by columns M through R.

Correlation Matrix for Part IV, 1929-34 to 1959-64

	H	I	J	K	L	M	N	O	P	Q	R
G	.718	.887*	.988**	.927*	.985**	-.013	.003	-.352	.443	-.040	.600
H		.637	.732	.612	.752	.174	.202	.147	.202	.348	.498
I			.811	.986**	.804	-.160	-.389	-.152	.113	.279	.286
J				.858	.999**	.063	.121	-.358	.535	-.143	.690
K					.852	-.136	-.287	-.248	.214	.207	.359
L						.070	.145	-.349	.532	-.124	.693
M							.627	.631	.725	.023	.717
N								.041	.653	-.233	.630
O									-.050	.595	.039
P										-.467	.947*
Q											-.317

One-tailed significance: *—.01;   **—.001.

Source: Calculated from Part I above and James W. Wilkie, *La revolución mexicana: Gasto federal y cambio social* (México, D.F.: Fondo de Cultura Económica, 1978).

TABLE 13. Engineering Degrees Granted, Egresados, and Degrees Registered, 1929-89

Year	Number of Degrees Granted	Percentage Share of Total	Number of Egresados	Percentage Share of Total	Number of Degrees Registered	Percentage Share of Total
1929	79	17.8				
1930	117	22.3				
1931	62	12.8				
1932	98	16.8				
1933	65	12.0				
1934	92	10.5				
1935	87	11.1				
1936	124	13.1				
1937	128	13.1				
1938	170	16.6				
1939	148	13.7				
1940	148	14.1				
1941	137	11.3				
1942	142	10.2				
1943	299	18.3				
1944	287	16.6				
1945	253	15.1				
1946	348	17.9				
1947	337	15.8				
1948	320	16.4				
1949	495	23.0				

TABLE 13 (Continued)

Year	Number of Degrees Granted	Percentage Share of Total	Number of Egresados	Percentage Share of Total	Number of Degrees Registered	Percentage Share of Total
1950	256	13.5				
1951	401	16.6				
1952	461	18.3				
1953	434	13.7				
1954	554	18.9				
1955	651	18.1				
1956	480	16.6				
1957	1,164	26.3				
1958	894	25.9				
1959	705	26.4				
1960	1,013	30.4				
1961	1,048	26.6				
1962	1,349	31.9				
1963	1,305	25.6				
1964	1,648	28.8				
1965	2,127	31.9				
1966	2,289	31.0				
1967	2,539	33.0	3,583	23.5		
1968	2,543	28.2	4,495	26.5		
1969	2,871	29.2	5,580	26.1		

TABLE 13 (Continued)

Year	Number of Degrees Granted	Percentage Share of Total	Number of Egresados	Percentage Share of Total	Number of Degrees Registered	Percentage Share of Total
1970	3,348	30.3	6,647	29.4	2,920	35.1
1971	2,475	18.5	7,348	28.7	4,860	34.0
1972			9,660	33.0	3,280	30.5
1973			10,440	31.6	3,000	28.4
1974			12,230	31.3	4,640	26.4
1975			13,480	30.3	5,650	26.7
1976			13,828	26.3	7,120	27.5
1977			17,136	27.7	8,680	27.9
1978			16,605	24.8	9,080	28.0
1979			18,737	24.4	8,780	26.2
1980			20,798	25.1	8,580	24.1
1981			23,296	25.4	9,350	24.1
1982			25,538	25.3	10,470	24.1
1983			26,756	23.6	12,630	28.4
1984			28,150	24.4	13,630	26.7
1985			27,135	22.6	15,040	27.0
1986			31,278	24.9		
1987			33,817	25.4		
1988			34,885	25.1		
1989			32,694	23.3		

SOURCE: AE; CE; SEP-ESM; ANUIES-AE; ANUIES-ESM; DGP; Víctor Urquidi and Adrián Lajous Vargas, *Educacación superior, ciencia y tecnología en el desarrollo económico de México* (México, D. F.: El Colegio de México, 1967).

TABLE 14. Engineering Degrees Granted, Nine Specialties, 1928-71

PART I. Absoute Data

Year	Ag.	Civil	Mech./Elec.	Chem.	Extr.	Vet.	Top./Hyd.	Petrol.	Other	Total
1928	32	38	31	10	4	0	2	0	17	134
1929	31	12	12	6	3	0	4	0	11	79
1930	46	17	15	3	4	15	3	0	14	117
1931	9	18	1	0	4	10	6	0	14	62
1932	18	24	9	4	7	6	9	0	21	98
1933	1	23	22	7	2	3	7	0	0	65
1934	4	37	16	10	4	15	6	0	0	92
1935	13	24	17	10	3	12	5	3	0	87
1936	8	49	21	9	4	13	18	2	0	124
1937	27	45	19	6	4	9	11	2	5	128
1938	0	53	51	38	1	3	9	3	2	160
1939	4	52	56	7	12	6	5	3	3	148
1940	11	53	42	9	6	8	13	2	4	148
1941	32	38	20	18	7	5	8	5	4	137
1942	19	41	25	22	2	16	8	1	8	142
1943	59	88	46	21	11	9	35	3	27	299
1944	62	89	54	21	9	7	23	6	16	287

TABLE 14, PART I (Continued)

Year	Ag.	Civil	Mech./Elec.	Chem.	Extr.	Vet.	Top./Hyd.	Petrol.	Other	Total
1945	46	67	41	45	15	6	21	7	5	253
1946	109	71	57	37	12	7	33	1	21	348
1947	93	77	52	36	12	8	33	4	22	337
1948	76	82	46	34	11	9	33	7	22	320
1949	108	101	110	42	14	32	24	5	59	495
1950	51	102	14	34	6	10	8	7	24	256
1951	22	125	78	64	19	21	14	6	52	401
1952	45	111	54	104	14	22	20	9	82	461
1953	15	134	52	99	6	25	19	5	79	434
1954	86	181	90	91	10	27	13	12	44	554
1955	83	207	46	137	16	26	21	17	98	651
1956	167	89	88	48	1	16	10	16	45	480
1957	209	373	155	228	17	31	19	50	82	1,164
1958	159	254	169	123	15	40	18	30	86	894
1959	124	183	119	117	5	30	17	40	70	705
1960	245	294	174	103	23	21	19	69	65	1,013
1961	13	327	319	126	23	30	35	51	124	1,048
1962	66	365	374	221	54	50	54	71	94	1,349
1963	119	378	373	240	46	63	31	31	25	1,306
1964	97	468	347	168	40	92	50	80	170	1,507

TABLE 14, PART I (Continued)

Year	Ag.	Civil	Mech./Elec.	Chem.	Extr.	Vet.	Top./Hyd.	Petrol.	Other	Total
1965	91	618	468	177	50	119	60	110	210	1,903
1966	116	542	491	159	60	126	60	110	230	1,894
1967	179	577	442	215	60	218	70	130	250	2,141
1968	209	679	629	393	60	213	70	130	250	2,633
1969	114	-733	578	289	70	220	70	140	290	2,514
1970	206	755	694	318	80	312	90	170	340	2,965
1971	279	803	674	262	60	261	70	120	250	2,779

PART II. Percentage Data, Six Specialties

Year	Ag.+Vet.	Civil	Mech./Elec.	Chem.	Petrol. + Extr.	Top./ Hyd.	Other
1928	23.9	28.4	23.1	7.5	3.0	1.5	12.7
1929	39.2	15.2	15.2	7.6	3.8	5.1	13.9
1930	52.1	14.5	12.8	2.6	3.4	2.6	12.0
1931	30.6	29.0	1.6	0.0	6.5	9.7	22.6
1932	24.5	24.5	9.2	4.1	7.1	9.2	21.4
1933	6.2	35.4	33.8	10.8	3.1	10.8	0.0
1934	20.7	40.2	17.4	10.9	4.3	6.5	0.0

TABLE 14, PART II (Continued)

Year	Ag.+Vet.	Civil	Mech./Elec.	Chem.	Petrol. + Extr.	Top./ Hyd.	Other
1935	28.7	27.6	19.5	11.5	6.9	5.7	0.0
1936	16.9	39.5	16.9	7.3	4.8	14.5	0.0
1937	28.1	35.2	14.8	4.7	4.7	8.6	3.9
1938	1.9	33.1	31.9	23.8	2.5	5.6	1.3
1939	6.8	35.1	37.8	4.7	10.1	3.4	2.0
1940	12.8	35.8	28.4	6.1	5.4	8.8	2.7
1941	27.0	27.7	14.6	13.1	8.8	5.8	2.9
1942	24.6	28.9	17.6	15.5	2.1	5.6	5.6
1943	22.7	29.4	15.4	7.0	4.7	11.7	9.0
1944	24.0	31.0	18.8	7.3	5.2	8.0	5.6
1945	20.6	26.5	16.2	17.8	8.7	8.3	2.0
1946	33.3	20.4	16.4	10.6	3.7	9.5	6.0
1947	30.0	22.8	15.4	10.7	4.7	9.8	6.5
1948	26.6	25.6	14.4	10.6	5.6	10.3	6.9
1949	28.3	20.4	22.2	8.5	3.8	4.8	11.9
1950	23.8	39.8	5.5	13.3	5.1	3.1	9.4
1951	10.7	31.2	19.5	16.0	6.2	3.5	13.0
1952	14.5	24.1	11.7	22.6	5.0	4.3	17.8
1953	9.2	30.9	12.0	22.8	2.5	4.4	18.2
1954	20.4	32.7	16.2	16.4	4.0	2.3	7.9

TABLE 14, PART II (Continued)

Year	Ag.+Vet.	Civil	Mech./Elec.	Chem.	Petrol. + Extr.	Top./ Hyd.	Other
1955	16.7	31.8	7.1	21.0	5.1	3.2	15.1
1956	38.1	18.5	18.3	10.0	3.5	2.1	9.4
1957	20.6	32.0	13.3	19.6	5.8	1.6	7.0
1958	22.3	28.4	18.9	13.8	5.0	2.0	9.6
1959	21.8	26.0	16.9	16.6	6.4	2.4	9.9
1960	26.3	29.0	17.2	10.2	9.1	1.9	6.4
1961	4.1	31.2	30.4	12.0	7.1	3.3	11.8
1962	8.6	27.1	27.7	16.4	9.3	4.0	7.0
1963	13.9	28.9	28.6	18.4	5.9	2.4	1.9
1964	12.5	31.1	23.0	11.1	8.0	3.3	11.3
1965	11.0	32.5	24.6	9.3	8.4	3.2	11.0
1966	12.8	28.6	25.9	8.4	9.0	3.2	12.1
1967	18.5	27.0	20.6	10.0	8.9	3.3	11.7
1968	16.0	25.8	23.9	14.9	7.2	2.7	9.5
1969	13.3	29.2	23.0	11.5	8.4	2.8	11.5
1970	17.5	25.5	23.4	10.7	8.4	3.0	11.5
1971	19.4	28.9	24.3	9.4	6.5	2.5	9.0

SOURCE: AE; CE; ANUIES-ESM; ANUIES-AE; SEP-ESM.

TABLE 15. Engineering Egresados, Fourteen Specialties,[1] 1967-89

PART I. Absolute Data

Year	Ag.	Extr.	Indust.	Mech.+ Mech.-El.	Chem.	Top./ Hyd.	Vet.	Civil	El.	Comp.	Earth	Bio- chem.	Text.	Other	Total
1967	166	73	267	930	562	72	318	873	112	0	42	26	65	77	3,583
1968	441	120	291	864	695	97	276	1,153	150	0	26	62	143	177	4,495
1969	497	133	357	1,255	932	98	378	1,332	168	0	37	62	110	221	5,580
1970	555	107	404	1,791	757	91	429	1,229	893	0	40	66	130	155	6,647
1971	550	132	528	1,452	1,176	130	470	1,432	975	0	156	92	152	103	7,348
1972	960	220	670	1,440	1,380	200	680	1,460	1,210	0	100	40	190	200	8,750
1973	990	300	920	1,530	1,680	140	770	1,720	1,240	0	90	160	210	200	9,950
1974	1,100	360	1,130	1,820	2,060	80	700	1,760	1,280	0	160	30	220	200	10,900
1975	1,660	370	1,420	1,850	1,790	210	880	1,810	1,200	0	160	60	220	200	11,830
1976	1,657	245	1,714	2,226	2,048	200	872	2,431	1,207	47	270	207	232	472	13,828
1977	2,119	234	2,305	2,582	2,129	333	1,266	3,441	1,324	121	176	266	242	598	17,136
1978	2,192	234	2,193	2,300	1,971	304	1,454	3,543	1,480	201	247	101	94	291	16,605
1979	3,084	287	2,920	2,291	2,161	343	1,532	3,701	1,199	267	325	211	78	358	18,757
1980	3,944	295	3,045	2,159	1,648	285	1,765	4,069	1,918	384	381	246	77	582	20,798
1981	5,690	321	2,972	2,577	1,565	623	2,083	4,003	1,669	553	319	318	54	549	23,296
1982	6,711	312	3,403	2,379	1,798	500	2,350	4,336	1,643	645	297	264	68	832	25,538
1983	7,321	374	3,280	2,457	1,726	595	2,786	3,931	1,426	978	320	269	82	1,211	26,756
1984	7,359	353	3,558	2,436	2,170	452	2,757	4,368	1,459	1,367	292	238	94	1,247	28,150

TABLE 15, PART I (Continued)

Year	Ag.	Extr.	Indust.	Mech.+ Mech.-El.	Chem.	Top./ Hyd.	Vet.	Civil	El.	Comp.	Earth	Bio-chem.	Text.	Other	Total
1985	5,636	311	4,014	2,470	2,081	571	2,857	4,126	1,495	1,683	288	248	94	1,261	27,135
1986	9,543	420	3,599	2,569	2,312	534	2,635	4,289	1,302	1,814	289	261	136	1,575	31,278
1987	9,004	505	4,354	2,620	2,302	569	2,604	4,931	1,834	2,490	384	282	184	1,754	33,817
1988	8,139	422	4,222	3,272	2,201	441	2,747	4,589	3,066	3,375	194	331	148	1,738	34,885
1989	7,060	406	4,312	3,688	1,908	347	2,714	4,353	1,809	3,698	316	225	153	1,705	32,694

TABLE 15, PART II. Percentage Data

Year	Ag.	Extr.	Indust.	Mech.+ Mech.-El.	Chem.	Top./ Hyd.	Vet.	Civil	El.	Comp.	Earth	Bio-chem.	Text.	Other
1967	4.6	2.0	7.5	26.0	15.7	2.0	8.9	24.4	3.1	0.0	1.2	0.7	1.8	2.1
1968	9.8	2.7	6.5	19.2	15.5	2.2	6.1	25.7	3.3	0.0	0.6	1.4	3.2	3.9
1969	8.9	2.4	6.4	22.5	16.7	1.8	6.8	23.9	3.0	0.0	0.7	1.1	2.0	4.0
1970	8.3	1.6	6.1	26.9	11.4	1.4	6.5	18.5	13.4	0.0	0.6	1.0	2.0	2.3
1971	7.5	1.8	7.2	19.8	16.0	1.8	6.4	19.5	13.3	0.0	2.1	1.3	2.1	1.4
1972	11.0	2.5	7.7	16.5	15.8	2.3	7.8	16.7	13.8	0.0	1.1	0.5	2.2	2.3
1973	9.9	3.0	9.2	15.4	16.9	1.4	7.7	17.3	12.5	0.0	0.9	1.6	2.1	2.0
1974	10.1	3.3	10.4	16.7	18.9	0.7	6.4	16.1	11.7	0.0	1.5	0.3	2.0	1.8
1975	14.0	3.1	12.0	15.6	15.1	1.8	7.4	15.3	10.1	0.0	1.4	0.5	1.9	1.7
1976	12.0	1.8	12.4	16.1	14.8	1.4	6.3	17.6	8.7	0.3	2.0	1.5	1.7	3.4
1977	12.4	1.4	13.5	15.1	12.4	1.9	7.4	20.1	7.7	0.7	1.0	1.6	1.4	3.5
1978	13.2	1.4	13.2	13.9	11.9	1.8	8.8	21.3	8.9	1.2	1.5	0.6	0.6	1.8
1979	16.4	1.5	15.6	12.2	11.5	1.8	8.2	19.7	6.4	1.4	1.7	1.1	0.4	1.9

TABLE 15, PART II (Continued)

Year	Ag.	Extr.	Indust.	Mech.+ Mech.-El.	Chem.	Top./ Hyd.	Vet.	Civil	El.	Comp.	Earth	Bio- chem.	Text.	Other
1980	19.0	1.4	14.6	10.4	7.9	1.4	8.5	19.6	9.2	1.8	1.8	1.2	0.4	2.8
1981	24.4	1.4	12.8	11.1	6.7	2.7	8.9	17.2	7.2	2.4	1.4	1.4	0.2	2.4
1982	26.3	1.2	13.3	9.3	7.0	2.0	9.2	17.0	6.4	2.5	1.2	1.0	0.3	3.3
1983	27.4	1.4	12.3	9.2	6.5	2.2	10.4	14.7	5.3	3.7	1.2	1.0	0.3	4.5
1984	26.1	1.3	12.6	8.7	7.7	1.6	9.8	15.5	5.2	4.9	1.0	0.8	0.3	4.4
1985	20.8	1.1	14.8	9.1	7.7	2.1	10.5	15.2	5.5	6.2	1.1	0.9	0.3	4.6
1986	30.5	1.3	11.5	8.2	7.4	1.7	8.4	13.7	4.2	5.8	0.9	0.8	0.4	5.0
1987	26.6	1.5	12.9	7.7	6.8	1.7	7.7	14.6	5.4	7.4	1.1	0.8	0.5	5.2
1988	23.3	1.2	12.1	9.4	6.3	1.3	7.9	13.2	8.8	9.7	0.6	0.9	0.4	5.0
1989	21.6	1.2	13.2	11.3	5.8	1.1	8.3	13.3	5.5	11.3	1.0	0.7	0.5	5.2

1. Includes nonengineering degree fields in the applied sciences. Data for 1972-75 partially estimated owing to lack of comprehensive data in sources.

SOURCE: ANUIES-ESM; ANUIES-AE; unpublished data.

TABLE 16. Engineering Degrees Registered, Nine Specialities, 1966-70 to 1981-85

PART I. Absolute Data

Period	Total	Ag./Vet.	Chem.	Civil	Comp.	El.	Petrol.	Indust.	Mech./El.
1966-70	15,000	1,200	3,000	2,500	50	400	250	10	3,500
1971-75	22,460	2,430	3,210	4,340	120	810	410	40	4,700
1976-80	44,270	4,850	2,860	8,300	250	1,610	750	4,790	6,690
1981-85	55,060	10,820	2,910	9,190	2,900	1,850	830	4,110	6,020

PART II. Percentage Data

Period	Ag./Vet.	Chem.	Civil	Comp.	El.	Petrol.	Indust.	Mech./El.
1966-70	8.0	20.0	16.7	0.3	2.7	1.7	0.1	23.3
1971-75	10.8	14.3	19.3	0.5	3.6	1.8	0.2	20.9
1976-80	11.0	6.5	18.7	0.6	3.6	1.7	10.8	15.1
1981-85	19.7	5.3	16.7	5.3	3.4	1.5	7.5	10.9

SOURCE: DGP.

TABLE 17. Engineering Degrees Registered, Ten Specialties, 1970-86

PART I. Absolute Data

Year	Civil	Chem.	Arch.	Ag.	Petrol.	Vet.	Mech./El.	Mech.	El.	Indust.
1970	710	277	112	61	6	231	467	107	156	41
1971	968	421	217	91	33	377	764	243	304	75
1972	652	285	126	78	26	238	539	129	185	37
1973	617	277	74	72	17	292	438	102	156	45
1974	925	386	215	121	51	232	569	236	308	91
1975	974	594	390	170	35	276	791	242	291	69
1976	1433	655	485	197	40	357	794	298	352	106
1977	1737	721	541	202	56	291	842	443	558	149
1978	1804	749	424	169	42	530	806	403	491	125
1979	1710	685	347	149	42	469	760	427	535	149
1980	1517	682	266	198	29	546	785	371	602	139
1981	1468	544	239	146	41	636	756	311	552	168
1982	1835	593	361	137	33	695	735	451	782	250
1983	1665	574	315	89	70	861	894	397	691	240
1984	2052	718	487	158	72	1258	971	648	892	383
1985	1902	694	385	159	55	1203	856	545	842	321
1986	1803	692	342	171	88	1227	764	495	778	346

PART II. Percentage Data, Nine Specialties

Year	Civil	Chem.	Ag.	Petrol.	Vet.	Mech.	Mech./Elec.	El.	Indust.
1970	24.3	9.5	2.1	0.2	7.9	3.7	16.0	5.3	1.4
1971	19.9	8.7	1.9	0.7	7.8	5.0	15.7	6.3	1.5
1972	19.9	8.7	2.4	0.8	7.3	3.9	16.4	5.6	1.1
1973	20.5	9.2	2.4	0.6	9.7	3.4	14.6	5.2	1.5
1974	19.9	8.3	2.6	1.1	5.0	5.1	12.3	6.6	2.0
1975	17.2	10.5	3.0	0.6	4.9	4.3	14.0	5.2	1.2
1976	20.1	9.2	2.8	0.6	5.0	4.2	11.2	4.9	1.5
1977	20.0	8.3	2.3	0.6	3.4	5.1	9.7	6.4	1.7
1978	19.9	8.2	1.9	0.5	5.8	4.4	8.9	5.4	1.4
1979	19.5	7.8	1.7	0.5	5.3	4.9	8.7	6.1	1.7
1980	17.7	7.9	2.3	0.3	6.4	4.3	9.1	7.0	1.6
1981	15.7	5.8	1.6	0.4	6.8	3.3	8.1	5.9	1.8
1982	17.5	5.7	1.3	0.3	6.6	4.3	7.0	7.5	2.4
1983	13.2	4.5	0.7	0.6	6.8	3.1	7.1	5.5	1.9
1984	15.1	5.3	1.2	0.5	9.2	4.8	7.1	6.5	2.8

TABLE 17/PART II (Continued)

Year	Civil	Chem.	Ag.	Pet.	Vet.	Mec.	Mec./Elec.	El.	Indust.
1985	12.6	4.6	1.1	0.4	8.0	3.6	5.7	5.6	2.1
1986	10.9	4.2	1.0	0.5	7.4	3.0	4.6	4.7	1.9

SOURCE: DGP, unpublished data.

TABLE 18. **Index of Engineering Degrees Registered, Ten Specialties, 1970-86** (1980=100)

Year	Civil	Chem.	Arch.	Ag.	Extr.	Vet.	Mech./El.	Mech.	El./Electr-onic	Indust.
1970	46.8	40.6	42.1	30.8	20.7	42.3	59.5	28.8	25.9	29.5
1971	63.8	61.7	81.6	46.0	113.8	69.0	97.3	65.5	50.5	54.0
1972	43.0	41.8	47.4	39.4	89.7	43.6	68.7	34.8	30.7	26.6
1973	40.7	40.6	27.8	36.4	58.6	53.5	55.8	27.5	25.9	32.4
1974	61.0	56.6	80.8	61.1	175.9	42.5	72.5	63.6	51.2	65.5
1975	64.2	87.1	146.6	85.9	120.7	50.5	100.8	65.2	48.3	49.6
1976	94.5	96.0	182.3	99.5	137.9	65.4	101.1	80.3	58.5	76.3
1977	114.5	105.7	203.4	102.0	193.1	53.3	107.3	119.4	92.7	107.2
1978	118.9	109.8	159.4	85.4	144.8	97.1	102.7	108.6	81.6	89.9
1979	112.7	100.4	130.5	75.3	144.8	85.9	96.8	115.1	88.9	107.2
1980	100.0	100.0	100.0	100.0	100.0	100.0	100.0	100.0	100.0	100.0
1981	96.8	79.8	89.8	73.7	141.4	116.5	96.3	83.8	91.7	120.9
1982	121.0	87.0	135.7	69.2	113.8	127.3	93.6	121.6	129.9	179.9
1983	109.8	84.2	118.4	44.9	241.4	157.7	113.9	107.0	114.8	172.7
1984	135.3	105.3	183.1	79.8	248.3	230.4	123.7	174.7	148.2	275.5
1985	125.4	101.8	144.7	80.3	189.7	220.3	109.0	146.9	139.9	230.9
1986	118.9	101.5	128.6	86.4	303.4	224.7	97.3	133.4	129.2	227.3

SOURCE: Calculated from Table 17 above.

TABLE 19. **Economically Active Population by Economic Sector, 1900-90**

PART I. Ten Sectors

Sector	1900	1910	1921	1930	1940
Total	5,131,051	5,337,889	4,883,561	5,165,803	5,858,116
Agriculture, Ranching, Fishing, Hunting	3,177,840	3,584,191	3,488,102	3,626,278	3,830,871
Extractive Industries and Petroleum	107,348	104,093	26,890	51,246	106,706
Manufacturing	624,039	613,913	534,428	692,161	639,607
Construction	62,997	74,703	~	~	~
Electric Energy	8,910	10,553	~	~	~
Commerce	261,455	293,753	273,902	273,841	552,467
Transportation	59,666	55,091	58,974	107,052	149,470
Services	491,781	508,084	58,343	52,694	223,749
Government	25,189	27,661	63,074	153,343	191,588
Insufficiently Specified	311,826	65,847	379,848	209,188	163,658

	1950	1960	1970	1980	1990
Total	8,272,093	11,332,016	12,955,057	22,066,084	23,403,413
Agriculture Ranching, Fishing, Hunting	4823,901	6,143,540	5,103,519	5,700,860	5,300,114
Extractive Industries and Petroleum	97,143	141,530	180,175	513,339	260,515
Manufacturing	972,542	1,556,091	2,169,074	2,580,199	4,493,279
Construction	224,512	408,279	571,006	1,307,767	1,594,961
Electric Energy	24,966	41,443	53,285	116,197	154,469
Commerce	684,092	1,075,174	1,196,878	1,471,578	3,108,128
Transportation	210,592	356,939	368,813	683,640	1,045,392
Services	879,379	1,527,229	2,158,175	3,142,354	5,714,325
Government	~	~	406,607	~	928,358
Insufficiently Specified	354,966	81,791	747,525	6,425,759	803,872

PART II. Three Sectors

Year	Total	Absolute	Primary Sector Percentage Share	Absolute	Secondary Sector Percentage Share
1900	5,131,051	3,177,840	61.93	803,294	15.66
1910	5,337,889	3,584,191	67.15	803,262	15.05
1921	4,883,561	3,488,102	71.43	61,318	1.26
1930	5,165,803	3,626,278	70.20	743,407	14.39
1940	5,858,116	3,830,871	65.39	746,313	12.74
1950	8,272,093	4,823,901	58.32	1,319,163	15.95
1960	11,332,016	6,143,540	54.21	2,147,343	18.95
1970	12,955,057	5,103,519	39.39	2,973,540	22.95
1980[a]	22,066,084	5,700,860	25.83	4,516,934	20.47
1990	23,403,413	5,300,114	22.65	6,503,224	27.79

Year	Absolute	Tertiary Sector Percentage Share	Absolute	Not Specified Percentage Share
1900	838,091	16.33	311,826	6.08
1910	884,589	16.57	65,847	1.23
1921	454,293	9.30	379,848	7.78
1930	586,930	11.36	209,188	4.05
1940	1,117,274	19.07	163,658	2.79
1950	1,774,063	21.45	354,966	4.29
1960	2,959,342	26.11	81,791	0.72
1970	4,130,473	31.88	747,525	5.77
1980[a]	5,297,572	24.01	6,425,759	29.12
1990	10,796,203	46.13	803,872	3.43

a. Cf. totals in Table 23. The 1980 census gives different totals for EAP by occupation and EAP by sector of activity.

SOURCE: EHM; Census.

TABLE 20. Professionals and Technicians, 1900-40

PART I. Public Administration and Liberal Professions in Economically Active Population,[1] 1900-30

Division	1900	1910	1920	1930
Public Administration	64,004	64,384	63,074	153,343
Liberal Professions	38,764	67,653	58,343	52,694
Total	102,768	132,037	121,417	206,037
EAP[1]	4,691,729	5,395,263	5,025,770	5,327,530
Public Administration/EAP	1.36	1.19	1.26	2.88
Liberal Professions/EAP	0.83	1.25	1.16	0.99
Total/EAP	2.19	2.45	2.42	3.87

1. EAP = Total - (Div 8 + Div 10) + .03(Div 8)
    Division 8: Domestic Workers.
    Division 10: Persons with non-productive occupations, without an occupation, and whose occupation is unknown.
    .03(Division 8) = The number of paid domestic workers was estimated at 3 percent of all domestic workers.

SOURCE: Census, 1930.

PART II. Public Administration and Liberal Professions in Economically Active Population, 1930 and 1940

Division	1930	1940
Agriculture, Ranching, Hunting	3,634,713	3,830,871
Mining, Petroleum, Gas	47,991	106,706
Industry	523,927	639,607
Communications and Transportation	103,333	149,470
Commerce	273,812	552,467
Public Administration	147,301	191,588
Liberal Occupations	52,678	42,719
Paid Domestic Workers[1]	161,000	181,030
Not Specified	367,475	163,658
Unknown Occupations	6,011,048	7,492,408
Total Domestic Workers	5,390,444	6,484,058

TABLE 20, PART II (Continued)

Division	1930	1940
EAP[2]	5,312,230	5,858,116
Public Administration +		
Liberal Professions	199,979	234,307
Public Administration/EAP	2.77	3.27
Liberal Professions/EAP	0.99	0.73
Public Administration +		
Liberal Professions/ EAP	3.76	4.00

1. Paid Domestic Workers calculated for 1930 as 3 percent of Total
Domestic Workers.

2. Does not include Unknown Occupations or unpaid domestic workers.

SOURCE: Census, 1940.

PART III. **Public Administration and Liberal
Professions in Economically Active Population (Alternate Data),
1910, 1921, and 1930**

Sector	1910	1921	1930
Public Administration	27,664	8,769	
		}	65,086
Teachers	21,007	26,708	
Medical Services	7,837	11,846	14,696
Legal Services	~	4,969	5,125
Religious Professionals	4,690	3,421	3,206
Literary, Scientific, and			
Artistic Professionals	22,786	28,226	29,667
Photography and Cinema	1,206	1,491	2,240
Diversions	2,162	2,114	1,706
Total	87,352	87,544	121,726

SOURCE: Census.

TABLE 21. **Professionals, Technicians, and Management in Economically Active Population, 1950-90**

Area of Principal Occupation	1950	1960	1970	1980	1990
EAP	8,272,093	11,332,016	12,955,057	21,393,250	23,403,413
Professionals and Technicians	206,939	408,639	733,209	1,582,237	2,473,498
Management	65,108	95,132	319,828	260,681	569,561
Total	272,047	503,771	1,053,037	1,842,918	3,043,059

As Percentage of EAP

Professionals and Technicians	2.50	3.61	5.66	7.40	10.57
Management	0.79	0.84	2.47	1.22	2.43
Total	3.29	4.45	8.13	8.61	13.00

SOURCE: Census.

TABLE 22. **Professionals, Technicians, and Management, by Sector, 1950-90**

PART I. Professionals and Technicians by Sector, 1950-90

Sector	1950	1960	1970	1980	1980 Est.	1980 Rounded	1990
Agriculture	1,197	16,100	18,966	23,161	29,317	29,000	33,787
Extractive Industries	2,990	11,785	14,874	18,856	23,868	24,000	24,038
Manufacturing	17,594	46,968	97,957	231,812	293,429	293,000	209,115
Construction	5,700	18,237	23,145	61,094	77,333	77,000	60,828
Utilities	1,794	3,557	4,987	26,476	33,513	36,000	16,135
Commerce	3,257	22,359	21,881	20,563	26,029	26,000	89,192
Transportation	2,139	6,523	8,185	6,554	8,296	8,000	32,130
Services	168,050	280,304	529,291	798,969	1,011,339	1,011,000	1,946,970
Not Specified	4,218	2,806	13,923	394,752	79,112	79,000	61,303
Total	206,939	408,639	733,209	1,582,237	1,582,237	1,582,000	2,473,498
EAP Total	8,272,093	11,332,016	12,955,057	21,393,250	21,393,250	21,393,250	23,403,413
Agriculture	0.6	3.9	2.6	1.5	1.9	1.8	1.4
Extractive Industries	1.4	2.9	2.0	1.2	1.5	1.5	1.0
Manufacturing	8.5	11.5	13.4	14.7	18.5	18.5	8.5
Construction	2.8	4.5	3.2	3.9	4.9	4.9	2.5
Utilities	0.9	0.9	0.7	1.7	2.1	2.3	0.7
Commerce	1.6	5.5	3.0	1.3	1.6	1.6	3.6
Transportation	1.0	1.6	1.1	0.4	0.5	0.5	1.3
Services	81.2	68.6	72.2	50.5	63.9	63.9	78.7
Not Specified	2.0	0.7	1.9	24.9	5.0	5.0	2.5

PART II. Management by Sector, 1950-90

Sector	1950	1960	1970	1980	1980 Est.	1980 Rounded	1990
Agriculture	0	0	23,850	27,726	38,038	38,000	21,996
Extractive Industries	2,448	1,746	5,152	13,161	18,056	18,000	4,511
Manufacturing	14,942	26,499	86,336	41,443	56,856	57,000	123,410
Construction	2,525	7,743	12,357	8,839	12,126	12,000	20,765
Utilities	355	800	2,069	3,204	4,396	4,000	3,496
Commerce	15,856	25,505	59,767	33,971	46,605	47,000	113,791
Transportation	1,909	3,463	10,538	6,947	9,531	10,000	21,622
Services	22,533	27,943	101,456	35,721	49,006	49,000	237,694
Not Specified	4,540	1,433	18,303	89,669	26,068	26,000	22,276
Total	65,108	95,132	319,828	260,681	260,681	261,000	569,561
EAP Total	8,272,093	11,332,016	12,955,057	21,393,250	21,393,250	21,393,250	23,403,413
Agriculture	0.0	0.0	7.5	10.6	14.6	14.6	3.9
Extractive Industries	3.8	1.8	1.6	5.0	6.9	6.9	0.8
Manufacturing	22.9	27.9	27.0	15.9	21.8	21.8	21.7
Construction	3.9	8.1	3.9	3.4	4.7	4.6	3.6
Utilities	0.5	0.8	0.6	1.2	1.7	1.5	0.6
Commerce	24.4	26.8	18.7	13.0	17.9	18.0	20.0
Transportation	2.9	3.6	3.3	2.7	3.7	3.8	3.8
Services	34.6	29.4	31.7	13.7	18.8	18.8	41.7
Not Specified	7.0	1.5	5.7	34.4	10.0	10.0	3.9

SOURCE: Census.

TABLE 23. **Occupational Structure of Economic Sectors, 1950-90**

PART I. **Total Economically Active Population**

	1950	1960
Professionals and Technicians	206,939	408,639
Management	65,108	95,132
Office Personnel	384,814	693,665
Merchants	647,165	1,023,723
Workers in Agriculture	4,811,710	6,067,679
Workers in Mining	80,997	109,284
Workers in Goods and Services	1,481,477	2,142,010
Domestic Workers	593,883	791,884
Total	8,272,093	11,332,016

	1970	1980	1990
Professionals and Technicians	733,209	1,582,237	2,473,498
Professionals		393,016	630,621
Technicians		508,456	767,997
Teachers		551,537	874,411
Artists		129,228	200,469
Management	319,828	260,681	569,561
Public Functionaries		20,770	
Private Sector Management		219,324	
Agricultural Administration		20,587	
Office Personnel	977,179	1,993,830	2,186,582
Merchants	967,267	1,584,373	2,706,935
Dependent Vendors		1,489,957	2,200,975
Vendors Ambulantes		94,416	505,960
Agricultural Workers	4,952,200	5,342,495	5,173,725
Foremen		13,513	
Farmers		5,249,771	
Equipment Operators		79,211	

TABLE 23, PART I (Continued)

	1970	1980	1990
Non-Agricultural Workers	2,768,780	4,764,935	6,354,901
Foremen		127,155	388,548
Artisans and Laborers		4,176,929	3,728,668
Assistants and Apprentices		460,851	1,055,628
Operators of fixed machinery			1,182,057
Workers in Services	1,560,614	1,644,646	2,787,512
Employees		640,361	1,137,735
Transportation Drivers		755,026	1,171,619
Security		249,259	478,158
Domestic Workers		888,857	646,199
Not Specified	675,980	3,331,196	504,500
Total	12,955,057	21,393,250	23,403,413

PART II. **Agriculture**

	1950	1960
Professionals and Technicians	1,197	16,100
Management		
Office Personnel	3,626	25,966
Merchants	6,222	29,784
Workers in Agriculture	4,810,053	6,065,008
Workers in Mining		
Workers in Goods and Services	14	
Domestic Workers	2,789	8,072
Total	4,823,901	6,144,930

	1970	1980	1990
Professionals and Technicians	18,966	23,161	33,787
Professionals		8,132	13,907
Technicians		10,144	19,109
Teachers		3,167	309
Artists		1,718	462

TABLE 23, PART II (Continued)

	1970	1980	1990
Management	23,850	27,726	21,996
Public Functionaries		909	
Private Sector Management		10,401	
Agricultural Administration		16,416	
Office Personnel	16,819	44,875	18,589
Merchants	8,754	45,332	21,071
Dependent Vendors		43,372	19,748
Vendors Ambulantes		1,960	1,323
Agricultural Workers	4,878,524	5,063,181	5,046,485
Foremen		7,532	
Farmers		4,996,442	
Equipment Operators		59,207	
Non-Agricultural Workers	57,936	146,561	28,633
Foremen		3,281	1,775
Artisans and Laborers		125,748	17,015
Assistants and Apprentices		17,532	7,677
Operators of fixed machinery			2,166
Workers in Services	30,951	114,318	111,185
Employees		22,220	13,779
Transportation Drivers		84,985	84,202
Security		7,113	13,204
Domestic Workers		25,498	915
Not Specified	67,719	29,327	17,453
Total	5,103,519	5,519,979	5,300,114

TABLE 23, PART III. **Extractive Industries**

	1950	1960
Professionals and Technicians	2,990	11,785
Management	2,448	1,746
Office Personnel	7,692	15,228
Merchants	1,011	2,109
Workers in Agriculture		
Workers in Mining	80,462	109,026
Workers in Goods and Services	13	
Domestic Workers	2,527	1,907
Total	97,143	141,801

	1970	1980	1990
Professionals and Technicians	14,874	18,856	24,038
Professionals		8,155	11,518
Technicians		8,307	11,921
Teachers		484	365
Artists		1,910	234
Management	5,152	13,161	4,511
Public Functionaries		417	
Private Sector Management		12,716	
Agricultural Administration		28	
Office Personnel	19,359	75,927	34,307
Merchants	2,653	159,869	2,649
Dependent Vendors		150,186	2,566
Vendors Ambulantes		9,683	83
Agricultural Workers	1,703	2,455	1,324
Foremen		55	
Farmers		2,173	
Equipment Operators		227	
Non-Agricultural Workers	115,645	196,178	154,505
Foremen		6,664	16,716
Artisans and Laborers		174,630	76,570
Assistants and Apprentices		14,884	32,856
Operators of Fixed Machinery			28,363

TABLE 23, PART III (Continued)

	1970	1980	1990
Workers in Services	14,245	17,861	34,870
Employees		5,519	6,177
Transportation Drivers		9,649	19,714
Security		2,693	8,979
Domestic Workers		905	222
Not Specified	6,544	19,976	4,089
Total	180,175	505,188	260,515

PART IV. **Manufacturing**

	1950	1960
Professionals and Technicians	17,594	46,968
Management	14,942	26,499
Office Personnel	43,871	108,837
Merchants	27,277	52,399
Workers in Agriculture		
Workers in Mining		
Workers in Goods and Services	838,132	1,296,622
Domestic Workers	30,726	24,990
Total	972,542	1,556,315

	1970	1980	1990
Professionals and Technicians	97,957	231,812	209,115
Professionals		68,512	63,446
Technicians		70,734	108,781
Teachers		75,688	4,683
Artists		16,878	32,205
Management	86,336	41,443	123,410
Public Functionaries		1,221	
Private Sector Management		39,956	
Agricultural Administration		266	
Office Personnel	227,660	196,518	309,315

TABLE 23, PART IV (Continued)

	1970	1980	1990
Merchants	98,647	108,807	263,202
Dependent Vendors		104,159	247,208
Vendors Ambulantes		4,648	15,994
Agricultural Workers	15,911	23,440	82,593
Foremen		255	
Farmers		20,977	
Equipment Operators		2,208	
Non-Agricultural Workers	1,473,623	1,760,084	3,171,101
Foremen		45,585	242,700
Artisans and Laborers		1,630,559	1,397,844
Assistants and Apprentices		83,940	433,810
Operators of Fixed Machinery			1,096,747
Workers in Services	117,109	109,732	280,819
Employees		57,587	64,843
Transportation Drivers		36,054	159,401
Security		16,091	56,575
Domestic Workers		6,162	2,397
Not Specified	51,831	55,521	51,327
Total	2,169,074	2,533,519	4,493,279

TABLE 23, PART V. **Construction**

	1950	1960
Professionals and Technicians	5,700	18,237
Management	2,525	7,743
Office Personnel	3,291	9,951
Merchants	756	1,840
Workers in Agriculture		
Workers in Mining		
Workers in Goods and Services	209,827	366,768
Domestic Workers	2,413	3,863
Total	224,512	408,402

TABLE 23, PART V (Continued)

	1970	1980	1990
Professionals and Technicians	23,145	61,094	60,828
Professionals		17,206	39,622
Technicians		40,802	19,945
Teachers		761	332
Artists		2,325	929
Management	12,357	8,839	20,765
Public Functionaries		800	
Private Sector Management		7,988	
Agricultural Administration		51	
Office Personnel	20,482	37,513	36,065
Merchants	4,380	7,520	2,185
Dependent Vendors		7,253	2,034
Vendors Ambulantes		267	151
Agricultural Workers	3,834	10,957	4,388
Foremen		78	
Farmers		9,086	
Equipment Operators	1,793		
Non-Agricultural Workers	480,273	1,103,485	1,416,450
Foremen		11,705	54,885
Artisans and Laborers		856,040	997,782
Assistants and Apprentices		157,380	353,912
Operators of Fixed Machinery			9,871
Workers in Services	19,964	39,180	49,000
Employees		27,712	5,810
Transportation Drivers		7,913	32,081
Security		3,555	11,109
Domestic Workers		74,668	454
Not Specified	6,571	6,999	4,826
Total	571,006	1,271,895	1,594,961

PART VI. Utilities

	1950	1960
Professionals and Technicians	1,794	3,557
Management	355	800
Office Personnel	5,163	12,877
Merchants	906	1,172
Workers in Agriculture		
Workers in Mining		
Workers in Goods and Services	15,101	22,313
Domestic Workers	1,647	726
Total	24,966	41,445

	1970	1980	1990
Professionals and Technicians	4,987	26,476	16,135
Professionals		3,381	7,111
Technicians		6,984	8,561
Teachers		983	315
Artists		15,128	148
Management	2,069	3,204	3,496
Public Functionaries		381	
Private Sector Management		2,821	
Agricultural Administration		2	
Office Personnel	13,539	23,307	39,396
Merchants	814	4,438	1,641
Dependent Vendors		3,546	1,597
Vendors Ambulantes		892	44
Agricultural workers	292	286	542
Foremen		7	
Farmers		227	
Equipment Operators		52	

TABLE 23, PART VI (Continued)

	1970	1980	1990
Non-Agricultural Workers	24,240	44,314	75,819
Foremen		2,996	8,292
Artisans and Laborers		35,636	47,419
Assistants and Apprentices		5,682	12,145
Operators of Fixed Machinery			7,963
Workers in Services	4,707	5,992	14,405
Employees		2,590	3,188
Transportation Drivers		2,281	7,442
Security		1,121	3,775
Domestic Workers		81	35
Not Specified	2,637	6,126	3,000
Total	53,285	114,224	154,469

PART VII. **Commerce**

	1950	1960
Professionals and Technicians	3,257	22,359
Management	15,856	25,505
Office Personnel	59,492	103,515
Merchants	580,040	875,807
Workers in Agriculture		
Workers in Mining		
Workers in Goods and Services	10,015	37,829
Domestic Workers	15,432	9,578
Total	684,092	1,074,593

	1970	1980	1990
Professionals and Technicians	21,881	20,563	89,192
Professionals		4,956	26,463
Technicians		12,792	57,460
Teachers		774	1,430
Artists		2,041	3,839

TABLE 23, PART VII^a (Continued)

	1970	1980	1990
Management	59,767	33,971	113,791
Public Functionaries		646	
Private Sector Management		32,845	
Agricultural Administration		480	
Office Personnel	157,606	151,883	314,118
Merchants	757,330	1,056,384	2,130,840
Dependent Vendors		991,179	1,738,141
Vendors Ambulantes		65,205	392,699
Agricultural Workers	19,756	26,378	12,017
Foremen		168	
Farmers		25,802	
Equipment Operators		408	
Non-Agricultural Workers	88,278	85,793	191,266
Foremen		2,235	8,817
Artisans and Laborers		76,503	146,722
Assistants and Apprentices		7,055	27,242
Operators of Fixed Machinery			8,485
Workers in Services	71,241	40,356	241,655
Employees		16,690	97,874
Transportation Drivers		20,120	113,198
Security		3,546	30,583
Domestic Workers		1,935	3,458
Not Specified	21,019	27,931	11,791
Total	1,196,878	1,445,194	3,108,128

PART VIII. **Transportation**

	1950	1960
Professionals and Technicians	2,139	6,523
Management	1,909	3,463
Office Personnel	41,282	63,194
Merchants	1,551	3,552
Workers in Agriculture		
Workers in Mining		
Workers in Goods and Services	157,892	275,043
Domestic Workers	5,819	5,282
Total	210,592	357,057

	1970	1980	1990
Professionals and Technicians	8,185	6,554	32,130
Professionals		1,853	9,293
Technicians		3,978	21,184
Teachers		232	882
Artists		491	771
Management	10,538	6,947	21,622
Public Functionaries		835	
Private Sector Management		6,026	
Agricultural Administration		86	
Office Personnel	41,782	67,535	191,070
Merchants	4,073	15,197	12,085
Dependent Vendors		14,611	11,073
Vendors Ambulantes		586	1,012
Agricultural Workers	1,310	8,580	2,748
Foremen		94	
Farmers		7,219	
Equipment Operators		1,267	
Non-Agricultural Workers	71,091	130,268	87,640
Foremen		2,286	7,610
Artisans and Laborers		80,014	59,773
Assistants and Apprentices		47,968	17,554
Operators of Fixed Machinery			2,703

TABLE 23, PART VIII (Continued)

	1970	1980	1990
Workers in Services	221,791	424,212	691,592
Employees		5,178	57,908
Transportation Drivers		415,215	610,612
Security		3,819	23,072
Domestic Workers		1,996	194
Not Specified	10,043	9,421	6,311
Total	368,813	670,710	1,045,392

a. Includes communications.

PART IX. Services

	1950	1960
Professionals and Technicians	168,050	280,304
Management	22,533	27,943
Office Personnel	139,388	331,292
Merchants	25,687	56,188
Workers in Agriculture		
Workers in Mining		
Workers in Goods and Services	44,393	105,862
Domestic Workers	479,328	724,093
Total	879,379	1,525,682

	1970	1980	1990
Professionals and Technicians	529,291	798,969	1,946,970
Professionals		112,248	435,805
Technicians		234,244	486,589
Teachers		386,575	864,334
Artists		65,902	160,242

TABLE 23, PART IX (Continued)

	1970	1980	1990
Management	101,456	35,721	237,694
Public Functionaries		5,242	
Private Sector Management		30,228	
Agricultural Administration		251	
Office Personnel	398,212	341,218	1,087,015
Merchants	77,754	59,625	261,148
Dependent Vendors		54,235	167,241
Vendors Ambulantes		5,390	93,907
Agricultural Workers	26,859	9,347	15,184
Foremen		2,028	
Farmers		6,475	
Equipment Operators		844	
Non-Agricultural Workers	345,410	496,563	1,163,799
Foremen		13,092	38,951
Artisans and Laborers		423,919	950,964
Assistants and Apprentices		59,552	154,554
Operators of Fixed Machinery			19,330
Workers in Services	1,027,252	554,278	1,275,130
Employees		384,517	856,522
Transportation Drivers		18,859	103,141
Security		150,902	315,467
Domestic Workers		753,604	610,616
Not Specified	58,548	32,483	45,127
Total	2,564,782	3,081,808	6,642,683

PART X. Insufficiently Specified

	1950	1960
Professionals and Technicians	4,218	2,806
Management	4,540	1,433
Office Personnel	81,009	22,805
Merchants	3,715	872
Workers in Agriculture	1,657	2,671
Workers in Mining	535	258
Workers in Goods and Services	206,090	37,573
Domestic Workers	53,202	13,373
Total	354,966	81,791

	1970	1980	1990
Professionals and Technicians	13,923	394,752	61,303
Professionals		168,573	23,456
Technicians		120,471	34,447
Teachers		82,873	1,761
Artists		22,835	1,639
Management	18,303	89,669	22,276
Public Functionaries		10,319	
Private Sector Management		76,343	
Agricultural Administration		3,007	
Office Personnel	81,720	1,055,054	156,707
Merchants	12,862	127,201	12,114
Dependent Vendors		121,416	11,367
Vendors Ambulantes		5,785	747
Agricultural Workers	4,011	197,871	8,444
Foremen		3,296	
Farmers		181,370	
Equipment Operators		13,205	
Non-Agricultural Workers	112,284	880,049	65,688
Foremen		39,311	8,802
Artisans and Laborers		773,880	34,579
Assistants and Apprentices		66,858	15,878
Operators of Fixed Machinery			6,429

TABLE 23, PART X (Continued)

	1970	1980	1990
Workers in Services	53,354	338,717	88,856
Employees		118,348	31,634
Transportation Drivers		159,950	41,828
Security		60,419	15,394
Domestic Workers		24,008	27,908
Not Specified	451,068	3,143,412	360,576
Total	747,525	6,250,733	803,872

SOURCE: Census.

TABLE 24. **Professional and Technician Economically Active Population, by Economic Sector,** [1] **1950-90**

(%)

Year	Primary	Secondary	Tertiary
1950	0.6	13.6	83.8
1960	3.9	19.7	75.7
1970	2.6	18.5	76.3
1980	1.8	27.2	66.1
1990	2.4	19.4	74.1

1. These are are unmodified census categories; cf. Table 30.

SOURCE: Calculated from census.

TABLE 25. **Professional Degrees Granted, by Economic Sector, 1928-71**

(%)

Year	Primary	Secondary	Tertiary
1928	7.2	11.0	81.7
1929	8.7	6.6	84.7
1930	13.3	6.3	80.4
1931	6.4	3.3	90.3
1932	7.2	6.1	86.7
1933	2.5	5.6	91.9
1934	3.5	3.1	93.4
1935	4.7	3.5	91.7
1936	4.8	3.2	92.0
1937	5.7	3.2	91.0
1938	1.6	9.3	89.1
1939	3.0	6.6	90.3
1940	4.2	5.7	90.1
1941	5.0	3.7	91.4
1942	3.5	4.2	92.3
1943	7.8	6.2	86.0
1944	6.5	5.5	88.0

TABLE 25 (Continued)

Year	Primary	Secondary	Tertiary
1945	6.1	5.8	88.1
1946	9.2	6.5	84.3
1947	7.8	5.7	86.6
1948	7.6	5.7	86.7
1949	9.3	10.8	79.9
1950	4.5	4.0	91.5
1951	3.9	9.2	87.0
1952	4.9	10.7	84.4
1953	2.4	8.0	89.5
1954	5.5	8.3	86.2
1955	4.9	8.4	86.7
1956	7.5	6.5	86.0
1957	8.1	11.5	80.4
1958	8.1	11.7	80.1
1959	9.0	12.7	78.3
1960	12.2	11.1	76.7
1961	4.2	15.6	80.2
1962	7.2	16.9	75.8
1963	6.1	13.4	80.5
1964	6.1	11.8	82.1
1965	5.8	13.1	81.2
1966	5.9	12.2	81.9
1967	8.5	11.9	79.7
1968	6.7	14.7	78.6
1969	6.5	12.3	81.2
1970	6.5	13.0	80.5
1971	6.1	13.5	80.4

SOURCE: Calculated from Table 1.

TABLE 26. **University Egresados, by Economic Sector, 1967-89**

(%)

Year	Primary	Secondary	Tertiary
1967	4.1	12.9	83.0
1968	5.5	13.0	81.5
1969	5.2	13.5	81.4
1970	5.2	17.9	76.9
1971	5.0	17.1	77.9
1972	7.3	17.4	75.4
1973	6.8	17.6	75.6
1974	5.9	17.3	76.8
1975	7.3	15.3	77.5
1976	5.7	14.5	79.8
1977	6.4	14.3	79.3
1978	6.3	12.2	81.6
1979	6.8	11.5	81.6
1980	7.6	11.0	81.4
1981	9.5	10.0	80.5
1982	9.8	9.5	80.7
1983	9.7	8.1	82.1
1984	9.5	8.6	81.9
1985	7.8	8.7	83.5
1986	10.5	8.1	81.4
1987	9.5	8.7	81.7
1988	8.4	9.5	82.0
1989	7.5	8.6	83.9

SOURCE: Calculated from Table 3.

TABLE 27. Professional Employment and Degrees Granted, 1950,
and Professional Employment and Egresados, 1980

(%)

Year	Employment				Degrees/Egresados			
	ENG	HEALTH	Law	TEACH	ENG	HEALTH	Law	TEACH
1950	10.2	39.1	17.0	5.5	13.5	45.5	12.5	15.3
1980	22.1	23.7	~	15.1	25.1	21.8	~	17.1

SOURCE: Census and Tables 1 and 3.

TABLE 28. Various Measures of Demand for Professionals in
Nuevo León State

PART I. Professionals Employed in Nuevo León (A) and Egresados
of UANL and ITESM (B), 1979 and 1980

(%)

(A)

Year	BUS	ENG	HEALTH	Law	Other
1979	19.9	28.7	21.5	10.7	19.2
			(B)[1]		
1980	18.4	36.8	13.3	9.7	21.8

1. UANL and ITESM accounted for 77.0 percent of all egresados in the state.

TABLE 28 (continued)

PART II. **Employer Demand for BUS and ENG Professionals,**
1980-83

(% of Total Demand)

Year	BUS	ENG
1980	34.9	51.3
1981	38.4	56.7
1982	37.7	57.3
1983	43.9	50.0
Averages	38.7	53.8

PART III. **Percent of UANL Graduates Employed Within One Year**
of Graduation, Five Fields, 1980

(% Employed)

BUS	ENG	HEALTH	Law	Econ.
93.9	79.5	65.0	79.7	100.0

SOURCE: Programa de Seguimiento de Egresados UANL, *Estudio sobre el egresado al titularse en la Universidad Autónoma de Nuevo León 1980/81* (Monterrey: [UANL], [1981]); UANL and Cámera de la Industria de Transformación de Nuevo León, *La demanda de técnicos y profesionistas en el estado de Nuevo León* (Monterrey, Nuevo León: UANL, 1981); ANUIES-AE.

TABLE 29. **Professions of Public-Sector Employees, Centralized and Decentralized Sectors, Five Fields, 1975**

(%)

Field	Centralized Sector	Decentralized Sector	Average
Law	12.4	7.1	9.8
Med.	11.0	16.1	13.6
ENG	28.0	30.4	29.2
BUS	16.5	20.1	18.3
Econ.	4.7	4.6	4.7

SOURCE: Comisión de Recursos Humanos del Sector Público del Gobierno Federal, *Censo de recursos humanos del sector público federal: Administración central 1975* and *Administración decentralizada y de participación estatal mayoritaria 1975* (México, D. F.: Comisión de Recursos Humanos del Sector Público del Gobierno Federal, 1976).

TABLE 30. **Professionals and Technicians in Economically Active Population and Percentage Change, 1950, 1980, and 1990**

PART I. **Professionals and Technicians in Census Data**

1950	
A. Engineers (and related technicians)	17,793
B. Chemists (and related technicians)	8,966
C. Primary School Teachers[1]	79,234
D. Secondary School and University Teachers	3,241
E. Researchers (and related technicians)	1,175
F. Lawyers	11,604
G. Doctors	17,260
H. Nurses	9,206
I. Writers/Artists	34,131
J. Other Professionals	24,329
K. Public Officials at Director's Level	17,691
L. Directors of Commercial Establishments	19,833
M. Owners/Operators of Industries	17,792
N. Other Directors and Administrators	9,792
O. Typists	58,510
P. Office Accountants	51,818

TABLE 30, PART I (Continued)

1980 and 1990	1980	1990
Q. Professionals	395,987	630,621
R. Artists	132,108	200,469
S. Public Officials	20,927	29,384[a]
T. Directors General, Area Directors	110,557	193,993[a]
U. Secondary School and University Teachers	70,230	110,176[a]
V. Primary School Teachers[1]	485,636	764235[a]
W. Technicians	515,045	767,997
X. Skilled Offfice Workers[2]	972,440	1,053,933[a]

1. Includes preschool, special, and sports instructors, school inspectors, and other education workers.
2. Includes office chiefs, accountants, machinery operators, library and archival workers, and public relations personnel.
a. Estimated from census data.

PART II. **Aggregate Professionals and Technicians Calculated from Census Data in Part I**

1950	Professionals		Technicians	
	Wide	Narrow	Wide	Narrow
	Definition[1]	Definition[2]	Definition[3]	Definition[4]
	150,680	106,040	207,986	128,752

1980	Professionals		Technicians	
	Wide	Narrow	Wide	Narrow
	Definition[5]	Definition[6]	Definition[7]	Definition[8]
	729,809	549,022	1,973,121	1,487,485

1990	Professionals		Technicians	
	Wide	Narrow	Wide	Narrow
	Definition[5]	Definition[6]	Definition[7]	Definition[8]
	1,164,643	860,474	2,990,892	2,226,657

1. 1950 wide definition of professionals = $2/3A + 2/3B + D + 2/3 E + F + G + I + J + K + 1/2L + 1/2M$.
2. 1950 narrow definition of professionals = $2/3A + 2/3B + 2/3 E + F + G + I + J$.
3. 1950 wide definition of technicians = $1/3A + 1/3B + C + 1/3E + H + O + P$.
4. 1950 narrow definition of technicians = $1/3A + 1/3B + 1/3E + H + O + P$.
5. 1980 and 1990 wide definition of professionals = $Q + R + S + T + U$.
6. 1980 and 1990 narrow definition of professionals = $Q + R + S$.
7. 1980 and 1990 wide definition of technicians = $V + W + X$.
8. 1980 and 1990 narrow definition of technicians = $W + X$.

TABLE 30 (Continued)

PART III: **Summary Statistics on Professionals and Technicians in Census Data**

A. Professionals and Technicians as Percent of Economically Active Population, 1950, 1980, and 1990

Year	Professionals		Technicians	
	Wide Definition	Narrow Definition	Wide Definition	Narrow Definition
1950	1.8	1.3	2.5	1.6
1980	3.3	2.5	8.9	6.7
1990	5.0	3.7	12.8	9.5

B. Percentage Change, 1950-80

Period	Professionals		Technicians	
	Wide Definition	Narrow Definition	Wide Definition	Narrow Definition
1950-80	384.3	417.8	848.7	1055.3

C. Implicit Annual Rates of Change

Period	Professionals		Technicians	
	Wide Definition	Narrow Definition	Wide Definition	Narrow Definition
1950-80	5.4	5.6	7.8	8.5
1980-90	4.8	4.6	4.3	4.1

Source: Censuses of 1950 and 1980.

TABLE 31. **Increase in Degrees Granted, Egresados, and Degrees Registered, 1950-89**

(Percentage Change by Ten- and Five-Year Periods)

Period	Degrees Granted	Egresados	Degrees Registered
Ten-Year			
1950-60	75.1		
1960-70	232.1		
1970-80		267.9	149.1
Five-Year			
1940-45	59.7		
1945-50	81.2		
1950-55	88.7		
1955-60	-7.2		
1960-65	100.2		
1965-70[a]	65.9	48.0	
1970-75[b]		97.3	48.2
1975-80		85.9	68.1
1980-85		45.0	56.2
1985-89		16.9	

a. Egresados data are for 1967-70.
b. Degrees Registered data are for 1971-75.

SOURCE: Calculated from Tables 1, 3, and 5.

TABLE 32. **Estimated Expenditure per University Student in Mexico, 1930-80**

Year	Pesos of 1970 per Student	Index (1970=100)
1930	1,013	62
1935	2,535	156
1940	1,830	112
1945	1,754	108
1950	1,815	111
1955	1,614	99
1958	4,641	285
1965	2,161	133
1970	1,628	100
1975	1,993	122
1980	2,084	128

SOURCE: CE; AE; ANUIES-ESM; SEP-OE; EHM; OELM; PROIDES; SEP, *Información estadística*, 1958-70; Pedro Aspe and Paul Sigmund, eds., *The Political Economy of Income Distribution in Mexico* (New York: Holmes and Meier Publishers, 1984). Data for 1930-55 were estimated from data on SEP expenditures. Expenditure data were deflated with the Macro Price Index from James W. Wilkie, "From Economic Growth to Economic Stagnation in Mexico," in SALA, vol. 26, p. 924.

TABLE 33. **UNESCO Data on Expenditure per University Student in Mexico, 1961-85**

Year	Pesos of 1970 per Student	Index (1970=100)
1961	5,344	178
1965	5,306	177
1970	3,002	100
1975	3,332	111
1980	6,683	223
1985	4,949	165

SOURCE: Derived from UNESCO-SY, various years. UNESCO data in current pesos deflated with the Macro Price Index (James W. Wilkie, "From Economic Growth to Economic Stagnation in Mexico," SALA, vol. 26, p. 924).

Table 34.   **Students per Faculty at Mexican Universities, 1928-90**

Year	Average Students per Faculty	Index (1970=100)
1928	21.8	223
1929	16.4	167
1930	15.3	156
1931	18.1	185
1932	14.8	151
1933	10.7	109
1934	7.9	81
1935	9.3	95
1936	8.3	85
1937	9.7	99
1938	6.8	70
1939	7.3	75
1949	7.1	73
1950	4.9	50
1951	4.4	45
1952	5.6	57
1953	5.3	54
1954	5.5	56
1955	7.8	80
1956	4.8	49
1957	8.8	89
1958	7.2	74
1959	5.9	60
1960	7.3	75
1961	7.7	79
1962	7.9	80
1963	7.4	75
1964	7.6	78
1965	10.3	105
1966	10.8	110
1967	10.3	105
1968	10.6	108
1969	9.7	99

TABLE 34 (Continued)

Year	Average Students per Faculty	Index (1970=100)
1970	9.8	100
1971	10.9	111
1972	10.9	111
1973	10.8	111
1974	11.1	114
1975	11.4	116
1976	12.3	126
1977	11.7	119
1978	11.9	121
1979	12.1	123
1980	11.6	119
1981	12.1	124
1982	10.9	111
1983	11.0	112
1984	10.1	103
1985	10.1	103
1986	10.8	111
1987	10.2	104
1988	10.2	104
1989	10.3	105
1990	10.3	105

SOURCE: CE; AE; EHM; ANUIES-AE; ANUIES-ESM; SEP-EBSEN.

TABLE 35. **Full-Time, Part-Time, and Hourly Faculty at Mexican Universities, 1965-90**

(%)

Year	Full-Time	Part-Time	Hourly
1965	6.9	4.3	88.9
1967	9.0	5.3	85.7
1968	7.2	4.1	88.7
1969	8.0	4.7	87.3
1970	8.2	5.1	86.7
1971	8.8	5.2	86.0
1976	8.6	7.6	83.8
1979	18.4	9.4	72.2
1980	17.2	7.9	75.0
1981	18.1	8.1	73.9
1982	18.8	8.0	73.2
1983	20.8	8.4	70.8
1984	19.6	8.2	72.2
1985	20.9	8.3	70.9
1986	22.1	8.0	69.9
1987	23.2	7.8	69.0
1988	22.7	8.2	69.1
1989	24.6	8.2	67.1
1990	25.1	8.3	66.6

SOURCE: Calculated from ANUIES-AE, ANUIES-ESM, and SEP, *Guia de la enseñanza superior 1965* (México, D. F.: SEP, 1966).

TABLE 36. **Estimated Expenditure per Student at UNAM,**[1] **1924-85**

Year	Pesos of 1970 per Student	Index (1970=100)
1924	3,036	35
1925	2,811	32
1926	2,736	32
1927	2,461	28
1928	2,744	32
1929	3,468	40
1930	~	~
1931	13,594	157
1932	3,979	46
1933	4,616	53
1934	3,066	35
1935	3,148	36
1936	3,428	40
1937	5,635	65
1938	3,577	41
1939	3,369	39
1940	3,198	37
1941	3,010	35
1942	2,860	33
1943	2,254	26
1944	1,935	22
1944-45	1,670	19
1945-46	1,988	23
1946-47	2,231	26
1947-48	2,568	30
1948-49	2,476	29
1949-50	2,578	30
1950-51	1,990	23
1951-52	1,912	22
1952-53	2,093	24
1953-54	2,103	24
1954-55	2,648	31
1955-56	2,765	32
1956-57	2,666	31
1957-58	2,919	34
1958-59	3,553	41
1959-60	3,617	42

TABLE 36 (Continued)

Year	Pesos of 1970	Index
1960-61	4,030	47
1962	4,650	54
1963	6,092	70
1964	6,952	80
1965	6,469	75
1966	7,500	87
1967	9,517	110
1968	10,967	127
1969	10,086	116
1970	8,664	100
1971	7,494	86
1972	9,668	112
1973	11,551	133
1974	~	~
1975	11,898	137
1976	12,759	147
1977	~	~
1978	~	~
1979	13,456	155
1980	13,172	152
1981	17,424	201
1982	15,873	183
1983	14,015	162
1984	11,988	138
1985	12,508	144

1. Sources generally give data for total expenditure at UNAM and thus include the roughly 15 percent of UNAM's expenditure which is devoted to the preparatory level. Budget data have been modified to take this factor into account. For series on expenditure for all levels, see FU, p. 83, and HEU, p. 61.

SOURCE: Data derived from HEU; *50 años de revolución;* OELM; ANUIES-ESM; FU; UNAM-PP; Carlos Muñoz Izquierdo, "Evaluación del desarrollo educativo en México (1958-1970) y factores que lo han determinado," *Revista del Centro de Estudios Educativos* 3: 3 (1973); SEP-EBSEN. Expenditure data were deflated with the Macro Price Index from James W. Wilkie, "From Economic Growth to Economic Stagnation in Mexico," SALA, vol. 26, p. 924.

Table 37. **Students per Faculty Member at UNAM,[1] 1931-90**

Year	Average Students per Faculty Member	Index (1970=100)
1931	8.2	61
1932	9.1	68
1933	8.2	61
1934	6.7	50
1935	7.0	52
1936	6.5	49
1937	6.1	46
1938	8.4	63
1939	7.2	54
1940	7.7	57
1941	7.8	58
1942	7.5	56
1943	8.5	63
1944	8.3	62
1945	7.9	59
1946	7.2	54
1947	6.8	51
1948	7.1	53
1949	7.5	56
1950	7.7	57
1951	7.7	57
1952	7.6	57
1953	7.1	53
1954	6.9	51
1955	7.6	57
1956	7.6	57
1957	7.6	57
1958	7.9	59
1959	12.1	90
1960	9.8	73
1961	10.1	75
1962	10.7	80
1963	10.5	78
1964	10.7	80

TABLE 37 (Continued)

Year	Average Students per Faculty Member	Index (1970=100)
1965	10.5	78
1966	9.6	72
1967	8.8	66
1968	8.8	66
1969	9.7	73
1970	8.7	65
1971	8.3	62
1972	8.9	67
1973	8.6	64
1974	9.8	73
1975	9.7	73
1976	10.0	74
1977	~	~
1978	~	~
1979	10.0	75
1980	6.6	49
1981	6.6	49
1982	5.8	44
1983	7.8	58
1984	5.7	42
1985	5.1	38
1986	7.0	52
1987	6.0	45
1988	6.1	46
1989	6.5	49
1990	6.1	46

1. Includes ENEP's after 1980.

SOURCE: Calculated from NAFINSA-EMC; AE; CE; UNAM-AE; HEU; ANUIES-AE; Alberto Menéndez Guzmán, *Tendencias del presupuesto universitario (1967-76)* (México, D. F.: UNAM, Dirección General de Presupuesto por Programación, n.d.). Data from these sources, which vary within generally similar parameters, were averaged in overlapping years.

TABLE 38. **Full-Time, Part-Time, and Hourly Faculty at UNAM,**[1] **1969-90**

Year	Full-Time	Part-Time	Hourly
1969	3.0	3.2	93.8
1970	3.8	4.4	91.8
1971	4.0	3.9	92.1
1976	4.2	2.3	93.5
1979	8.1	3.7	88.2
1980	7.0	3.0	90.1
1981	7.6	2.8	89.6
1982	8.4	3.1	88.5
1983	13.8	3.7	82.5
1984	9.8	3.3	82.5
1985	10.2	3.1	86.8
1986	10.1	2.7	87.2
1987	11.7	2.7	85.5
1988	7.5	1.9	90.6
1989	10.1	2.6	87.3
1990	12.0	2.9	85.0

1. Main campus only.

SOURCE: Calculated from ANUIES-AE and ANUIES-ESM.

TABLE 39. **Percentage Share of UNAM Budget Devoted to Faculty Support, 1967-88**

Year	Percentage of Budget
1967	30.6
1968	49.7
1969	51.3
1970	50.2
1971	52.7
1972	53.3
1973	44.0
1974[a]	48.0

TABLE 39 (Continued)

Year	Percentage of Budget
1975	52.1
1976	57.3
1977	58.9
1978	64.8
1979	61.9
1980	61.2
1981	62.7
1982	62.5
1983	61.1
1984	62.2
1985	64.1
1986	65.8
1987	65.1
1988	64.6

a. Estimated.

SOURCE: HEU; ANUIES-AE; UNAM-PP.

TABLE 40. Quality Measures, Sample Public and Private Universities[1]

PART I. 1970

	% Full-Time Faculty	Students per Faculty	Students per Full-Time Faculty
Public			
IPN	11.3	12	102
MICHSN	7.5	20	266
UABC	1.7	6	332
UACH	10.0	9	87
UACO	1.7	10	560
UAEM	3.8	6	157
UANL	23.2	11	49
UAP	4.7	10	212
UASIN	17.5	9	51
UASLP	5.1	6	115
UAT	1.6	10	648
UG	13.1	14	105
UGUAN	6.4	6	101
UNAM[2]	3.8	9	227
UV	15.5	11	71
Unweighted Averages	8.5	10	205
Private			
Anahuác	3.1	3	95
Ibero[2]	3.9	6	144
ITAM	5.7	4	77
ITESM[2]	58.6	12	21
UAG	18.7	17	89
Unweighted Averages	18.0	8	85

PART II. 1980

	% Full-Time Faculty	Students per Faculty	Students per Full-Time Faculty
Public			
IPN	27.5	9	33
MICHSN	15.8	21	135
UABC	17.7	12	66
UACH	18.2	11	60
UACO	7.6	14	186
UAEM	9.7	11	118
UAM	66.3	15	22
UANL	20.7	17	84
UAP	23.8	27	112
UASIN	43.7	24	55
UASLP	13.7	13	98
UAT	16.6	13	81
UG	14.6	25	171
UGUAN	21.6	7	31
UNAM[2]	6.7	7	99
UV	23.3	22	95
Unweighted Averages	21.7	16	90
Private			
Anahuác	25.4	6	23
Ibero[2]	0.0	8	
ITAM	25.2	10	41
ITESM[2]	25.5	11	42
UAG	72.3	18	25
UDLA	52.4	13	25
Unweighted Averages	33.5	11	31

PART III. 1990

	% Full-Time Faculty	Students per Faculty	Students per Full-Time Faculty
Public			
IPN	41.9	9	22
MICHSN	17.1	17	77
UABC	24.6	10	39
UACH	27.4	11	40
UACO	10.7	10	94
UAEM	19.6	12	59
UAM	61.2	13	21
UANL	43.9	19	42
UAP	46.9	37	80
UASIN	51.4	14	28
UASLP	19.3	11	56
UAT	25.7	8	31
UG	12.8	18	138
UGUAN	29.5	6	22
UNAM[2]	12.0	5	45
UV	18.2	7	41
Unweighted Averages	28.9	13	52
Private			
Anahuác	4.1	8	190
Ibero[2]	10.7	7	
ITAM	25.1	9	65
ITESM[2]	21.7	12	34
UAG	64.0	18	29
UDLA	27.7	9	33
Unweighted Averages	25.6	10	67

1. Abbreviations for universities in the sample are as follows:

Anahuác	Universidad Anahuác
Ibero	Universidad Iberoamericana
IPN	Instituto Politécnico Nacional
ITAM	Instituto Tecnológico Autónomo de México
ITESM	Instituto Tecnológico y de Estudios Superiores de Monterrey

MICHSN	Universidad Michoacana de San Nicolás
UABC	Universidad Autónoma de Baja California
UACH	Universidad Autónoma de Chihuahua
UACO	Universidad Autónoma de Coahuila
UAEM	Universidad Autónoma de Estado de México
UAG	Universidad Autónoma de Guadalajara
UAM	Universidad Autónoma Metropolitana
UANL	Universidad Autónoma de Nuevo León
UAP	Universidad Autónoma de Puebla
UASIN	Universidad Autónoma de Sinaloa
UASLP	Universidad Autónoma de San Luis Potosí
UAT	Universidad Autónoma de Tamaulipas
UDLA	Universidad de las Américas-Puebla
UG	Universidad de Guadalajara
UGUAN	Universidad de Guanajuato
UNAM	Universidad Nacional Autónoma de México
UV	Universidad Veracruzana

2. Central campus only.

SOURCE: ANUIES-ESM; ANUIES-AE.

TABLE 41. **Enrollment in Sample Fields of Study at Public and Private Universities, Five Fields, 1959 and 1964**

PART I. **Absolute Data**

| | 1959 | | | 1964 | | |
Field	Public	Private	Total	Public	Private	Total
BUS	8,556	2,932	11,488	14,762	8,974	23,706
ENG	16,182	2,074	18,256	23,360	3,017	26,377
HEALTH	13,787	548	14,335	17,679	1,010	18,689
Law	9,123	395	9,518	14,255	974	15,229
TEACH	3,105	377	3,482	6,007	468	6,475

PART II. **Public and Private Shares of Enrollment
in Sample Fields, 1959 and 1964**

Field	1959 Public/Total	1959 Private/Total	1964 Public/Total	1964 Private/Total
BUS	74.5	25.5	62.3	37.9
ENG	88.6	11.4	88.6	11.4
HEALTH	96.2	3.8	94.6	5.4
Law	95.8	4.2	93.6	6.4
TEACH	89.2	10.8	92.8	7.2

PART III. **Enrollment in Sample Fields as Share of Total
Enrollment, 1959 and 1964**

Field	Public 1959	Public 1964	Private 1959	Private 1964
BUS	13.4	14.8	37.8	52.7
ENG	25.4	23.5	26.7	17.7
HEALTH	21.6	17.7	7.1	5.9
Law	14.3	14.3	5.1	5.7
TEACH	4.9	6.0	4.9	2.7

SOURCE: Calculated from OELM, Appendix D.

TABLE 42. **UNAM and IPN Share of Total Enrollment, 1928-60**

Year	UNAM/ Total	IPN/ Total	UNAM+IPN/ Total
1928	32.2		32.2
1929	32.8		32.8
1930	40.9		40.9
1931	37.4		37.4
1932	57.7		57.7
1933	76.4		76.4
1934	72.0		72.0
1935	63.5		63.5
1936	53.0	13.0	66.0
1937	43.7	9.6	53.3
1938	60.9	11.9	72.7
1939	55.2	11.9	67.1

TABLE 42 (Continued)

Year	UNAM/ Total	IPN/ Total	UNAM+IPN/ Total
1940	54.9	11.4	66.3
1941	51.3	12.1	63.4
1942	46.4	11.6	58.0
1943	50.3	11.1	61.4
1944	47.2	9.3	56.5
1945	45.8	10.4	56.2
1946	41.0	10.3	51.3
1947	37.2	10.5	47.7
1948	34.0	9.6	43.6
1949	36.1	8.8	44.9
1950	36.1	7.2	43.3
1951	48.6	10.7	59.2
1952	36.5	8.5	44.9
1953	39.0	9.5	48.5
1954	45.9	12.1	58.0
1955	44.2	9.7	53.9
1956	50.7	13.3	64.1
1957	54.8	12.8	67.7
1958	56.0	14.5	70.5
1959	55.3	14.2	69.5
1960	55.2	12.6	67.8

SOURCE: NAFINSA-EMC.

TABLE 43.   **Enrollment in Private Universities, UNAM, and IPN, 1959-64**

| Total University | | Percentage | | | UNAM-IPN as |
Year	Enrollment	Private	Private	UNAM	IPN	% of Total
1959	71,525	7,357	10.3	33,264	8,899	58.9
1960	78,787	9,205	11.7	37,241	7,769	57.1
1961	88,202	9,780	11.1	40,922	9,372	57.0
1962	100,519	12,599	12.5	43,387	10,783	53.9
1963	110,378	15,374	13.9	45,141	10,806	50.7
1964	116,628	17,412	14.9	42,256	12,017	46.5

SOURCE: OELM, Appendix C.

Table 44.   **UNAM and IPN Share of Total University Enrollment (Alternate Data), 1961-66**

Year	UNAM	IPN	UNAM+IPN
1961	30.7	7.0	37.7
1962	29.2	6.7	35.9
1963	28.4	6.9	35.3
1964	27.5	7.4	35.0
1965	23.7	6.9	30.6
1966	23.0	7.8	30.8

SOURCE: OELM.

TABLE 45. **Egresados of Public and Private Universities, 1967-89**

Year	Total Egresados	Public	Private	UNAM	ENEPs[1]	Total UNAM	IPN
1967	15,443			5,752	0	5,752	1,151
1968	16,483			5,190	0	5,190	1,883
1969	20,797			6,464	0	6,464	2,456
1970	22,904			6,191	0	6,191	4,304
1971	25,793			6,579	0	6,574	4,598
1972	29,396			6,895	0	6,895	4,598
1973	33,106			7,756	0	7,756	5,411
1974	39,186			8,607	0	8,607	6,610
1975	44,186			11,012	0	11,012	5,605
1976	48,674	41,683	6,991	11,960	0	11,960	7,206
1977	55,446	47,059	8,387	10,653	1,437	12,090	8,361
1978	59,294	50,349	8,945	11,989	2,396	14,385	7,192
1979	66,656	56,550	10,106	9,678	2,794	12,472	10,355
1980	69,572	59,040	10,532	9,060	3,287	12,347	8,005
1981	78,644	66,368	12,276	11,340	3,818	15,158	7,139
1982	85,505	71,496	14,009	10,297	5,894	16,191	7,165
1983	96,572	78,502	18,070	10,794	4,834	15,628	5,978
1984	98,788	79,839	18,949	8,951	5,592	14,543	6,212
1985	103,280	82,869	20,411	9,939	5,050	14,989	6,815
1986	106,693	87,283	19,410	9,939	6,378	16,317	5,805
1987	117,378	95,714	21,664	10,137	7,011	17,148	7,113
1988	115,670	94,597	21,073	9,236	6,129	15,365	7,094
1989	115,407	93,107	22,300	7,982	6,890	14,872	7,701

1. The ENEPs (Escuela Nacional de Estudios Profesionales) function as decentralized campuses of UNAM.

SOURCE: ANUIES-ESM and ANUIES-AE.

TABLE 46. Egresados of Eleven Sample Public Universities,[1] 1967-89

Year	UACO	UACH	UAEM	UANL	UAP	UASLP	UAS	UAT	UG	MICHSN	UV
1967	240	108	144	939	293	276	86	77	1,053	266	517
1968	264	163	182	1,038	375	229	51	139	854	301	737
1969	385	185	223	1,101	393	378	132	192	1,267	397	919
1970	386	244	136	1,295	423	466	124	251	1,146	472	1053
1971	326	315	199	1,471	1,157	541	163	239	1,488	521	987
1972	401	248	227	1,448	1,188	714	306	364	2,151	625	947
1973	431	322	247	1,409	1,419	613	306	440	2,627	754	1,053
1974	812	422	299	1,746	1,737	586	440	515	2,805	906	1,626
1975	649	658	342	1,452	1,738	813	581	622	2,764	1,033	1,628
1976	829	572	471	2,198	2,273	963	1,150	935	3,568	1,271	1,744
1977	902	852	723	2,362	2,390	1,272	1,086	872	3,993	1,739	2,381
1978	1,068	1,087	777	2,709	2,806	1,159	1,155	878	3,681	2,026	2,233
1979	1,014	1,102	991	4,439	2,350	1,190	1,387	1,808	3,731	2,410	2,891
1980	1,260	1,158	1,565	3,942	2,762	1,287	1,866	1,475	3,820	2,462	3,601
1981	1,373	1,233	1,427	3,787	2,629	1,343	2,786	1,269	4,411	2,932	4,400
1982	1,415	1,502	1,504	4,384	2,679	1,289	2,942	1,310	5,389	2,836	4,041
1983	1,596	1,490	1,635	4,938	2,905	1,515	3,176	2,270	5,468	3,090	6,599
1984	1,638	1,470	1,916	4,856	3,531	1,831	3,176	2,480	5,227	3,076	6,048
1985	2,075	1,142	1,900	4,675	2,051	1,497	4,269	3,420	5,971	3,200	5,856
1986	2,312	1,102	3,348	4,384	2,438	1,441	4,083	2,943	5,971	3,208	5,856
1987	2,844	1,133	2,804	4,503	3,362	1,454	4,443	3,514	6,386	3,410	6,130
1988	3,310	1,050	2,148	5,080	3,312	1,558	4,216	2,418	6,971	3,420	6,170
1989	2,776	1,230	2,516	4,637	3,473	1,534	2,276	3,466	6,420	3,494	5,028

TABLE 46 (Continued)

1. Universities in sample are:

MICHSN	Universidad Michoacana de San Nicolás
UACH	Universidad Autónoma de Chihuahua
UACO	Universidad Autónoma de Coahuila
UAEM	Universidad Autónoma de Estado de México
UANL	Universidad Autónoma de Nuevo León
UAP	Universidad Autónoma de Puebla
UASIN	Universidad Autónoma de Sinaloa
UASLP	Universidad Autónoma de San Luis Potosí
UAT	Universidad Autónoma de Tamaulipas
UG	Universidad de Guadalajara
UV	Universidad Veracruzana

SOURCE: ANUIES-ESM; ANUIES-AE.

TABLE 47. **Egresados of Three Sample Private Universities, 1967-89**

Year	IBERO	UAG	ITESM	Decentralized[1] ITESM	Total ITESM
1967	371	350	416	0	416
1968	290	440	608	0	608
1969	541	606	325	0	325
1970	503	669	325	0	325
1971	510	532	455	0	455
1972	641	~	654	0	654
1973	762	~	778	0	778
1974	1,143	~	470	0	470
1975	1,345	~	740	0	740
1976	1,219	1,257	747	84	831
1977	724	2,106	1,118	115	1,233
1978	720	2,354	1,058	37	1,095
1979	857	2,193	1,054	158	1,212
1980	435	2,053	1,165	210	1,375
1981	622	2,292	1,292	320	1,612
1982	623	2,017	1,355	461	1,816
1983	1,404	2,541	1,496	645	2,141
1984	1,516	2,254	1,540	578	2,118
1985	1,683	2,357	1,769	309	2,078
1986	1,378	1,282	1,867	901	2,768
1987	1,173	2,346	1,766	1,043	2,809
1988	1,709	2,083	1,764	833	2,597
1989	1,428	1,884	1,323	645	1,968

1. The ITESM has decentralized campuses in several states and the Federal District.

SOURCE: ANUIES-ESM; ANUIES-AE.

TABLE 48. **Summary Percentage Data on Egresados of
Public and Private Universities
and in Sample,[1] 1967-89**

PART I. **Public and Private Shares**

Year	UNAM+IPN as % of Total	Private[2] as % of Total	Public[2] as % of Total
1967	44.7	11.6	88.4
1968	42.9	13.2	86.8
1969	42.9	11.8	88.2
1970	45.8	11.2	88.8
1971	43.3	10.3	89.7
1972	39.1	12.5	87.5
1973	39.8	13.4	86.6
1974	38.8	12.6	87.4
1975	37.6	14.2	85.8
1976	39.4	14.4	85.6
1977	36.9	15.1	84.9
1978	36.4	15.1	84.9
1979	34.2	15.2	84.8
1980	29.3	15.1	84.9
1981	28.4	15.6	84.4
1982	27.3	16.4	83.6
1983	22.4	18.7	81.3
1984	21.0	19.2	80.8
1985	21.1	19.8	80.2
1986	20.7	18.2	81.8
1987	20.7	18.5	81.5
1988	19.4	18.2	81.8
1989	19.6	19.3	80.7

PART II. Data on Sample

Year	Sample as % of Total Egresados	Sample Private as % of Total Egresados of Private Universities	Sample Public as % of Total Egresados of Public Universities
1967	78.0	61.7	95.1
1968	77.3	60.1	93.9
1969	76.8	58.5	92.7
1970	78.5	56.9	91.5
1971	77.8	55.3	90.3
1972	72.8	53.7	89.1
1973	73.5	52.1	87.9
1974	73.3	50.5	86.7
1975	70.1	48.9	85.5
1976	79.0	47.3	84.3
1977	77.7	48.4	82.9
1978	76.4	46.6	81.7
1979	75.6	42.2	81.6
1980	71.0	36.7	77.2
1981	69.2	36.9	75.2
1982	66.8	31.8	73.6
1983	64.6	33.7	71.7
1984	62.7	31.1	70.1
1985	61.9	30.0	69.8
1986	60.6	28.0	67.8
1987	60.1	29.2	67.1
1988	59.2	30.3	65.7
1989	57.0	23.7	65.0

1. See absolute data on universities in sample in Tables 46 and 47.
2. Private and public shares are estimated 1967-75.

SOURCE: ANUIES-ESM; ANUIES-AE.

TABLE 49. **Mexico's Class Structure,**[1] **1895-1980**

(% and Percentage Change [PC])

Year	Upper	PC	Middle	PC	Lower	PC
1895	1.5	~	7.8	~	90.7	~
1940	2.9	93.3	12.6	61.5	84.5	-6.8
1950	1.7	-41.4	18.0	42.9	80.3	-5.0
1960	3.8	123.5	21.0	16.7	75.2	-6.4
1970	5.7	50.0	27.9	32.9	66.4	-11.7
1980[a]	5.2	-8.8	31.5	12.9	63.5	-4.4

1. The categories "upper," "middle," and "lower" are adopted from the sources.

a. The assumption in QMCS that all persons who did not or could not specify their occupation on the census form for 1980 were from the popular sector cannot be correct. Some large fraction of this number should be evenly spread back across all occupational groups. I estimated for this table that the number of persons in unspecified occupational groups belonging to the popular sector was 10 percent in 1980 (rising from 5.2 percent in 1970). I divided the rest of the number of persons of unspecified occupation equally among all other class strata. This manipulation leads to a few significant changes in the data for 1980 but does not affect the most important secular trends in Mexico's class structure.

SOURCE: For 1895 and 1940, adapted from Howard F. Cline, *Mexico: Revolution to Evolution, 1940-1960* (New York: Oxford University Press, 1963), p. 124; for 1950-1970, QMCS; for 1980, modified from data in QMCS as in Table 23, Part I.

TABLE 50. **Mexico's Class Structure, by Income and Occupation,
1950-80**

(%)

	1950			1960		
	Income	Occu-pation	Combined	Income	Occu-pation	Combined
UPPER	1.8	1.6	1.7	5.6	2.0	3.8
Leisure	0.2	0.8	0.5	1.0	0.8	0.9
Semi-Leisure	1.6	0.8	1.2	4.6	1.2	2.9
MIDDLE	19.4	16.6	18.0	21.8	20.2	21.0
Stable	3.2	6.6	4.9	4.8	8.5	6.7
Marginal	16.2	10.0	13.1	17.0	11.7	14.4
LOWER	78.8	81.8	80.3	72.6	77.8	75.2
Transitional	25.4	20.0	22.7	15.8	20.9	18.4
Popular	53.4	61.8	57.6	56.8	56.9	56.9
Total	100	100	100	100	100	100

	1970			1980		
	Income	Occu-pation	Combined	Income	Occu-pation	Combined
UPPER	7.0	4.4	5.7	6.7	3.7	5.2
Leisure	1.5	2.5	2.0	2.4	1.2	1.8
Semi-Leisure	5.9	1.9	3.9	4.3	2.5	3.4
MIDDLE	32.5	23.4	28.0	36.3	26.7	31.5
Stable	7.9	10.0	9.0	11.1	12.1	11.6
Marginal	24.6	13.4	19.0	25.2	14.6	19.9
LOWER	60.5	72.2	66.4	57.0	70.0	63.5
Transitional	12.4	24.8	18.6	12.0	22.6	17.3
Popular	48.1	47.4	47.8	45.0	47.5	46.3
Total	100	100	100	100	100	100

SOURCE: Calculated from QMCS with data for 1980 as in Table 22, Part I.

TABLE 51. **Percentage Change in Absolute Data for Four
Selected Classes, 1950-60, 1960-70, and 1970-80**

UPPER

	Income	Occupation	Combined
1950-60	177.4	72.9	127.8
1960-70	113.9	143.4	124.5
1970-80	39.8	39.6	39.7

Semi-Leisure

	Income	Occupation	Combined
1950-60	164.3	98.2	141.2
1960-70	1.2	78.8	95.7
1970-80	13.6	115.6	40.4

MIDDLE

	Income	Occupation	Combined
1950-60	-0.3	67	30.7
1960-70	153.3	32.5	73.6
1970-80	65.2	88.0	74.9

Stable

	Income	Occupation	Combined
1950-60	31.7	76.1	61.5
1960-70	178.4	35.2	73.6
1970-80	109.0	98.6	103.1

SOURCE: Calculated from QMCS with data for 1980 as in Table 22, Part I.

TABLE 52. **Change in Percentage Data for Four Selected Classes, 1950-60, 1960-70, and 1970-80**

(% and Percentage Change [PC])

PART I. **Combined Occupation and Income**

Year	Middle	PC	Stable Middle	PC	Upper	PC	Leisure	PC
1950	18.0	~	4.9	~	1.7	~	1.2	~
1960	21.0	16.7	6.7	36.7	3.8	123.5	2.9	141.7
1970	28.0	33.3	9.0	34.3	5.7	50.0	3.7	27.6
1980	31.5	12.5	11.6	28.9	5.2	-8.8	3.4	-8.1

PART II. **Income**

Year	Middle	PC	Stable Middle	PC	Upper	PC	Semi-Leisure	PC
1950	19.4	~	3.2	~	1.8	~	1.6	~
1960	21.8	12.4	4.8	50.0	5.6	211.1	4.6	187.5
1970	32.5	49.1	7.9	64.6	7.0	25.0	5.9	28.3
1980	36.3	11.7	11.1	40.5	6.7	-4.3	4.3	-27.1

PART III. **Occupation**

Year	Middle	PC	Stable Middle	PC	Upper	PC	Semi-Leisure	PC
1950	16.6	~	6.6	~	1.6	~	0.8	~
1960	20.2	21.7	8.5	28.8	2.0	25.0	1.2	50.0
1970	23.4	15.8	10	17.6	4.4	120.0	1.9	58.3
1980	26.7	14.1	12.1	21.0	3.7	-15.9	2.5	31.6

SOURCE: Calculated from QMCS with data for 1980 as in Table 22, Part I.

TABLE 53. **Percentage Change in Class Structure, 1950-80**

PART I. **Absolute Data**

	Income	Occupation	Combined
UPPER	729.5	487.4	614.6
Semi-Leisure	507.7	663.8	562.3
MIDDLE	317.1	315.7	316.5
Stable	666.3	372.7	469.3
LOWER	60.7	120.3	91.1

PART II. **Percentage Data**

	Income	Occupation	Combined
UPPER	272.2	131.3	205.9
Semi-Leisure	168.8	212.5	183.3
MIDDLE	87.1	60.8	75.0
Stable	246.9	83.3	136.7

SOURCE: Calculated from QMCS with data for 1980 as in Table 22, Part I.

Table 54. **Comparison of Growth Rates of University Degrees Granted, Egresados, and Degrees Registered with Growth of Social Classes, 1950-90**

(PC per Decade)

		Professionals		Classes[1]	
Period	Degrees Granted	Egresados	Degrees Registered	Stable Middle	Semi-Leisure
1950-60	75.1	~	~	76.1	98.2
1960-70	232.1	~	~	35.2	78.8
1970-80	~	266.5	149.1	98.6	115.6
1980-90[a]	~	69.6	~	41.2	8.1

1. Gauged by occupation.

a. Egresados data for 1980-89.

SOURCE: Calculated from Tables 1, 3, 5, and 51.

TABLE 55. Highest Level of Schooling Attained by Fathers of
UNAM Students, 1949, 1963, 1970, and 1980

(%)

	Professional	Preparatory Vocational	Technical	Secondary	Primary	Total
1949	23.6	~	~	~	9.5	~
1963	20.8	~	~	~	14.3	~
1970[a]	19	4	3	7	19	52.0
1980	17.4	4.4	2.1	10.4	27.3	61.6

a. Rounded figures are given in source.

SOURCE: Adapted from UNAM-CU; UNAM-CEAL; UNAM-EAE; UNAM-
AE.

TABLE 56. **Monthly Income of Families of UNAM Students,[1] 1963, 1970, and 1980**

Part I. **1963**

Pesos of 1970	0-748	749-999	1000-1498	1499-1998	1199-2497	2498-3121	3122-4120	4121-5119	5120-6117	6118-7116	7117-8115	8116-10112	10113-12110	12110+
Percent of Families	2.0	2.6	9.6	13.2	6.7	12.6	18.3	11.0	3.6	7.3	3.6	4.6	1.5	3.9

Part II. **1970**

Pesos of 1970	0-600	600-1000	1000-1500	1500-2000	2000-2500	2500-3000	3000-4000	4000-5000	5000-6000	6000-7000	7000-8000	8000-10000	10000-12000	12000+	No Response
Percent of Families	1.1	3.2	9	10.4	10.1	12.5	13.5	11.0	7.7	4.7	3.6	4.2	2.9	3.7	3.7

Part III. **1980**

Pesos of 1970	0-820	821-1230	1231-1639	1640-2049	2050-2459	2460-3279	3280-4098	4099+	No Response
Percent of Families	7.1	13.4	16.8	13.8	13.2	12.9	9.4	11.3	2.1

1. Data for 1963 and 1980 deflated to derive pesos of 1970 using Micro Price Index from James W. Wilkie, "From Economic Growth to Economic Stagnation in Mexico," in SALA, vol. 26, p. 924. Because the original data had three different base years, the peso categories used in this table differ slightly.

SOURCE: UNAM-AE; UNAM-CU.

TABLE 57. **Class Background of UNAM Students, 1963, 1970,**
and 1980

(%)

Class	1963	1970	1980
LOWER	4.6	4.3	7.1
MIDDLE	29.5	29.5	57.2
UPPER	66.4	62.5	33.6
No Response	~	3.7	2.1
LOWER+			
Transitional Middle	14.2	13.3	37.3

SOURCE: Calculated from Table 56 using QMCS class breakdown by
income.

TABLE 58. **Women Professionals and Technicians in**
Economically Active Population, 1900-90

(%)

Year	Percent
1900	30.8
1910	27.4
1921	37.7
1930	36.5
1940	32.8
1950	32.8
1960	37.7
1970	33.8
1980	40.7
1990	36.2

SOURCE: Calculated from AE; CE; census.

TABLE 59. **UNAM Degrees Granted to Women, 1910-66, and Women Enrolled, 1930-66**

Year	Degrees Granted	(%) Enrollment
1910	12.3	
1911	3.5	
1912	15.0	
1913	32.5	
1914	18.3	
1915	16.7	
1916	38.0	
1917	18.5	
1918	14.0	
1919	15.2	
1920	14.9	
1921	30.4	
1922	27.3	
1923	20.0	
1924	26.7	
1925	16.7	
1926	19.8	
1927	28.5	
1928	25.2	
1929	33.3	
1930	33.1	28.8
1931	28.9	28.7
1932	26.9	29.0
1933	26.8	27.7
1934	24.3	20.1
1935	23.2	20.1
1936	17.2	19.7
1937	16.8	21.6
1938	18.0	22.4
1939	18.0	21.6
1940	14.4	20.7
1941	18.8	22.4
1942	19.1	21.6
1943	19.5	21.0
1944	19.8	22.8

TABLE 59 (Continued)

Year	Degrees Granted	Enrollment
1945	21.2	21.9
1946	20.6	20.3
1947	21.2	20.2
1948	23.9	19.2
1949	20.1	18.0
1950	19.5	18.3
1951	26.1	16.8
1952	23.1	17.2
1953	19.3	16.7
1954	21.9	16.1
1955	18.9	16.6
1956	17.1	17.0
1957	20.0	16.9
1958	22.2	17.0
1959	18.4	17.2
1960	18.4	17.0
1961	19.1	17.1
1962	18.6	17.8
1963	20.5	19.2
1964	20.0	19.6
1965	18.0	20.7
1966	21.6	21.5
Average	21.1	20.3
Standard Deviation	5.8	3.5

SOURCE: HEU.

TABLE 60. **Women Enrolled, Women Egresados, and Degrees Granted to Women, Selected Fields, 1968**

(%)

Field	Enrollment	Egresados	Degrees Granted
Bus. Ad.	8.5	9.3	8.9
Accot.	17.0	16.8	9.9
Arch.	7.7	7.2	6.9
Law	13.1	13.5	11.3
Indust. Chemistry	46.2	43.2	47.8
Pharm. Chem.	72.9	81.9	76.9
Physics	11.6	16.7	15.4
Physics/Math	7.1	4.3	4.3
Math	32.2	33.1	15.0
Biology	52.0	45.9	48.9
History	60.6	58.1	60.0
Art History	100.0	100.0	100.0
Languages	85.3	66.7	100.0
Philosophy	39.7	42.4	39.1
Letters	67.4	70.0	64.5
Ag. Eng.	1.1	0.9	1.1
Civil Eng.	0.7	0.6	0.8
Com./El. Eng.	0.1	0.0	0.0
Indust. Eng.	4.8	4.2	2.6
Chem. Eng.	7.1	9.3	8.4
Med.	19.6	17.7	15.8
Dent.	43.8	46.2	35.1
Psych.	63.6	62.9	64.1
Averages	33.1	32.6	32.0

SOURCE: Calculated from ANUIES-ESM.

TABLE 61. **Women Enrolled, Women Egresados, and Degrees Granted to Women, Selected Fields, 1969**

(%)

Field	Enrollment	Egresados	Degrees Granted
Acct.	17.8	17.9	9.3
Arch.	9.5	13.0	5.6
Bus. Ad.	10.7	9.6	15.8
Communications	33.3	36.0	50.0
Dent.	44.9	47.5	45.8
Econ.	12.7	10.0	13.4
ENG	2.8	2.4	2.0
HUM	61.5	64.8	73.0
Law	14.3	13.8	12.8
Nursing	88.3	~	~
Med.	20.6	18.1	15.6
Pharm. Chem.	76.6	79.7	83.1
Psych./SW	70.5	69.8	62.8
SCI	60.1	30.9	40.1
Ed.	58.6	56.8	78.1
Percent Accounted for by Sample Fields	76.9	56.8	78.1
Average of Women in Each Category	18.3	18.6	14.6

SOURCE: Calculated from ANUIES-ESM.

TABLE 62. **Women Enrolled in Selected Fields as Share of Total Enrollment in Those Fields, 1969, 1980, and 1990**

(%)

Field	1969	1980	1990
Account.	17.8	37.2	50.2
Arch.	9.5	20.7	35.0
Bus. Ad.	10.7	33.7	48.8
Communications	33.3	50.2	65.5
Dent.	44.9	54.7	64.8
Econ.	12.7	26.3	37.1
ENG	2.8	9.0	21.6
HUM	61.5	57.2	55.0
Law	14.3	27.8	39.1
Med.	20.6	33.0	43.9
Nursing	88.3	88.0	92.4
Pharm. Chem.	76.6	64.6	68.3
Psych./SW	70.5	73.5	76.0
SCI	60.1	37.0	39.8
TEACH	76.9	64.7	63.4

SOURCE: Calculated from ANUIES-ESM; ANUIES-AE.

TABLE 63. **Women Enrolled in Selected Fields as Share of Total Women Enrolled, 1969, 1980, and 1990**

(%)

Field	1969	1980	1990
Acct.	11.4	6.1	12.7
Arch.	1.3	2.5	3.6
Bus. Ad.	2.3	4.8	8.4
Communications	0.6	2.7	3.2
Dent.	4.4	7.2	3.2
Econ.	1.9	2.0	1.4
ENG	3.0	7.1	16.8
HUM	7.7	2.4	1.9
Law	6.4	6.4	8.1
Med.	11.0	11.4	4.9
Nursing	0.3	0.7	.8
Pharm. Chem.	3.9	2.8	2.1
Psych./SW	5.2	4.7	5.1
SCI	5.3	3.2	2.2
TEACH	21.3	20.0	17.2
Percentage of Female Enrollment Represented in These Fields	86.0	84.0	91.6

SOURCE: Calculated from ANUIES-ESM; ANUIES-AE.

Table 64. **Degrees Registered by Women Professionals, 15 Sample Fields, 1970-85**

Year	All	Bus. Ad.	Acct.	Ag./Vet.	Arch.	Engineering Civil	Engineering Indust.	Engineering Chem.
1970	8.6	~	10.3	3.8	0.0	1.0	2.4	7.2
1975	8.0	14.7	16.6	3.8	7.2	1.4	4.3	8.9
1980	18.4	23.2	28.1	10.9	12.5	3.4	7.2	12.5
1985	19.3	36.4	28.3	14.9	24.3	4.4	7.2	21.2

Year	Law	Med.	Dent.	Psych.	SW	SCI	Normal	NS
1970	9.7	15.8	46.3	~	~	0.0	72.1	46.4
1975	10.3	21.1	41.5	74.9	~	29.4	60.1	60.7
1980	18.2	25.9	55.7	72.8	95.2	38.1	71.7	51.3
1985	23.4	31.9	60.1	76.7	93.8	50.2	66.8	51.8

SOURCE: DGE, unpublished data.

BIBLIOGRAPHY

Primary Statistical Sources

Asociación Nacional de Universidades e Institutos de Enseñanza Superior (ANUIES). *Anuario estadístico.*

——. *La enseñanza superior en México* and *La educación superior en México.*

——. *Programa integral para el desarrollo de la educación superior.* México, D. F.: 1986.

Attolini, José. *Las finanzas de la universidad a través del tiempo.* México, D. F.: Escuela Nacional de Economía (UNAM), 1951.

Dirección General de Estadística. *Anuario estadístico.*

——. *Compendio estadístico.*

——. *Estadísticas para el sistema de educacion nacional.*

Dirección General de Profesiones. Unpublished data.

Estrada Campo, Humberto. *Historia de los cursos de postgrado de la UNAM.* México, D. F.: UNAM, 1983.

González Cosío, Arturo. *Historia estadística de la universidad, 1910–1967.* México, D.F.: UNAM, 1968.

Instituto de Estadística, Geografía, e Informática (INEGI). *Estadísticas Históricas de México.* México, D. F.: INEGI, 1985.

Mostkoff, Aída, and Stephanie Granato. "Quantifying Mexico's Class Structure." In *Society and Economy in Mexico.* James W. Wilkie, ed. Los Angeles: UCLA Latin American Center Publications, 1989.

Nacional Financiera, S. A. (NAFINSA). *La economía mexicana en cifras.*

Obra educativa de López Mateos. N.p.: N.p. [ANUIES], n.d. [1965].

Secretaría de Educación Pública (SEP). *La educación pública en México 1964/1970.* México, D. F.: SEP, 1970.

——. *Estadística básica del sistema educativo nacional, 1971–1972.*

205

México, D. F.: SEP, 1972.

———. *Obra Educativa, 1970–1976.* México, D. F.: SEP, n.d. [1976].

Secretaría de la Presidencia. *50 años de revolución mexicana en cifras.* México, D. F.: NAFINSA, 1963.

UAM. *Quince años de estadística.* México, D. F.: UAM, [1989].

UNAM. *Anuario estadístico.*

———. Dirección General de Administración, Departamento de Estadística. *Cuadernos estadísticos año lectivo 1979–1980.* México, D. F.: UNAM, n.d. [1980].

———. *Primer censo universitario.* México, D. F.: UNAM, 1953.

———. Dirección General de Administración. *Estadísticas del aspecto escolar, 1970.* México D.F.: UNAM, 1970.

———. *Exámenes profesionales practicados de 1841–1975.* México, D. F.: n.d. [1975].

———. Dirección General de Asuntos del Personal Académico. *Diagnóstico del personal académico de la UNAM* (1984) and *Censo del personal académico* (1986). México, D. F.: UNAM, 1984 and 1986.

———. *Presupuesto por programas.* Various years.

Reference

Asociación Nacional de Universidades e Institutos de Enseñanza Superior (ANUIES). *Carreras del área de la química en México: Planes de estudio.* México, D. F.: ANUIES, 1980.

———. *Catálogo de carreras 1986.* México, D. F.: ANUIES, 1986.

Oliver H., Rogelio. *Elección de carrera.* México, D. F.: Editorial LIMUSA, 1981.

Secretaría de Educación Pública (SEP). *Información profesional y subprofesional de México.* México, D. F.: SEP, Dirección General de Enseñanza Superior e Investigación Científica, 1958.

UNAM. *Educación medio superior.* México, D. F.: UNAM–SEP, 1984.

———. *Educación superior.* México, D. F.: UNAM, 1983.

Villa, Kitty. *Mexico: A Study of the Educational System of Mexico and a Guide to the Academic Placement of Students in Educational Institutions in the United States.* New York: World Education Series, American Association of College Registrars and Admissions Officers, 1982.

Books, Dissertations, Theses, and Manuscripts

American Chamber of Commerce of Mexico, A. C. *Mexico: Oportunidades de empleo 1987.* México, D. F.: American Chamber of Commerce of Mexico, 1987.

Asociación Nacional de Universidades e Institutos de Enseñanza Superior (ANUIES). *La enseñanza de la ingeniería en México: Estudio preliminar.* México, D. F.: ANUIES, 1962.

——. *Aspectos normativos de la educación superior.* México. D.F.: ANUIES, 1982.

——. *Planeación de la educación en México.* México, D. F.: ANUIES, 1979.

——. *Programa integral para el desarrollo de la educación superior (PROIDES).* México, D. F.: ANUIES, n.d. [1986].

Arizmendi Rodríguez, Roberto. *La decentralización de la educación superior.* México, D. F.: SEP/ANUIES, 1982.

Arrow, K. *Higher Education as a Filter.* Stanford: Stanford University Press, 1972.

Aspe, Pedro, and Paul E. Sigmund, eds. *The Political Economy of Income Distribution in Mexico.* New York: Holmes and Meier Publishers, 1984.

Banco de México. Departamento de Investigaciones Industriales. *El empleo de personal técnico en la industria de transformación.* México, D. F.: Banco de México, 1959.

——. *Programas de becas y datos profesionales de los becarios.* México, D. F.: Banco de México, 1964.

Becker, G. S. *Human Capital: A Theoretical and Empirical Analysis, with Special Reference to Education.* Princeton: Princeton University Press, 1964.

Bennett, Douglas C., and Kenneth E. Sharpe. *Transnational Corporations versus the State: The Political Economy of the Mexican Auto Industry.* Princeton: Princeton University Press, 1985.

Benveniste, Guy. *Bureaucracy and National Planning: A Sociological Case Study of Mexico.* New York: Praeger, 1970.

Berg, Ivar. *Education and Jobs: The Great Training Robbery.* Boston: Beacon Press, 1971.

Bialostozky, Clara J. de. *Recursos humanos: Tabulaciones con base en una muestra del censo de población de 1960*. México, D. F.: El Colegio de México, 1970.

Blaug, Mark. *The Economics of Education: An Annotated Bibliography*. Oxford: Pergamon Press, 1978.

———. *Education and the Employment Problem in Developing Countries*. Geneva: International Labor Office, 1974.

———. *An Introduction to the Economics of Education*. London: Penguin, 1970.

Brandenburg, Frank. *The Making of Modern Mexico*. Englewood Cliffs: Prentice-Hall, 1964.

Bravo Ahuja, Víctor. *Obra educativa, 1970–1976*. México, D. F.: SEP, 1976.

Bravo Ugarte, José. *La educación en México*. México, D. F.: Editorial Jus, 1966.

Brooke, Nigel, John Oxenham, and Angela Little. *Qualifications and Employment in Mexico*. International Development Studies Research Report. Sussex: University of Sussex, 1978.

Camp, Roderic A. *Intellectuals and the State in Twentieth-Century Mexico*. Austin: University of Texas Press, 1985.

———. *Mexico's Leaders: Their Education and Recruitment*. Tucson: University of Arizona Press, 1980.

———. *Mexican Political Biographies, 1935–75*. Tucson: University of Arizona Press, 1976.

———. *The Role of Economists in Policy–Making: A Comparative Case Study of Mexico and the United States*. Tucson: University of Arizona Press, 1977.

Carmino Ruiz, Gilardo, et al. *Estudio comparativo de la oferta y demanda actual para profesores con nivel de postgrado para las instituciones de educación agropecuaria superior en México (1983–1985)*. Chapingo: Colegio de Postgrado, 1986.

Carnoy, Martin. "The Costs and Returns to Schooling in Mexico." Ph.D. Diss. University of Chicago, 1964.

———. *Education and Employment: A Critical Appraisal*. Paris: UNESCO, International Institute for Educational Planning, 1977.

———. *Education and Employment: A Method for Local Policy Research*. Studies Series 71. Paris: UNESCO, Division of Educational Policy and Planning, 1979.

——, Henry Levin, et al. *Economía política del financiamiento educativo en países en vías de desarrollo*. México, D. F.: Ediciones Gérnika, 1986.

Castillo, Isidro. *México: Sus revoluciones sociales y la educación*. Volumes 2 and 4. N.p.: Gobierno del Estado de Michoacán, 1976.

Castillo Miranda, Wilfrido. *Asi nació la carrera de administración de empresas*. México, D. F.: Colegio de Licenciados en Administración de Empresas, 1970.

Castrejón Diez, Jaime. *La educación superior en ocho países de América Latina y el Caribe*. México, D. F.: Asociación Nacional de Universidades e Institutos de Enseñanza Superior (ANUIES), 1978.

——. *La educación superior en México*. México, D. F.: Editorial Edicol, S.A., 1979.

—— y Marisol Pérez Lizaur. *Historia de las universidades estatales*. 2 vols. México, D. F.: SEP, 1976.

Center for Latin American Studies. *Viewpoints on Education and Social Change in Latin America*. Occasional Publications No. 5. Lawrence: University of Kansas Press, 1965.

Centro de Investigación para el Desarrollo, A. C. (CIDAC). *Tecnología e industria en el futuro de México: Posibles vinculaciones estratégicas*. México, D. F.: Editorial Diana, 1989.

Clark, Burton R., ed. *The Academic Profession: Nations, Disciplines, and Institutional Settings*. Berkeley and Los Angeles: University of California Press, 1987.

Cleaves, Peter S. *Las profesiones y el estado: El caso de México*. México, D. F.: El Colegio de México, 1985.

——. *Professions and the State: The Mexican Case*. Tucson: University of Arizona Press, 1987.

Cline, Howard F. *Mexico: Revolution to Evolution, 1940-1960*. New York: Oxford University Press, 1963.

Cockcroft, James. *Intellectual Precursors of the Mexican Revolution, 1900–1913*. Austin: University of Texas Press, 1968.

Comisión de Recursos Humanos del Sector Público del Gobierno Federal. *Censo de recursos humanos del sector público federal: Administración central 1975*. México, D. F.: Comisión de Recursos Humanos del Sector Público del Gobierno Federal, 1976.

——. *Administración decentralizada y de participación estatal mayoritaria 1975*. México, D. F.: Comisión de Recursos Humanos del Sector Público del Gobierno Federal, 1976.

CONACYT. *La ciencia y la tecnología en el sector medicina y salud: Diagnóstico y política*. México, D. F.: CONACYT, 1976.

——. *Programa nacional de ciencia y tecnología, 1978–1982*. México, D. F.: CONACYT, 1978.

COPLAMAR. *Necesidades esenciales en México*. México, D.F.: Siglo XXI, 1982, Vol. 2 (La Educación).

Correa, Hector, and Ana María Chávez. *Planificación de recursos humanos para la industria siderúrgica*. México, D. F.: n.p., 1976.

Cypher, James M. *State and Capital in Mexico: Development Policy since 1940*. Boulder, CO: Westview Press, 1990.

Davis, Russell G. *Science, Engineering, and Technical Education in Mexico*. New York: Education and World Affairs, 1967.

——, ed. *Planning Education for Development: Volume I, Issues and Problems in the Planning of Education in Developing Countries*. Cambridge, MA: Center for Education and Development, Harvard University, 1980.

Derossi, Flavia. *The Mexican Entrepreneur*. Paris: Development Centre of the Organisation for Economic Co–operation and Development, 1971.

Dirección de Enfermería de la Secretaría de Salud y Asistencia. *Estudio de recursos de enfermería y obstétricia en México*. México, D. F.: Dirección de Enfermería de la Secretaría de Salud y Asistencia, 1979.

Domínguez, Jorge I. *The Political Economy of Mexico: Challenges at Home and Abroad*. Beverly Hills: Sage, 1982.

Domínguez, Raúl. *El proyecto universitario del rector Barros Sierra (estudio histórico)*. México, D. F.: UNAM, CESU (Centro de Estudios sobre la Universidad), 1986.

Dore, Ronald. *The Diploma Disease: Education, Qualification, and Development*. London: George Allen and Unwin, 1976.

Eaton, David J., and John Michael Andersen. *The State of the Rio Grande/Río Bravo*. Tucson: University of Arizona Press, 1987.

ECLA. *Education, Human Resources, and Development in Latin America*. New York: United Nations, 1968.

Figueroa, Rodolfo. *Prioridades nacionales y reclutamiento de funcionarios públicos*. México, D. F.: El Colegio de México, 1981.

Fuentes Molinar, Olac. *Educación y política en México*. México, D.F.: Nueva Imagen, 1983.

Gallo, María. *Las políticas educativas en México como indicadores de una situación nacional (1958–1976)*. México, D.F.: CIESAS (Centro de Investigación y Estudios Superiores en Antropología Social), 1987.

García Esquivel, Alfonso, et al. *Los recursos humanos en la fabricación de productos metálicos*. México, D. F.: Servicio Nacional de Adiestramiento Rápido de la Mano de Obra en la Industria, 1976.

García Sancho, Francisco, and Leoncio Hernández. *Educación superior, ciencia y tecnología en México, 1945–1975: Un diagnóstico de la educación superior y de la investigación científica y tecnológica en México*. México, D.F.: SEP, 1977.

Garza, Graciela. *La titulación en la UNAM*. México, D.F.: UNAM, CESU (Centro de Estudios sobre la Universidad), 1986.

Gil, Clark C. *Education in a Changing Mexico*. Washington, D.C.: Office of Education, U.S. Department of Health, Education, and Welfare, 1969.

Ginneken, Wouter van. *Socioeconomic Groups and Income Distribution in Mexico*. New York: St. Martin's Press, 1980.

Glade, William P., Jr., and Charles W. Anderson. *The Political Economy of Mexico*. Madison: University of Wisconsin Press, 1963.

Gleason Galicia, Rubén. *Las estadísticas y censos de México: Su organización y estado actual*. México, D.F.: UNAM, IIS (Instituto de Investigaciones Sociales), 1968.

González Casanova, Pablo. *Democracia en México*. México, D.F.: Ediciones Era, 1965.

González Salazar, Gloria. *Subocupación y estructura de clases sociales en México*. México, D. F.: UNAM, 1972.

Grayson, George. *The Politics of Mexican Oil*. Pittsburgh: University of Pittsburgh Press, 1980.

Greenberg, Martin H. *Bureaucracy and Development: A Mexican Case Study*. Lexington: D.C. Heath, 1970.

Gregory, Peter. *The Myth of Market Failure: Employment and the Labor Market in Mexico.* Baltimore: Johns Hopkins University Press, 1986.

Guevara Niebla, Gilberto. *La democracia en la calle: Crónica del movimiento estudiantil mexicano.* México, D. F.: Siglo XXI, 1988.

——, ed. *Las luchas estudiantiles en México.* 2 vols. México, D.F.: Editorial Línea, 1983.

——. *La rosa de los cambios: Breve historia de la UNAM.* México, D.F.: Cal y Arena, 1990.

Haber, Stephen H. *Industry and Underdevelopment: The Industrialization of Mexico, 1890-1940.* Stanford: Stanford University Press, 1989.

Harbison, Frederick, and Charles A. Myers. *Education, Manpower, and Economic Growth: Strategies of Human Resource Development.* New York: McGraw–Hill, 1964.

——. *Manpower and Education: Country Studies in Economic Development.* New York: McGraw–Hill, 1965.

Harris Rivera, Yolanda Aguirre. *Características socioacadémicas de las escuelas de trabajo social en la república mexicana.* México, D.F.: UNAM, 1984.

Heyduk, Daniel, ed. *Education and Work: A Symposium.* New York: Institute of International Education (IIE), Council on Higher Education in the American Republics (CHEAR), 1979.

Historia de las profesiones en México. México, D. F.: El Colegio de México, 1982.

Institute of International Education (IIE). *Profile of Foreign Students in the United States.* New York: IIE, 1981.

———. *Profiles: Detailed Analyses of the Foreign Student Population 1983/84.* New York: IIE, 1985.

——. Council on Higher Education in the American Republics (CHEAR). *La agricultura y la universidad.* Buenos Aires: N.p., 1966.

Institutos Mexicanos de Educación Superior Privada (IMESP). *La educación privada en México, 1980–81: Su aportación al desarrollo de la nación (Anteproyecto).* [México, D. F.: N.p., n.d. [1979].

Instituto Nacional de Estadística, Geografía, e Informática (INEGI). *Participación del sector público en el producto interno bruto de*

México, 1975-1983. México, D. F.: Secretaría de Programación y Presupuesto (SPP), 1984.

Instituto Tecnológico Regional de Ciudad Juárez. *Estudio de la demanda social de carreras profesionales de nivel técnico y de licenciatura.* Juárez: Instituto Tecnológico Regional de Ciudad Juárez, 1977.

Jaffe, A. J. *People, Jobs, and Economic Development: A Case History of Puerto Rico Supplemented by Recent Mexican Experiences.* Glencoe, Il: The Free Press of Glencoe Illinois, 1959.

Jérez Jiménez, Cuauhtémoc. *Vasconcelos y la educación nacionalista.* México, D.F.: SEP, 1986.

Jiménez Mier y Terán, Fernando. *El autoritarismo en el gobierno de la UNAM.* México, D. F.: Foro Universitario, 1982.

Kelly, Guillermo. *Politics and Administration in Mexico: Recruitment and Promotion of the Politico–Administrative Class.* Technical Paper Series (33). Austin: Institute of Latin American Studies, University of Texas, 1981.

Kicza, John E. "Business and Society in Late Colonial Mexico City." Ph.D. Diss. University of California, Los Angeles, 1979.

——. *Colonial Entrepreneurs: Families and Business in Bourbon Mexico City.* Albuquerque: University of New Mexico Press, 1983.

King, Richard G., Alfonso Rangel Guerra, David Kline, and Noel F. McGinn. *Nueve universidades mexicanas: Un análisis de su crecimiento y desarrollo.* México, D.F.: ANUIES, 1972.

King, Richard G., et al. *The Provincial Universities of Mexico: An Analysis of Growth and Development.* New York: Praeger, 1971.

Knight, Alan. *The Mexican Revolution. Vol. I: Porfirians, Liberals, and Peasants.* Cambridge: Cambridge University Press, 1986.

Krauze, Enrique. *Caudillos culturales en la revolución mexicana.* México, D.F.: SEP; Siglo XXI Editores, 1985.

Labastida, Horacio. *Banco de datos censales para el desarrollo social.* México, D.F.: UNAM, 1972.

LaBelle, Thomas J. *Nonformal Education and Social Change in Latin America.* Los Angeles: UCLA Latin American Center, University of California, Los Angeles, 1976.

Lajous, Alejandro. *Los orígenes del partido único en México.* México, D.F.: El Colegio de México, 1981.

Lajous Vargas, Adrián. "Aspectos de la educación superior y el empleo de profesionistas en México 1959–1967." Licenciate Thesis, UNAM, Escuela Nacional de Economía, 1967.

Latapí, Pablo. *Análisis de un sexenio de educación en México, 1970–1976.* México, D.F.: Editorial Nueva Imagen, 1980.

——. *Diagnóstico educativo nacional: Balanza y progreso escolar de México durante los últimos seis años.* México, D.F.: Centro de Estudios Educativos, 1964.

——. *Mitos y verdades de la educación mexicana/1971–1972 (Una opinión independiente).* México, D.F.: Centro de Estudios Educativos, 1973.

——. *Temas de la política educativa (1976–1978).* México, D.F.: SEP, Fondo de Cultura Económica, 1982.

Leff, Nathaniel H. *The Brazilian Capital Goods Industry, 1929-1964.* Cambridge, MA: Harvard University Press, 1968.

León López, Enrique G. *La ingeniería en México.* México, D.F.: SEP/Setentas, 1974.

Leonardo R., Patricia de. *La educación superior privada en México: Bosquejo histórico.* México, D.F.: Editorial Línea, 1983.

Lerner, Victoria. *La educación socialista.* México, D. F.: El Colegio de México, 1979.

Levy, Daniel C. *Higher Education and the State in Latin America: Private Challenges to Public Dominance.* Chicago: University of Chicago Press, 1986.

——. *University and Government in Mexico: Autonomy in an Authoritarian System.* New York: Praeger, 1980.

——. "University Autonomy versus Government Control: The Mexican Case." Ph.D. Diss. University of North Carolina, 1977.

Liebman, Arthur, Kenneth N. Walker, and Myron Glazer. *Latin American University Students: A Six Nation Study.* Cambridge, MA: Harvard University Press, 1972.

Looney, Robert E. *Economic Policymaking in Mexico: Factors Underlying the 1982 Crisis.* Durham, NC: Duke University Press, 1985.

——. *Mexico's Economy: A Policy Analysis with Forecasts to 1990.* Boulder, CO: Westview Press, 1978.

Lorentzen, Anne. *Capital Goods and Technological Development in*

Mexico. Copenhagen: Centre for Development Research, 1986.

Lorey, David E. *The University System and Economic Development in Mexico since 1929.* Stanford: Stanford University Press, forthcoming.

——. *United States-Mexico Border Statistics since 1900.* Los Angeles: UCLA Latin American Center Publications, 1990.

Mabry, Donald J. *The Mexican University and the State: Student Conflicts, 1910–1971.* College Station: Texas A & M Press, 1982.

Malo, Salvador, Jonathan Garst, and Graciela Garza. *El egresado del posgrado de la UNAM.* México, D.F.: UNAM, 1981.

Malo, Salvador, R. G. Davis, and Richard King. *The Technology of Instruction in Mexican Universities.* New York: Education and World Affairs, 1968.

Martínez Della Rocca, Salvador. *Estado y universidad en México 1920–1968: Historia de los movimientos estudiantiles en la UNAM.* México, D. F.: Joan Boldó i Climent Editores, 1986.

——, and Imano Ordorika Sacristán. "UNAM: Espejo del mejor México posible: La universidad en el contexto educativo nacional." Manuscript of November 1991.

McGinn, Noel F., and Susan L. Street. *Higher Education Policies in Mexico.* Austin: Institute of Latin American Studies, University of Texas at Austin, 1980.

Medina Lara, Beatriz, et al. *Oferta y demanda de profesionales, 1980–82.* Mérida: Centro de Desarrollo Universitario, Universidad Autónoma de Yucatán, 1983.

Mendieta y Nuñez, Lucio, and José Gómez Robledo. *Problemas de la universidad.* México, D.F.: UNAM, 1948.

Mendoza Avila, Eusebio. *La educación tecnológica en México.* México, D.F.: IPN, 1980.

Menéndez Guzmán, Alberto. *Tendencias del presupuesto universitario (1967–1976).* México, D.F.: UNAM, Dirección General de Presupuesto por Programación, n.d.

Meneses, Ernesto. *La Iberoamericana en el contexto de la educación superior contemporánea.* México, D.F.: Universidad Iberoamericana, 1979.

Meyer, Lorenzo, Rafael Segovia, and Alejandra Lajous. *Los inicios de la institucionalización: La política del maximato.* México D.F.: El Colegio de México, 1978.

Mohar B., Oscar. *Crisis y contradicciones en la educación técnica de México*. México, D.F.: Editorial Gaceta, 1984.

Morales–Gómez, Daniel, and Carlos Alberto Torres. *The State, Corporatist Politics, and Educational Policy Making in Mexico*. New York: Praeger, 1990.

Mosk, Sanford. *Industrial Revolution in Mexico*. Berkeley and Los Angeles: University of California Press, 1950.

Muñoz Izquierdo, Carlos, and Pedro Gerardo Rodríguez. *Costos, financiamiento y eficiencia de la educación formal en México*. México, D.F.: Centro de Estudios Educativos, 1977.

Myers, Charles Nash. *Education and National Development*. Princeton: Industrial Relations Section, Princeton University, 1965.

——. *U.S. University Activity Abroad: The Mexican Case*. New York: Education and World Affairs, 1968.

Myers, R. G. *Education and Emigration: Study Abroad and the Migration of Human Resources*. New York: David McKay, 1972.

Organization for Economic Cooperation and Development (OECD). *Industry and University*. Paris: OECD, 1984.

Osborn, Thomas Noel. *Higher Education in Mexico: History, Growth, and Problems in a Dichotomized Industry*. El Paso: Texas Western Press, 1976.

Padua, Jorge. *Educación, industrialización y progreso técnico en México*. México, D.F.: El Colegio de México, 1984.

Pan American Health Organization. *Migration of Health Personnel, Scientists, and Engineers from Latin America*. Washington, D. C.: World Health Organization, 1966.

Pantoja Morán, David. *Notas y reflexiones acerca de la historia del bachillerato*. México, D.F.: Colegio de Ciencias y Humanidades, UNAM, 1983.

Pellicer de Brody, Olga, and Esteban L. Mancilla. *El entendimiento con los Estados Unidos y la gestacíon del desarrollo estabilizador*. México, D. F.: El Colegio de México, 1978.

Pérez, Raúl, et al. *Características de la ocupación de los profesionales en las empresas de la península de Yucatán*. N.p. [Mérida]: Centro de Desarrollo Universitario, Universidad Autónoma de Yucatán, 1983.

Pérez Lizaur, Marisal. *Historia de las universidades estatales*, 2 vols. México, D. F.: SEP, 1976.

Pescador Osuna, José Angel and Carlos Alberto Torres. *Poder político y educación en México*. México, D. F.: Unión Tipográfica Editorial Hispano Americana, 1985.

Philip, George. *The Mexican Economy*. New York: Routledge, 1988.

——. *Oil and Politics in Latin America*. Cambridge: Cambridge University Press, 1982.

Potash, Robert A. *Mexican Government and Industrial Development in the Early Republic: The Banco de Avío*. Amherst: University of Massachusetts Press, 1983.

Programa de Seguimiento de Egresados UANL. *Estudio sobre el egresado al titularse en la Universidad Autónoma de Nuevo León 1980/81*. Monterrey: N.p. [UANL], n.d.[1981].

Proyecto para la Planeación de Recursos Humanos. *La estructura ocupacional de México 1930–80*. México, D.F.: Comisión Consultiva del Empleo y la Productividad, Subcomisión de Recursos Humanos, 1982.

——. *La estructura ocupacional de México 1930–80: Anexo metodológico, anexo estadístico*. México, D.F.: Comisión Consultiva del Empleo y la Productividad, Subcomisión de Recursos Humanos, 1982.

——. *Necesidades de recursos humanos de México, 1980–2000*. México, D.F.: Comisión Consultiva del Empleo y la Productividad, Subcomisión de Recursos Humanas, n.d.

Psacharopoulos, George, and Bikas C. Sanyal. *Higher Education and Employment: The IIEP Experience in Five Less Developed Countries*. Paris: UNESCO, 1981.

Quirk, Robert E. *Mexico*. Englewood Cliffs: Prentice-Hall, 1971.

Ramírez, Celia. *La formación profesional en la UNAM*. Pensamiento Universitario 67 (Nueva Epoca). México, D. F.: Centro de Estudios sobre la Universidad, 1986.

Ramírez, Miguel D. *Mexico's Economic Crisis*. New York: Praeger, 1989.

Ramírez, Ramón. *El movimiento estudiantíl de México: Julio–diciembre 1968*. México, D. F.: Ediciones Era, 1969.

Randall, Laura. *The Political Economy of Mexican Oil*. New York: Praeger Press, 1989.

Rangel Guerra, Alfonso. *La educación superior en México*. México, D. F.: El Colegio de México, 1979.

——. *Systems of Higher Education: Mexico*. New York: International Council for Educational Development, 1978.

——, and Alma Chapoy Bonifaz. *Estructura de la Universidad Nacional Autónoma de México: Ensayo socioeconómico*. México, D. F.: Fondo de Cultura Popular, 1970.

Reynolds, Clark. *The Mexican Economy: Twentieth-Century Structure and Growth*. New Haven and London: Yale University Press, 1970.

Reynolds, Clark W., and Blanca M. de Petricioli. *The Teaching of Economics in Mexico*. New York: Education and World Affairs, 1967.

Reyes Heroles González Garza, Jesús. *Política macroeconómica y bienestar en México*. México, D. F.: Fondo de Cultura Económica, 1983.

Rice, Jaqueline Ann. "The Porfirian Political Elite: Life Patterns of the Delegates to the 1892 Unión Liberal Convention." Ph.D. Diss. University of California, Los Angeles, 1979.

Robles, Martha. *Educación y sociedad en la historia de México*. México, D. F.: Siglo XXI Editores, 1977.

Rodríguez, Valdemar. "National University of Mexico: Rebirth and Role of the Universitarios (1910–1957)." Ph.D. Diss. University of Texas at Austin, 1958.

Ruiz Massieu, Mario. *El cambio en la universidad*. México, D. F.: UNAM, 1987.

Sánchez, George. *Mexico: A Revolution by Education*. New York: Viking Press, 1936.

Schultz, Theodore. *The Economic Value of Education*. New York: Columbia University Press, 1963.

Schumacher, August. *Agricultural Development and Rural Employment: A Mexican Dilemma*. La Jolla: Program in United States–Mexican Studies, University of California, San Diego, 1981.

Secretaría de Educación Pública (SEP). *Aportaciones al estudio de los problemas de la educación*. México, D.F.: N.p., n.d.

——. *Manual de estadísticas básicas: IV, sector educativo*. México, D. F.:

SEP, n.d.[1979].

——. *Información profesional y subprofesional de México.* México, D. F.: SEP, 1958.

——. Dirección General de Profesiones (DGP). *Análisis del mercado nacional de profesionistas y técnicos: Oferta 1967–1978, demanda 1967–1978, y proyecciones a 1990.* México, D. F.: SEP, 1982.

Secretaría de Programación y Presupuesto (SPP). *Antología de la planeación en México (1917–1985).* México, D. F.: Fondo de Cultura Económica, 1985.

Shearer, J. C. *High–Level Manpower in Overseas Subsidiaries: Experience in Brazil and Mexico.* Princeton: Industrial Relations Section, Princeton University, 1960.

Silva Herzog, Jesús. *Una historia de la Universidad de México y sus problemas.* México, D. F.: Siglo XXI Editores, 1986.

Smith, Peter H. *Labyrinths of Power: Political Recruitment in Twentieth–Century Mexico.* Princeton: Princeton University Press, 1979.

Solana, Fernando, et al. *Historia de la educación pública en México.* México, D. F.: SEP and Fondo de Cultura Económica, 1981.

Solís M., Leopoldo. *Controversias sobre el crecimiento y la distribución.* México, D. F.: Fondo de Cultura Económica, 1972.

——. *La realidad económica mexicana: Retrovisión y perspectivas.* México, D.F.: Siglo XXI, 1987.

Strassmann, Paul W. *Technological Change and Economic Development: The Manufacturing Experience in Mexico and Puerto Rico.* Ithaca, NY: Cornell University Press, 1968.

Tamayo, Jorge, ed. *Ley orgánica de la instrucción pública en el Distrito Federal de 1867.* México, D. F.: UNAM, 1967.

Tannenbaum, Frank. *Mexico: The Struggle for Peace and Bread.* Englewood Cliffs: Prentice-Hall, 1950.

Thomas, Brinley. *Migration and Urban Development: A Reappraisal of British and American Long Cycles.* London: Methuen and Company, 1972.

UAP. *Perspectivas de la educación superior en México.* Puebla: UAP, 1984.

UANL. *La demanda de profesionistas en el estado de Nuevo León.* Monterrey: UANL, n.d. [1977].

UANL and Cámera de la Industria de Transformación de Nuevo León. *La demanda de técnicos y profesionistas en el estado de Nuevo León.* Monterrey: UANL, 1981.

UNAM. *Bibliografía sobre educación superior en América Latina.* México, D. F.: UNAM, 1983.

——. *Evaluación y marco de referencia para los cambios académicos administrativos.* México, D. F.: UNAM, 1984.

——. *Fortaleza y debilidad de la UNAM: Respuesta de la comunidad universitaria: Propuestas y alternativa.* Suplemento Extraordinario No. 16. Ciudad Universitaria: UNAM, 1986.

——. *Modificaciones académicas en la Universidad Nacional Autónoma de México.* México, D. F.: UNAM, 1986.

——. Instituto de Investigaciones Sociales (IIS). *Historia estadística de la universidad (1910–1967).* México, D. F.: UNAM, 1968.

——. FCPS. *La questión de registro de los títulos y de las cédulas profesionales.* México, D. F.: UNAM, 1968.

——. Facultad de Ingeniería. *Visión histórica del posgrado en la facultad de ingeniería.* México, D. F.: UNAM, 1984.

UNESCO. *Higher Education: International Trends, 1960–70.* New York: UNESCO, 1975.

——. *New Trends and New Responsibilities for Universities in Latin America.* Paris: UNESCO, 1980.

Urquidi, Víctor, and Adrián Lajous Vargas. *Educación superior, ciencia y tecnología en el desarrollo económico de México.* México, D. F.: El Colegio de México, 1967.

van Genneken, Wouter. *Socioeconomic Groups and Income Distribution in Mexico: A Study Prepared for the ILO World Employment Programme.* New York: St. Martin's Press, 1980.

Vaughan, Mary Kay. *The State, Education, and Social Class in Mexico, 1880–1928.* DeKalb: Northern Illinois University Press, 1982.

Vernon, Raymond. *The Dilemma of Mexico's Development: The Roles of the Private and Public Sectors.* Cambridge, MA: Harvard University Press, 1963.

——, ed. *Public Policy and Private Enterprise in Mexico.* Cambridge, MA: Harvard University Press, 1964.

Villaseñor García, Guillermo. *Estado y universidad, 1976–1982.* México, D. F.: UAM, 1988.

Villegas, Abelardo. *Positivismo y porfirismo.* México, D. F.: SEP, 1972.

Wences Reza, Rosalío. *La universidad en la historia de México.* México, D. F.: Editorial Línea, 1984.

Wilkie, James W. *The Mexican Revolution: Federal Expendtiure and Social Change.* Berkeley and Los Angeles: Univerity of California Press, 1967.

——. *La revolución mexicana: Gasto federal y cambio social, 1910–1970.* México, D. F.: Fondo de Cultura Económica, 1978.

Witker, Jorge V. *Universidad y dependencia científica y tecnológica en América Latina.* México, D. F.: UNAM, 1979.

Zermeño, Sergio. *México: Una democracia utópica. El movimiento estudiantil del 68.* México, D. F.: Siglo XXI Editores, 1985.

Articles and Book Chapters

Almond, Gabriel A. "The Development of Political Development." In *Understanding Political Development.* Ed. Samuel P. Huntington and Myron Weiner. Boston: Little, Brown and Company, 1987.

Amparo Casar, María. "La reestructuración de la participación del estado en la industria nacional." *El Cotidiano,* 23 (1988), 28-38.

Arce Gurza, Francisco. "El inicio de una nueva era, 1910–1945." In *Historia de las profesiones en México.* México, D. F.: El Colegio de México, 1982.

Ayala, Gustavo. "Ingeniería civil: Importancia y consecuencias." In *Ciencia y desarrollo, número especial: Los estudios de posgrado en México. Naturaleza, funciones, diagnóstico.* México, D. F.: CONACYT, 1987.

Baloyra, Enrique A. "Oil Policies and Budgets in Venezuela, 1938–1968." *Latin American Research Review,* 9, no. 2 (Summer, 1974), 28–72.

Barkin, David. "La educación: ¿Una barrera al desarrollo económico?" *El Trimestre Económico,* 33, no. 4 (October–December, 1971), 951–993.

Barrios, Maritza, and Russel G. Davis. "The Rate–of–Return Approach to Educational Planning." In *Planning Education for Development: Volume I, Issues and Problems in the Planning of Education in Developing Countries, USAID/Harvard.* Ed. Russell G. Davis. Cambridge, MA: Center for Education and

Development, Harvard University, 1980.

Bartolucci, Jorge. "Demanda de los sectores medios." *Revista Mexicana de Ciencias Políticas y Sociales*, NS 29 (Nueva Epoca), 129–142.

Beck, Robert E. "The Liberal Arts Major in the Bell System Management: Project Quill Report." Washington, D.C.: Association of American Colleges, 1981.

Behrman, Jere R. "Schooling in Latin America: What Are the Patterns and What Is the Impact?" *Journal of Interamerican Studies and World Affairs*, 27, no. 4 (Winter, 1985–1986).

Bortz, Jeffrey. "The Development of Quantitative History in Mexico since 1940: Socioeconomic Change, Income Distribution, and Wages." In *Statistical Abstract of Latin America*, vol. 27, pp. 1107-1127.

Brooke, Nigel. "Actitudes de los empleadores mexicanos respeto a la educación: Un test de la teoría de capital humano?" *Revista del Centro de Estudios Educativos*, 8, no. 4 (1978), 109–32.

Burke, Michael E. "The University of Mexico and the Revolution, 1910–1940." *Americas*, 34, no. 2 (1977), 252–273.

del Camino, Isidoro. "Gasto educativo nacional, desperdicio escolar y económico, pirámide escolar en México." *Revista del Centro de Estudios Educativos*, 1, no. 4 (1971), 1–34.

Camp, Roderic A. "The Cabinet and the Técnico in Mexico and the United States." *Journal of Comparative Administration*, no. 3 (August, 1971), 200–201.

——. "Intellectuals: Agents of Change in Mexico?" *Journal of Interamerican Studies and World Affairs*, 23, no. 3 (August, 1981).

——. "Mexican Governors since Cárdenas: Education and Career Contacts." *Journal of Interamerican Studies and World Affairs*, 16, no. 4 (November, 1974).

——. "The Middle–Level Technocrat in Mexico." *Journal of Developing Areas*, 6, no. 4 (July, 1972), 571–582.

——. "The Political Technocrat in Mexico and the Survival of the Political System." *Latin American Research Review*, 20, no. 1 (1985), 97–118.

Carnoy, Martin. "Education in Latin America: An Empirical Approach." In *Viewpoints on Education and Social Change in Latin America*. Center for Latin American Studies. Occasional

Publications no. 5. Lawrence: University of Kansas Press, 1965, pp. 41–54.

——. "Earnings and Schooling in Mexico." *Economic Development and Cultural Change*, 15, no. 4.

Cochrane, James D. "Mexico's New Científicos: The Díaz Ordaz Cabinet." *Interamerican Economic Affairs*, no. 21 (Summer, 1967), 61–72.

Coleman, Kenneth M., and John Wanat. "On Measuring Presidential Ideology through Budgets: A Reappraisal of the Wilkie Approach." *Latin American Research Review*, 10, no. 1 (Spring, 1975), 77–88.

Consejo Interamericano para Educación, Ciencia y Cultura (CIECC). "Exodo de profesionales y técnicos en los países latinoamericanos" *Revista del Centro de Estudios Educativos*, 2, no. 2 (1972), 61–83.

COPLAMAR, *Necesidades esenciales en México*. México, D.F.: Siglo XXI, 1982, Vol. 2 (*La educación*).

Covo, Milena. "Apuntes para el análisis de la trayectoría de una generación universitaria." In *Educación y realidad socioeconómica*. México, D. F.: Centro de Estudios Educativos, 1979.

Cravalta Franco, María Aparecida, and Claudia de Moura Castro. "La contribución de educación técnica a la movilidad social." *Revista Latinoamericana de Estudios Educativos*, 11, no. 1, 1–42.

Cruz Valverde, Aurelio. "Economía y educación: Una panorama." *Revista de Educación Superior*, NS 30, 32.

Davis, Russell G. "The Manpower Requirements Approach to Educational Planning." In *Planning Education for Development: Volume I, Issues and Problems in the Planning of Education in Developing Countries, USAID/Harvard*. Ed. Russell G. Davis. Cambridge, MA: Center for Education and Development, Harvard University, 1980.

de Ibarrola, María. "El crecimiento de la escolaridad superior en México como expresión de los proyectos socioeducativos del estado y la burguesía." *Cuadernos de Investigación Educativa*, 9.

——. "Estudio de producción, mercado de trabajo, y escolaridad en México." *Cuadernos de Investigación Educativa* 14.

——. "La formación de profesores y la producción nacional." *Revista de Educación e Investigación Técnica*, no. 14 (Autumn, 1984), 22–31.

"El progreso del país requiere que todos los técnicos tengan trabajo: Echeverría." *El Día*, July 23, 1971.

Espinosa, Evan D. "La explosión demográfica en México: Análisis y implicaciones educativas." *Revista de Educación Superior*, NS 25, 16–48.

Folger, John K., and Charles B. Nam. "Education of the American Population." In *Education and Jobs: The Great Training Robbery.* Ed. Ivar Berg. Boston: Beacon Press, 1971.

Foster, Edward, and Jack Rodgers. "Quality of Education and Student Earnings." *Higher Education*, no. 8 (1979), 21–37.

Fretz, Deirdre. "Wanted: Engineers." *Mexico Journal*, November 13, 1989, pp. 25-26.

Fuentes Molinar, Olac. "Universidad y democracia: La mirada hacia la izquierda." *Cuadernos Políticos*, 53 (January/April, 1981), 4-18.

García Sordo, Mario. "Desempleados o subempleados, más de 90 mil agrónomos." *El Financiero*, October 5, 1988, p. 39.

Glade, William P. "Revolution and Economic Development: A Mexican Reprise." In William P. Glade and Charles W. Anderson, *The Political Economy of Mexico*. Madison: University of Wisconsin Press, 1963, pp. 87-88.

Goldblatt, Phyllis. "The Geography of Youth Employment and School Enrollment Rates in Mexico." In *Education and Development: Latin America and the Caribbean.* Ed. Thomas J. LaBelle. Los Angeles: UCLA Latin American Center, 1972.

Gómez Campo, Víctor Manuel. "Educación superior, mercado de trabajo, y práctica profesional: Un análisis comparativo de diversos estudios en México." *Revista de Educación Superior*, NS 45, 5–48.

———. "Relaciones entre educación y estructura económica: Dos grandes marcos de interpretación." *Revista de Educación Superior*, NS 41 (January-March, 1982), 5-43.

Gómez Junco, Horacio. "Presente y futuro de cinco innovaciones en el Tecnológica de Monterrey." *Revista de Educación Superior*, OS 4, no. 1 (1975), 32–46.

———. "Teaching and Research in the Social Sciences." *Voices of Mexico* (June–August, 1987), 20–22.

González Casanova, Pablo. "México: El ciclo de una revolución agraria," *Cuadernos Americanos,* 120, no. 1 (January-February, 1962).

Gortari Rabiela, Rebeca de. "Educación y conciencia nacional: Los ingenieros después de la revolución mexicana." *Revista Mexicana de Sociología,* 49, no. 3.

Grindle, Merilee. "Power, Expertise and the 'Técnico': Suggestions from a Mexican Case Study." *Journal of Politics,* 39, no. 2 (May, 1977), 399–426.

Guardarrama H., José de Jesús. "México necesita multiplicar 20 veces su número de ingenieros antes de 25 años." *El Financiero,* April 19, 1988, p. 53.

Gruber, W. "Career Patterns of Mexican Political Elites." *Western Political Quarterly,* 24, no. 3 (September, 1971).

Hanson, James A. "Federal Expenditures and 'Personalism' in the Mexican 'Institutional' Revolution." In *Money and Politics in Latin America.* Ed. James W. Wilkie. Los Angeles: UCLA Latin American Center Publications, 1977.

Hinojosa, Oscar. "La universidad privada escala posiciones como proveedora de funcionarios." *Proceso,* March 31, 1986, pp. 6–11.

Hirsch Adler, Ana. "Panorama de la formación de profesores universitarios en México." *Revista de Educación Superior,* NS 46 (1983), 16–44.

Huntington, Samuel P. "The Goals of Development." In *Understanding Political Development.* Eds. Samuel P. Huntington and Myron Weiner. Boston: Little, Brown and Company, 1987.

Ibarra, María Esther. "Decide la SEP que se encojan las universidades," *Proceso,* September 29, 1986, p. 1.

"La investigación tecnológica, en crisis." *Unomásuno,* January 29, 1990, p. 3.

Jaksic, Iván. "The Politics of Higher Education in Latin America." *Latin American Research Review,* 20, no. 1 (1985), 209–221.

Keesing, Donald, B. "Employment and Lack of Employment in Mexico, 1900–70." In *Quantitative Latin American Studies: Methods and Findings.* Eds. James W. Wilkie and Kenneth Ruddle. Los Angeles: UCLA Latin American Center Publications, 1977.

——. "Structural Change Early in Development: Mexico's Changing Industrial and Occupational Structure from 1895 to 1950." *Journal of Economic History,* 29, no. 4 (December, 1969), 716–738.

de Leonardo Ramírez, Patricia. "Los cuadros de la derecha." *El Cotidiano,* 24 (July–August, 1988), 89–94.

León López, Enrique G. "La educación técnica superior." In *El perfil de México en 1980.* México, D.F.: Siglo XXI Editores, 1970.

Levy, Daniel. "Serving Private Enterprise and the State: A Comparison of Mexico's Private and Public Universities." Paper presented at XI Congreso Internacional de LASA (Mexico City, September 29–October 1, 1983) cited in José Angel Pescador and Carlos Alberto Torres, *Poder político y educación en México* (México, D. F.: Unión Tipográfica Editorial Hispano Americano, 1985).

Lipset, Martin. "Values, Education, and Entrepreneurship." In *Elites in Latin America.* Eds. Martin Lipset and Aldo Solari. New York: Oxford University Press, 1967.

Llinas Zárate, Isabel. "La universidad ha cumplido con creces después de la revolución: Luis E. Todd," *Unomásuno,* January 28, 1990, p. 2.

Lomnitz, Larissa. "Horizontal and Vertical Relations and the Social Structure of Urban Mexico." *Latin American Research Review,* 17, no. 2 (1982), 51–74.

Lomnitz, Larissa, Leticia Mayer, and Martha W. Rees. "Recruiting Technical Elites: Mexico's Veterinarians." *Human Organization,* 42, no. 1 (Spring, 1983), 23–29.

Lorey, David E. "The Development of Engineering Expertise for Economic and Social Modernization in Mexico since 1929." In *Society and Economy in Mexico.* Ed. James W. Wilkie. Los Angeles: UCLA Latin American Center Publications, 1989.

——. "Higher Education in Mexico: The Problems of Quality and Employment." In *Reciprocal Images: Education in U.S.–Mexican Relations.* México, D. F.: ANUIES, 1990.

——. "Mexican Professional Education in the United States and the Myth of 'Brain Drain'," *Ensayos* (Revista del Departamento de Relaciones Internacionales, Universidad de las Américas-Puebla), 4, no. 9 (1988), 56-59.

——. "Professional Expertise and Mexican Modernization: Sources, Methods, and Preliminary Findings." In *Statistical Abstract of Latin America,* vol. 26, pp. 899-912.

Mabry, Donald J. "Changing Models of Mexican Politics, a Review Essay." *The New Scholar*, 5, no. 1 (1975), 31–37.

Mabry, Donald J., and Roderic A. Camp. "Mexican Political Elites 1935–1973: A Comparative Study." *The Americas*, no. 31 (April, 1975), 456–467.

Marquis, Carlos. "Sobre los egresados de la UAM–Azcapotzalco." *Revista Latinoamericana de Estudios Educativos*, 14, no. 4 (1984), 87–108.

Medin, Tzvi. "La mexicanidad política y filosófica en el sexenio de Miguel Alemán, 1946–1952." *Estudios Interdisciplinarios de América Latina y el Caribe*, 1, no. 1 (January-June, 1990), 5–22.

Medina, Alberto Hernández, and Alfredo Rentería Agraz. "El perfil de personal docente en las universidades de provincia." *Revista Latinoamericana de Estudios Educativos*, 14, no. 3, 13–65.

Mendoza Rojas, Javier. "Política del estado hacia la educación superior, 1983–1988." *Pensamiento Universitario*, 68 (Nueva Epoca).

"Mexican Higher Education Degrees." Translation of article from *La Jornada*, October 6, 1989, in *U.S.-Mexico Report*, 8, no. 11 (November, 1989), p. 12.

"México necesita 300 mil profesionistas por año, para asegurar su crecimiento," *Ocho Columnas* (Guadalajara, Jalisco), October 15, 1989.

Moffett, Matt. "Brain Drain Slows Mexico's Development: Researchers, Professionals, Skilled Workers Are Lured Abroad." *Wall Street Journal*, May 5, 1989, p. A1.

Montavon, Paul. "Some Questions on Education and Economic Development." In *Viewpoints on Education and Social Change in Latin America*. Occasional Publications no. 5. Lawrence: University of Kansas Press, 1965.

Muñoz Izquierdo, Carlos. "El desempleo en México: Características generales." *El Trimestre Económica*, 62, no. 167 (1975).

———. "Evaluación del desarrollo educativo en México (1958–1970) y factores que lo han determinado." *Revista del Centro de Estudios Educativos*, 3, no. 3 (1973).

———."Observaciones críticas a una previsión de recursos humanos basada en el enfoque de Herbert Parnes." *Revista de Educación e Investigación Técnica*, no. 10 (1981), 66–73.

——, and José Lobo. "Expansión escolar, mercado de trabajo, y distribución de ingreso en México: Un análisis longitudinal, 1960–1970." *Revista del Centro de Estudios Educativos,* 4, no. 1, 9–30.

——, José Lobo, Alberto Hernández Medina, and Pedro Gerardo Rodríguez. "Educación y mercado de trabajo." *Revista del Centro de Estudios Educativos,* 8, no. 2 (1978), 1–90.

——, and Pedro Gerardo Rodríguez. "La eseñanza técnica: ¿Canal de movilidad social para los trabajadores?" *Revista de Educación e Investigación Técnica,* no. 6–7 (double issue) (July–August–September, 1980), 70–86.

Myers, Charles Nash. "Proyección de la demanda de médicos en México: 1965–1980." *Revista de Educación Superior,* 1, no. 3 (1972), 77–103.

Nava Díaz, Eduardo. "Perspectiva de complemento al financiamiento del sector público en materia de educación superior: El caso de México, 1967–1980." *Revista de Educación Superior,* NS 17 (1976), 48–86.

Osborn, Thomas Noel. "A Survey of Developments and Current Trends in Higher Education in Mexico." Boulder: University of Colorado International Economic Studies Center, n.d.

Oxenham, John. "The University and High–Level Manpower." *Higher Education,* no. 9 (1980), 643–655.

Padilla, Jorge Díaz. "El impacto de los planes de desarrollo económico en la demanda de servicios de ingenieros industriales." *Revista de Educación e Investigación Técnica,* no. 4 (January–February–March, 1980), 60–68.

Padua, Jorge A. "Movilidad social y universidad." In *La crisis de la educación superior en México.* Ed. Gilberto Guevara Niebla. México, D.F.: Nueva Imagen, 1981.

Peña de la Mora, Eduardo. "Evaluación de las actitudes de compromiso social en institutos de educación técnica superior." *Revista de Educación e Investigación Técnica,* no. 13 (March, 1982), 9–17.

Pérez Roche, Manuel. "Algunos aspectos de la restructuración académica de la enseñanza superior: Cursos semestrales, salidas laterales, y sistemas de titulación." *Revista de Educación Superior,* 1, no. 4 (1972), 9–16.

Pescador Osuna, José Angel. "El balance de la educación superior en el sexenio 1976-1982." In UAP, *Perspectivas de la educación superior en México*. Puebla: UAP, 1984.

——, and Carlos Alberto Torres. "Educación superior, cultural, política y socialización del personal del estado: El papel político contradictorio de la universidad pública y privada en México." In *Poder político y educación en México*. Eds. José Angel Pescador and Carlos Alberto Torres. México, D. F.: Unión Tipográfica Editorial Hispano Americano, 1985.

Philip, George. "Public Enterprise in Mexico." In *Public Enterprise and the Development World*. Ed. V. V. Ramanadham. London and Sydney: Croom Helm, 1984.

——. "Mexican Politics Under Stress: Austerity and After." In *Politics in Mexico*. Ed. George Philip. London: Croom Helm, 1985.

Portas Cabrera, Eduardo. "La demanda, el personal docente, y el financiamiento de la educación superior en México." Social Service Project for ANUIES, n.d.

Prysor–Jones, Susanne. "Education and Equality in Developing Countries." In *Planning Education for Development: Volume I, Issues and Problems in the Planning of Education in Developing Countries, USAID/Harvard*. Ed. Russell G. Davis. Cambridge, MA: Center for Education and Development, Harvard University, 1980.

Quintero H., José Luis. "Metas de igualdad y efectos de subsidio de la educación superior mexicana." *Revista del Centro de Estudios Educativos*, 8, no. 3 (1978), 59–92.

Rangel Guerra, Alfonso. "Higher Education and Employment." In *Education and Work: A Symposium*. Ed. Daniel Heyduk. New York: Institute of International Education (IIE), Council on Higher Education in the American Republics (CHEAR), 1979.

——. "La decentralización de la educación superior." *Revista de Educación Superior*, NS 19 (1976), 42–48.

——. "Objetivos de la enseñanza superior frente a los requerimientos del desarrollo y el avance técnico." *Revista de Educación Superior*, OS 1, no. 1 (1972), 33–38.

"Reflecciones sobre planeación, 1917–1985." In *Antología de la planeación en México (1917–1985)*. Vol. 1. México, D. F.: Fondo de Cultura Económica, 1985.

Requelme, Marcial Antonio, et al. "Educación y empleo en el

municipio de Naucalpa, Estado de México: Notas e indicadores para su estudio." *Revista de Educación e Investigación Técnica,* no. 9 (1981), 43–70.

Ribeiro, Darcy. "Universities and Social Development." In *Elites in Latin America.* Eds. Martin Lipset and Aldo Solari. New York: Oxford University Press, 1967.

Ríos Ierrusca, Herculano. "El análisis de los recursos humanos en la medicina." *Revista de Educación Superior,* no. 6 (1980), 67–82.

Rivero, Martha. "La política económica durante la guerra." In *Entre la guerra y la estabilidad política: El México de los 40.* Ed. Rafael Loyola. México, D.F.: Grijalbo, 1990.

Romero Bueno, Marcel, Manuel García Macías, and Francisco Reyes Araneo. "Historia de la educación secundaria técnica en México." *Revista de Educación e Investigación Técnica,* no. 12 (1982), 7–12.

Safford, Frank. "Politics, Ideology, and Society." In *Spanish America After Independence.* Ed. Leslie Bethell. Cambridge: Cambridge University Press, 1987.

Samaniego, Norma. "El desafío del empleo ante la modernización." In *Los profesionistas mexicanos y los desafíos de la modernidad.* México, D.F.: Editorial Diana, 1989.

Schiefelbein, Ernesto. "Un modelo de simulación del sistema educativo mexicano." *Revista del Centro de Estudios Educativos,* 1, no. 4 (1971).

Schmelkes de Valle, Corina. "¿Por qué no se titulan graduados en México: Una investigación sobre pasantes como profesionales. Alternativas y recomendaciones para su titulación." *Revista de Educación e Investigación Técnica,* no. 10 (1981), 45–65.

——, et al. "La participación de la comunidad en el gasto educativo: Conclusiones de 24 casos de estudio en México." *Revista Latinoamericana de Estudios Educativos,* 13, no. 1, 9–47.

Scott, Robert E. "The Government Bureaucrat and Political Change in Latin America." *Journal of International Affairs,* no. 20 (1966), 294–95.

"El sector educativo debe preparar cuadros técnicos acorde con las necesidades del país: CANACINTRA." *Unomásuno,* June 26, 1987, p. 14.

Skidmore, Thomas E., and Peter H. Smith. "Notes on Quantitative

History: Federal Expenditure and Social Change in Mexico since 1910." *Latin American Research Review*, 5, no. 1 (Spring, 1970), 71–85.

Smith, Peter H. "La movilidad política en el México contemporáneo." *Foro Internacional*, 15, no. 3 (1975), 399–427.

Snodgrass, Donald R. "The Distribution of Schooling and the Distribution of Income." In *Planning Education for Development: Volume I, Issues and Problems in the Planning of Education in Developing Countries, USAID/Harvard.* Ed. Russell G. Davis. Cambridge, MA: Center for Education and Development, Harvard University, 1980.

Solari, Aldo. "Secondary Education and the Development of Elites." In *Elites in Latin America.* Eds. Martin Lipset and Aldo Solari. New York: Oxford University Press, 1967.

Stern, Claudio, and Joseph A. Kahl. "Stratification since the Revolution." In *Comparative Perspectives on Stratification: Mexico, Great Britain, and Japan.* Ed. Joseph A. Kahl. Boston: Little, Brown, and Company, 1968.

Trujillo Cedillo, José Manuel. "Educación y capital humano." *Revista de Educación e Investigación Técnica*, no. 14 (Autumn, 1984), 32–57.

Urquidi, Víctor. "Technology Transfer between Mexico and the United States: Past Experience and Future Prospects." *Estudios Mexicanos*, 2, no. 2 (Summer, 1986), 179–193.

Vielle, Jean–Pierre. "Planeación y reforma de la educación superior en México, 1970–1976." *Revista del Centro de Estudios Educativos*, 6, no. 4, 9–31.

Villagómez, Rafael, and Herculano Ríos. "Recursos humanos para la industria siderúrgica." *Revista de Educación Superior*, NS 18 (1976), 3–26.

Villareal, René. "El desarrollo industrial de México: Una perspectiva histórica." In *México: 75 años de revolución. Desarrollo económico I.* México, D. F.: Fondo de Cultura Económica, 1988.

Waggoner, Barbara Ashton. "Latin American Universities in Transition." In *Viewpoints on Education and Social Change in Latin America.* Center for Latin American Studies. Occasional Publications no. 5. Lawrence: University of Kansas Press, 1965.

Wichtrich, A. R. "Manpower Planning: A Business Perspective." In

Education and Work: A Symposium. Ed. Daniel Heyduk. New York: Institute of International Education (IIE), Council on Higher Education in the American Republics (CHEAR), 1979.

Wilkie, James W. "From Economic Growth to Economic Stagnation in Mexico." In *Statistical Abstract of Latin America,* vol. 27, pp. 913–936.

———. "The Six Ideological Phases of Mexico's 'Permanent Revolution' since 1910." In *Society and Economy in Mexico.* Ed. James W. Wilkie. Los Angeles: UCLA Latin American Center Publications, 1990.